Seasonal Yoga

A fusion of yoga and tai chi combined with lifestyle tips for every season

Susan Woodd and Julie Hanson

Seasonal Yoga
Evolution for Everyone

3rd edition
Glasgow Scotland & Farnham, England

You can use this book in several ways:
It is a good idea to read the introduction first, so that you know the concept.

1. Read the season you are in at present and just dip in and out when you need more facts.
2. Use it to support the organs or system that needs attention.
3. Go to the index at the back and look for the ailment or problem of the moment.

What if I live outside the UK?

Usually there is some seasonal change wherever you live in the world. Adapt this book around your own seasons. Remember, that wherever you live, eat locally grown produce in season if possible.

Contents

How To Use This Book 5

Part 1—The Season of Spring 9

The Feeling of Spring 9
Eight Priorities for Spring 11
Eight Daily Habits for Spring................ 11
Spring is About Being Cleaner............ 12
The Mental Detox 14
The Physical Detox.............................. 14
The Home Detox 15

Food Section 16
Food for the Spring Energy 17
Eight Food and Nutrition Tips 19

Exercise and Movement Section 20
Exercise for Spring 20
Qigong for Spring 22
T'ai Chi Moves for Spring 31
Yoga for Spring.................................... 33
Meditations and Contemplations for
    Spring... 47

Home and Lifestyle Section................ 51

Spring Summary.................................. 52

Part 2— The Season of Early Summer 53

The Feeling of Early Summer............. 53
Eight Priorities for Early Summer 56
Eight Things to Avoid
for Early Summer................................. 57
Eight Daily Habits for Early Summer 58
The season to work on self! 58
The five essential energy evolves! 58
Five essential energy enemies 59

Food Section 62
Health and longevity 63

The Body Clock 72
Conclusion... 78

Dao-yin of the Dragon 78

Early Summer practice in a circle 90

Mental contemplations for Early Summer
Yoga Nidra (conscious sleep)............. 98

Here is the Seasonal yoga

Early Summer Yoga Nidra script 100

Final questionnaire: 108

Part 3—The Season of Summer.... 109

The Feeling of Summer......................109
Eight Priorities for Summer................ 111
Eight Daily Habits for Summer 112

Food Section 113
Food for the Summer Energy 115

Seven Food and Nutrition Tips 116

Exercise and Movement Section 118
Exercise for Summer 120
Qigong for Summer 121

T'ai Chi Moves for Summer 130
Yoga for Summer................................131
Meditations and Contemplations
    for Summer...................................147

Home and Lifestyle Section................155

Summer Summary...............................156

Part 4—The Season of Late Summer 157	Exercise and Movement Section 205
	Exercise for Autumn 205
The Feeling of Late Summer 157	Qigong for Autumn 208
Eight Priorities for Late Summer 159	T'ai Chi Moves for Autumn 221
Eight Daily Habits for Late Summer 160	Yoga for Autumn 224
Eight Ways to Help Your Immune System 161	Meditations and Contemplations for Autumn 238
Food Section 162	Home and Lifestyle Section 243
Food for the Late Summer Energy .. 162	Autumn Summary 244
Eight Food and Nutrition Tips 163	
Exercise and Movement Section 164	Part 6—The Season of Winter 245
Exercise for Late Summer 164	The Feeling of Winter 245
Qigong for Late Summer 166	Eight Priorities for Winter 247
T'ai Chi Moves for Late Summer 178	Eight Daily Habits for Winter 248
Yoga for Late Summer 182	The Art of Meditation 249
Meditations and Contemplations for Late Summer 191	Food Section 253
	Food for the Winter Energy 253
Home and Lifestyle Section 195	Eight Food and Nutrition Tips 254
Late Summer Summary 196	Exercise and Movement Section 255
	Exercise for Winter 255
Part 5—The Season of Autumn 197	Cleansing the Chakras 256
The Feeling of Autumn 197	Qigong for Winter 263
Eight Priorities for Autumn 199	T'ai Chi Moves for Winter 275
Eight Daily Habits for Autumn 200	Yoga for Winter 279
The Menopause 200	Meditations and Contemplations for Winter 288
The 'Man-o-pause'? 202	
Food Section 203	Home and Lifestyle Section 292
Food for the Autumn Energy 203	Winter Summary 294
Eight Food and Nutrition Tips 204	**Quick Reference Guide for Body, Mind, and Emotions 238**

How To Use This Book

This book is about living in tune with nature. Read the short introduction, then go to the season you are currently in, and follow the guidelines on how to balance your energy in season. This book will explain how you can reacquaint yourself with living in season in an easy-to-understand way. Expanding awareness is most successfully achieved by keeping things simple.

> *"Life is a state of maintaining a balance between various states of constantly changing imbalances."* Achim Eckert

Seasonal Living—Living In Tune With Nature's Changes

Seasonal living is something that would never have been talked about 250 years ago, or even 150 years ago. We got up when it was light, we went to bed when it was dark, we ate local produce when it was in season, and we joined in with the energy and the festivals of the local community; we were totally in tune with energy and its natural cycles.

However, now we can shop, eat, or bank sitting in front of our computers twenty-four hours a day. We pay no attention to our energy fluctuations, and through the use of electric light continue to work until late into the night, and at the same pace throughout the year; often in high rise buildings far removed from the natural world. We ignore the early warning signs of tiredness as a precursor to sickness, before our bodies take over and finally make us so ill we are forced to listen!

Nothing in the natural world exists in isolation. We can clearly see this in the opposites of day/night, light/dark, cold/hot, wet/dry, expansion/contraction, movement/stillness and even summer and winter. Balanced energy flowing through the body equates to improved health. **When the body is in a state of dynamic coherent energy, there is a reduced risk of disease.**

The concept of energy in season is distilled from ancient wisdom and applied to the way we live today. It dates back over three thousand years ago when the ancient Chinese invented a system of illness prevention through observing nature, energy and the seasons. We decided to take the wonderful gems of information within that philosophy and simplify them into a form which could be used and easily fitted into today's fast-paced life, developing a system that is accessible to everyone.

By living this concept and teaching it to others in a simpler way, we have developed the knowledge and practice that is set out in *Energy in Season*. Seasonal Yoga we honour with extreme respect the origins of both traditional Chinese medicine and yoga; hopefully through an introduction to these practices you will want to know more and make them part of your daily life

Spring is the Wood Element

This time of year is **March /April** with 21st of March the official first day of spring in the UK. The energy of spring, like sap rising, is forceful, determined to rise up and move forward, yet it remains supple and flexible like a tree's ability to bend in the wind, secure in its strong roots. *The linked organs for this time of year are the Liver and Gallbladder*. The seasonal energy measure for spring is 3 out of 5.

Early Summer is the Space Element

This time of year is **May/June** the first day of early Summer 21 May. The Energy of early summer is about connection, connective tissue in the body and connecting with others. The secondary part of the fire element, which comes before summer as a warm up, energetically less extreme, considered to be more preparation for the full potential of summer. *The linked organs are the Pericardium and Triple Heater*. **The seasonal energy measure is 4 out of 5**.

Summer is the Fire Element

This time of year is **July / August** the first day of summer being the 21st of June. With the energy of fire, summer likes to be spontaneous, vibrant, active, and expressive; it loves to communicate and disperse its energy. *The linked organs are the Heart and Small Intestine*. **The seasonal energy measure for summer is 5 out of 5**.

Late Summer is the Earth Element

This time of year is **September/October**, late summer is the season to return to, and operate from, with a strong sense of centre and self-worth. Like the soil that feeds us and the ground that locates us in space, the earth element imparts stability, the power to think, nurture and sustain. *The linked organs are the Stomach and Spleen.* **The seasonal energy measure for late summer is 4 out of 5.**

Autumn is the Metal Element

This time of year is **November/December**, The start of the autumn being 21st October although in the traditional four season calendar it would begin on the 22nd or 23rd of September! Metal is the element of autumn, a time of consolidation; keeping what is of value and letting go of the rest. This element has the capacity to shape and refine with high principles, values and expectations. *The linked organs are the Lung and Large Intestine.* **The seasonal energy measure for autumn is 2 out of 5.**

Winter is the Water Element

This time of year is **January/February**. The official start to winter is the 21st of December, but everyone is too busy celebrating Christmas to make a serious start to living in tune with the winter energy. The water element has the capacity to withdraw, repair, rejuvenate, concentrate, conserve and listen. It gives us time to discover our hidden depths and the source of our inherited intelligence. Winter is the worst time to diet; yet this is just the time that all of the magazines and the media promote it! *The linked organs are the Kidney and Bladder.* **The seasonal energy measure for winter is 1 out of 5.**

Achieving balanced health is dependent upon three factors:

1. Keeping the body as free of toxins as possible.
2. Keeping the body as fit and exercised as physically possible.
3. Keeping uncluttered access to your brain/pure consciousness.

Practicing these three factors will allow your body cells to remember the perfect state of health they were once in. The following pages will show you:

- How to check if you are in or out of balance for the season.
- The ideal exercises for the season.
- Lifestyle changes for the season.
- A balanced eating plan suitable for the season.
- T'ai chi/qigong or energy moves for the season.
- A short yoga flow for the season.
- How to change things at home for the season.
- How to check out the way you are thinking in the season

A Few Key Points to Help You With the Concept

Qi or Prana
Qi or Prana is the vital energy (or life force), which is present in all things in a more or less dense form. It is an unseen force that moves throughout creation, through our bodies, our homes and landscape, and throughout the entire universe. It is an invisible dynamic energy known by its effects and is recognised indirectly by what it fosters, generates and protects; it acts as your own personal battery.

Meridians or Nadis
These are the channels or pathways of energy through which the Qi or Prana flows, and are regarded as a primary functional energetic network in the human system, which nourish the body's organs, glands and their related systems. Movement, stretching, breathing and mental focus can direct and unblock these channels (a blockage being the cause of stiffness and pain) to re-balance and establish the smooth flow of this vital life-giving force. Some meridians act as reservoirs of energy, while another twelve have different bi-lateral paths conducting energy to and from their associated organ. Each organ also has a time of year when it resonates with the particular energy of that season. Therefore individual organs/meridians require more focus at different times of year in order to re-charge them and maintain the energy homoeostasis of the entire body. This corrects any deficiencies or imbalances that may have occurred, thereby activating the body's own healing responses. This book shows you the location of these lines and the associated programmes for each season.

Qigong
Qigong is a method of managing health that has been practiced since ancient times in China. Qi in Chinese means air, breath or steam but also vitality, life force or energy. Gong means a skill acquired over time through diligent practice, therefore its goal is the systematic development of vital energy. Qi is also spelt Chi, and Qigong is also spelt, in earlier texts, Chi Gung/Chi Kung. These three types of spelling are used interchangeably throughout the book.

T'ai Chi
T'ai Chi (Taiji) is the way of nature, enabling us to have a greater understanding of the laws of nature and the universe, and thereby living in harmony with them. Based on Chi Kung (Qigong), sequences of soft martial movements are composed, based on the concept that every living and non-living thing is a small universe in its own right. A lifetime study helps to develop an understanding of health, social science, psychology and philosophy. The literal translation of T'ai is 'big' or 'great' while Chi means 'ultimate energy or life force', the same energy that powers everything in the universe. Therefore it is all about generating, maintaining and cultivating energy through movement and mind training.

Yoga
Yoga is the science of right and balanced living and as such is intended to be incorporated into daily life, working on all aspects of the person, from the physical to the energetic, the mental to the emotional and including the spiritual. The word 'yoga' means 'to unify' or facilitate oneness, which is derived from the Sanskrit word 'yuj' which means to join. This can be applied to the more physical level of balancing mind, body and emotions or in the more spiritual context of linking the individual consciousness with the universal.

The season of spring

The Wood Element

With the first smell of spring comes the suggestion that you are about to emerge from the gloom. The long dark grey days are about to end, being replaced by fresh, dewy mornings, that fill you full of the anticipation of warmth and sunshine. The smell of spring has a freshness that you do not get in any other season; provided by the new oxygen that comes from the young shoots and leaves growing around us at this time of year. We see the first daffodil shoot up through the ground, which spells a cheery yellow future.

The beginning of spring is March 21st, the spring equinox, when day equals night, after which the hours of daylight out-number the hours of darkness; in the Medieval calendar, spring was the start of the year. Spring is the time of year for new challenges and personal growth as we stretch ourselves out of winter toward new beginnings.

The Feeling of Spring

It is the time of the emergence of the new, and a time to be more energetic, flexible, spontaneous, creative, thoughtful, patient, sensitive and humorous. As the days get longer and there is more demand to get things started, so we need fresh approaches to our diet, lifestyle, exercise, and outlook. Even our home environment needs a spring clean to make changes in harmony with a natural feeling of expectation in the air. With the first taste of new, crispy green vegetables you just know that your body is getting re-energized with the vibrant energy of spring foods.

The feeling of new energy sends you into a purge of cleansing your body, house, car, and wardrobe, in fact anything that is surrounding you, so that you can match the external new energy with a new fresh cleaner feeling.

Anticipation of great things hang in this new air making you want to plan ahead, and to start new projects — even business plans flood your brain with a renewed energy and enthusiasm.

Part One

At last you can now see the way ahead for a great new year. If you do not feel like this, turn to the following pages to help you find this new energy.

If spring was a person, their nature would be that of a pioneer, entrepreneur or inventor, the one to put forward ideas that leads the rest of the team or gives them direction. They excel at goal setting, forward planning, motivating, organizing, devising action plans, being creative, and having a clear vision of how things will look. They love nothing better than to have a challenge to get their teeth into, possessing a sense of adventure and zest for life, and having the ability to inspire and share their enthusiasm with others. **So it makes sense to develop these qualities at this time of year to match the energy of the season.**

Information You Need to Know—a Reminder!

Each season is linked with a pair of organs, associated with tastes and particular flavours, colours, emotions, temperatures and activity — all of which have a relevance to health. Although it is a very complex system, we will cover the most basic of information in this book, keeping it simple enough to easily implement into your everyday life.

As each season changes to the next you need time to refine your life by increasing your awareness, and by looking at the priorities for that season. As humans we need a basic understanding of why we do things, so we believe that what we apply to our lives will work for our maximum benefit and potential.

If you are out of balance at the moment, these are the issues that might come up in spring to be dealt with:

- ☐ Do you have regular periods of depression or moodiness?
- ☐ Are you always planning, living in the future or have the desire to push forward at all costs?
- ☐ Do you have a problem with decision-making?
- ☐ Are you a highly competitive person, sometimes at the expense of others?
- ☐ Do you have feelings of being stuck or unable to move forward?
- ☐ Are you intolerant of lack of organization or get irritated regularly?
- ☐ Do you have a tendency to be over-controlling or dominating at certain times? (*Think about the answer.*)
- ☐ Are you easily frustrated or have the feeling of, 'I must get it done now'?
- ☐ Do you sometimes manifest anger not appropriate to the situation or become suddenly volatile?
- ☐ Do you have issues around rules and authority?
- ☐ Do you suffer from tired eyes or eye strain regularly?
- ☐ Are you frequently hung over or feel toxic?
- ☐ Do you suffer from bouts of extreme mental or physical tension?
- ☐ Do you have uneven energy levels; full on, then full off?

Eight Priorities for Spring

Resilience?

1. **Keep life flexible**, free and active, so that you are supple and strong in order to withstand the changing circumstances of life.
2. **Choose things to motivate you**, or be around people who do.
3. **Do not let anyone overpower you**. Take responsibility for yourself, build substance to your life, develop your creativity and then expand out to communicate with, and positively influence, others.
4. **Organize and decide** on a life plan for the year ahead. Set goals and forward plan, and even if you do not like the goal-setting concept, list some of the events you would like to create in the next few months.
5. **Take up activities with others**. If you are feeling pent up or bored, go away for a long weekend or do an energetic social activity that you enjoy.
6. **Detox and clean up your act**. It is time to simplify and lighten your diet, drink less alcohol, tea and coffee. (*See page 14.*)
7. **Safely release anger**, frustration, and irritation, which may have accumulated in the winter season, and replace it with patience, humour, gentleness, and human kindness. Shadow boxing, body combat/martial arts classes are all good for this.
8. **Start to move again**, and stretch your body. Go out for a walk, and create a feeling of being renewed with new energy and positive expectations.

Eight Daily Habits for Spring

1. **Be kind** to someone!
2. Do something toward **detoxifying your life**. You have a choice of five areas: food, thoughts, physical, home or outdoor environment.
3. Practise **making decisions**, being cordial, affectionate, enthusiastic and humorous.
4. When was the last time you **laughed heartily**? Increase the amount of joy and laughter in your life. Think of a friend who makes you laugh and spend some time with them.
5. Be aware of an area of your life you may be **stuck in**. Scan your life for issues that might be creating tension or discord, or making you feel uneasy, and make a change.
6. Set yourself a **challenge** in the morning but avoid rushing ahead or being too impulsive; instead practice living in the moment.
7. Do something **outside** if only for a short time (*weather permitting*). A brisk walk, wash the car, clean gutters, tidy the garden, or get off the bus/train one stop earlier and walk to work.
8. **Rest your eyes for ten minutes** and practise eye exercises.

Spring is the season to work on your eyesight. Tools for eyesight improvement:

- The **Bates Method** was designed by William H. Bates, a prominent New York eye specialist to improve the eyesight.
- **Palming**. Rub the palms together, and place them over the closed eyes to exclude all light, without applying pressure. This rests, relaxes and rejuvenates the eyes.
- **Splashing**. Splash the eyes with water, twenty times in the morning and evening.
- **Swinging**. Swing the whole body, rotating from right to left; the aim is to allow the eyes to remain still, sweep across the scene without stopping and staring.
- **Near and far focusing.** Hold a pencil twelve inches from your face. Focus on a distant object, e.g. a tree. Look for two seconds, blink, and then focus on the pencil. Blink, and focus back onto the tree; repeat several times.

Modern social conditions require far less eye movement than living in the natural environment; we need to make sure we keep the eye muscles strong and active. Keeping the neck straight and the head still, repeat each of the following ten times:

- Look up and down.
- Look as far as you can to the left and then to the right.
- Move the eyes diagonally up to the left then down to the right.
- Move the eyes diagonally up to the right then down to the left.
- Make wide circles, moving clockwise then anti-clockwise, then in a figure of 8.
- Open and close the eyes.
- Then rub your hands till they are warm and place them over your eyes again for thirty seconds.

Another treatment for the eyes:

Candle gazing (*tratak*)
This is used to cleanse the eyes and the tear ducts. It can be done by placing a candle an arm's length away and gazing into the black part of the flame without blinking for 1–3 minutes until your eyes water. Close the eyes and visualize the flame at the point between the eyebrows; this illuminates the third eye, and improves memory and concentration. It can be used as a preliminary exercise for meditation and is easy to do at home without any fuss or setting up.

Spring is About Being Cleaner

Because this season is basically about spring-cleaning your life, this section is about what you do in life that could be toxic. It can fall into five categories:

1. Food.
2. Thoughts.
3. Body.
4. Home environment.
5. Outdoor environment.

But first, a word of warning: Only go on a detox diet if you are in full health, but not if you are frail, unwell or pregnant. If in any doubt, check with your doctor.

Food
Spring is a great time to detox as we need to cleanse the body of the heavier sustaining foods of winter.

Drink
Good detox drinks are; nettle, fresh ginger, lemon and lime juice or fennel tea. Cut back on alcohol and coffee, as they overwhelm the liver, and when trying to lose weight or build immunity, they can play havoc with blood sugar levels. Most importantly, drink plenty of water. A simple way to start is with a five-day detox:

> ### Day one
> Just vegetable juices (*home-made if possible*) to which you can add barley or wheat grasses, as the chlorophyll helps to cleanse, and a teaspoon of physillium powder, which provides bulk, lines the gut and binds the unwanted substances in the alimentary canal to prevent them from being absorbed by intestinal lining.
>
> ### Day two
> Include the above and introduce some fruits to the juices. Be aware that vegetables are more favourable.
>
> ### Day three
> Vegetables and fruits can be included without juicing; be as imaginative as possible.
>
> ### Day four
> Rice or other light unbaked and unrefined carbohydrates.
>
> ### Day five
> Include a meal of meat or fish if you are not vegetarian.

You will not feel hungry as long as your body is getting the nutrients it needs. This is why we so often crave more after indulging in highly processed foods. A detoxification programme can be as simple as the combination of eating apples and drinking plenty of water for one day to give your system a rest, or by using a detoxification pack bought from your local chemist. Another option is for you to consult your local nutritionist who can design a programme just for you.

The Mental Detox

Take a good look at your life. If you feel emotionally and physically balanced you will have healthy wood energy. If you do not feel quite right about life, look inward. Examine your life as it is. What do you like and dislike? What would you like to change? Make notes on what you would like for the coming year. Look at situations you can not change and see if you can re-frame them by changing how you view them.

What you are trying to do is make your life journey more enjoyable and worthwhile. So create a short sentence about your wishes and intentions and make sure you do not put time limitations on it. Be positive, not wishy-washy! Take some time to dwell on what you would like to change and include in your life. Remember planning a future takes some thought. Have patience, as circumstances do not change overnight.

Meditation is a very good way of taking yourself to a higher place of inspiration. Keep reminding yourself of your intentions and put them into your daily routine. Use them as your meditation. Type them out and put them in a place you look at every day, maybe the bathroom mirror or stuck at the side of your computer screen, and also say them quietly to yourself at bedtime, sowing them as seeds in the mind for the morning.

The Physical Detox

Lifestyle detoxification in the spring is for the same reasons you take a shower; you will feel refreshed, clean, rejuvenated and healthier. While detoxifying, you may choose to re-evaluate your life, clear abuses, make changes and re-dedicate yourself to a healthier lifestyle. Toxins are already inside you; most of them are simply a by-product of living in the world today so are difficult to avoid. A major source is from our highly processed and refined foods, and medications that we take also leave residue behind.

Even if you do not live in a city, there are days when you can see the pollution in the air. Energy efficient homes and offices hold air inside that could be dirtier than the air outside. Unfortunately, toxins are everywhere and if you have some bad habits of your own as well, you are only making things harder for your body. The good news is that the body is an extremely efficient detoxifying machine, and as you become cleaner and healthier, so do the choices you make. Conversely the bad news is that the body can become overburdened, so you detoxify to help your cleansing systems work better.

A few suggestions might be:

1. Detoxification bath
Use half a cup of baking soda, Epsom salts or sea salt in a bath of water. Soak for 15–20 minutes and then scrub the skin gently with soap or a natural fibre such as cotton. Within a few minutes the water will turn murky and dirty; the colour of the water is caused by heavy metals coming out of the skin (*aluminium and mercury*). Take a weekly bath during a detox and monthly for maintenance.

2. Sauna/steam bath
Turkish baths sweat out the impurities, and are readily available in most gyms and sports complexes. Do not forget to replace the fluid lost by drinking fresh filtered water.

3. Aromatherapy treatments
Have a detoxifying aromatherapy massage, using such oils as lavender for irritability or mandarin for emotional release, (*good for PMT too*). An aromatherapist will advise and carry out treatment, but the focus should be on detoxifying and cleansing for this time of year.

The Home Detox

Toxin-free cleansing products should be used to take the toxic load off the liver. Spring is an important time for cleaning and harmonizing the energy of your home.

- **Clear out** any unused items, reducing clutter so that you can fill your home once again with a new invigorated atmosphere.
- **Curb chemicals**; try to avoid spray cleaning products (*i.e. oven cleaner, air freshener*) insect killer, glue, perfumes, and polishes. Use water-based paint wherever possible and keep the home well-ventilated.
- **Avoid chemical-based products**; hair dyes, sunscreens, hairsprays and deodorisers, as prolonged use can cause headaches, dizziness or allergic reactions. Start using perfumes and body lotions made only from plant essences.
- **Reduce toxic vapours** through the way cleaning products are used; ensure windows are open for good ventilation and start using environmentally-friendly products.
- **Change any furniture** that does not correctly support the body, especially beds and chairs. Tiredness can be a symptom of a chair causing bad posture — it should be providing good lower back support. An uncomfortable bed can also cause bad sleep or back pain. Assess whether your bed supports your spine and allows the shoulders and hips to lie comfortably.
- **Dust and dirt** can release bacteria into the air, or emit toxins, so clean the house regularly by vacuuming and dusting. EMF (*Electro-magnetic fields*) generated by household electrical equipment can exacerbate stress levels, and trigger allergies.
- **Cut down** on the use of electricity as much as possible and remove electrical equipment from bedrooms.
- **Increase the number of house plants** in your home; they filter out air pollutants (*spider plants are especially effective*). Avoid plants in your bedrooms.

Food Section

Seasonal Eating for Spring

The secret of our daily diet is to find balance and the correct fuel suitable for our constitution, condition, activity and lifestyle.

Spring Cooking

In spring we should have a lighter diet, so stir-fry vegetables, especially new spring greens, eaten warm or hot, especially as the weather is still cool at this time of year. It is time to see things in new ways and a change of diet is not only helpful, but vital in order to do this.

As the first season of the year, spring represents youth, so choose small young vegetables and foods as opposed to larger, older or reheated ones. Remember, what you put in, you get out! Eat food as near to its natural state as possible so that you do not waste energy converting it back. You need a smooth flow of energy for moving forward.

When cutting back on alcohol and coffee, drink; nettle, fennel tea, lemon and ginger tea, or soda, and plenty of water.

Raw and sprouted foods can be consumed if there are signs of heat or after large amounts of heat-producing physical activity. Most people benefit from taking a little bit of raw food daily, which can be gradually increased in spring in preparation for the summer as the climate gets warmer. They are excellent for cleansing and renewing the mind and body, as they take us back to our ancient roots and times of eating more simply, but must not be used by those with a weak digestion or bowel inflammation.

The organs for this time of year are the liver and gallbladder. Food and nutrition play a major role in their health and ability to function.

The Liver Imbalance

In our modern and highly pressurised world, the liver, and subsequently the gallbladder, can easily become obstructed, congested or overloaded with too much fat, chemicals and toxic substances (*and even thoughts and emotions*), which can then disrupt their role within the body. When this happens, the energy flow in the body is hampered, which results in a wide range of physical and emotional symptoms.

The digestive system is also affected because stress on the liver can affect the function of the spleen, pancreas and stomach, causing; bloating, ulcers, diabetes, inflammation and gas. This in turn influences the intestines leading to inflammatory conditions such as colitis or enteritis.

What to do?
Less is more, do less and have more energy. Cut down on overload in all areas and reduce stress on the liver. **Food that is a blood tonic or cleanser** helps with the essential function of the liver. **Blood tonics are** chlorophyll-rich foods; anything that is green (*such as wheat grass, etc.*); spirulina, dark grapes, raspberries, beetroot and even organic animal livers are useful (*like is used to treat like*). There is also a wide range of excellent herbs available through a local herbalist, Chinese medicine or acupuncture clinics.

Food for the Spring Energy

Mung beans, seaweeds, sprouted foods are excellent for liver rejuvenation; parsley, kale, watercress and a course of essential fatty acids (*omega 3, 6 and 9*) is recommended. It is thought that infants not having mother's breast milk can also lead to allergies and a weaker liver or immune system later in life.

Top tips

* Nettle tea is a great blood cleanser. Another key component is not to eat late at night, so that you use the liver/gallbladder energy to cleanse rather than digest.

* **Watch out for heat in the liver**: (*caused by a highly competitive lifestyle, intoxicants, fats, meat, eggs and cheese*), symptoms are a red tongue with a yellow coating, red eyes, constipation, a desire for cold fluids, resulting in migraines and high blood pressure. Use raw and detoxifying foods, bitter and sour tastes, e.g. lemon and lime, which can also help. Try to identify areas of stress in your life and deal with them. Increase doing things for the fun of it, and include more spontaneity in your life.

* **If dealing with past addiction to drugs or alcohol**, use all the previously mentioned cleansers; chlorophyll, spirulina and seaweeds in vegetable juices (especially carrot), beetroot, apple, celery, fennel and lime. Regular short fasts once a month, on fruit and vegetables, are invaluable. Favour vegetables more than fruit, as they are easier on the blood sugar levels, which may have been upset because of the addictions.

Eat food in season, see the following list and look at your local fruit shop or farmers market for what is fresh and grown locally. Eating freshly picked, locally grown food gives you the right fuel for creating the correct internal climate for the external climate around you; buy organic if you can and avoid all processed foods. It also gives you more energy as refrigeration, transportation and microwave cooking rob the food of its vital life force.

The Food List

Each season has a particular taste said to harmonize the organ of the season.

Sour is the taste for the liver and gallbladder, bringing the sour taste into your diet in the springtime will support these organs. Examples of sour foods are; lemon, vinegar, sauerkraut, apples, pickles, plums, lime and green tea. Sour has a yin cooling quality and an astringent effect, which is most active in the liver and gallbladder, counteracting the effect of greasy food and helping the digestive system to dissolve minerals. Sour is good for the mind as it plays a role in organizing scattered mental patterns and for helping those people who have changing personalities.

[Handwritten note: Sour/Acid cuts through grease]

Be aware that too much of any one flavour can also have a reaction. In this case an excessive use of the sour flavour tends to toughen flesh or thicken skin, hence the expression to be 'thick skinned' as a description for someone who is insensitive.

Foods for the Wood Element

Artichokes	Endive	Lentils	Sweet potato
Beans	Fennel	Millet	Spelt
Beetroot	Green beans	Olive oil	Sesame seeds
Brown rice	Green vegetables	Parsley	Strawberries
Carrots	Kale	Peaches	Turmeric
Chicory	Leeks	Quinoa	Watercress
Chicken	Lemons	Radish	

Eat more

Brown and basmati rice (whole grain)	Home-made fruit juices	Rice milk
Clear consommé soups	Hummus	Rice pasta
Fresh herbs	Oatcakes	Salads
Fresh spring greens	Porridge	Sunflower seeds
Fruit	Pumpkin seeds	Vegetables in general
	Rice cakes	Vegetable soups

Cooking Style

The best cooking methods for spring are; steaming, marinating, boiling, stir frying or minimal simmering, as these keep the foods light. Not using heavy fats gives them a rising, aerated quality and supports nature's upward and expansive activity. Cook foods for a shorter time, at a higher temperature, so that they remain crisp and crunchy. (*Avoid all re-heated foods.*)

Eight Food and Nutrition Tips

1. **The morning** is an important time for cleansing since it is the time you have been without food the longest, so cleansing foods with high natural water content are great!
2. **Detox** one day, one week or the whole month. As usual, this means cutting down on alcohol, tea and coffee. Eat food as near to the way it was originally grown or as fresh as possible, and try to avoid processed, microwaved or re-heated food. Avoid plastic, take the wrapping off foods as soon as you buy them or avoid buying plastic wrapped products altogether; they are a source of oestrogenic nonylphenols, and are considered to promote weight gain and male fertility issues. As the weather becomes warmer, start eating spring greens, stir-fries and steam-fries.
3. **Take some** good quality omega oils and plenty of cleansing filtered water to help the system to get moving again. The water should be as close to room temperature as possible; so no ice. If you want to clean something, warm water is best: the same for internal cleansing.
4. **Include chlorophyll** (*found in green vegetables*) in your diet, because it helps to remove drug deposits, counteracts toxins and deactivates carcinogens.
5. **Eat organic food**: keep it real and not refined.
6. **Take milk thistle** to give the liver a boost. Have one daily tbsp of flax seed oil on salads, or steamed vegetables.
7. Some believe a **small amount of alcohol**, half a glass of red wine, or beer can help the gallbladder breakdown cholesterol.
8. **Enjoy good food and good company** so that your soul is satisfied too! **Introduce spirulina into your life;** it is one of the green super foods, full of vitamin B_{12}, which is great for liver support. (*It is available at your local health food shop or practitioner, in powder or tablet form.*)

Cut down or avoid alcohol, tea, coffee, saturated fats, (*cheese, cream, eggs and fat from meat*), chocolate, oranges, peanuts, refined convenience foods, oily greasy foods, excessively processed or baked wheat, chemical additives, artificial colourings, preservatives, ready-made meals and tinned foods, remember that the liver loves freshness!

Reduce dairy intake (*milk, yoghurt, cheese*) as the liver and gallbladder hate large amounts of cold fats, meat, sugar (*sweets, cakes or puddings*), white bread and white rice.

Exercise and Movement Section

This section will show you various ways to stimulate the energy lines appropriate for this time of year. As you read earlier, each season has a pair of organs that are complementary and particular to it. The diagrams below show how the lines run down the sides of the body and up the inner thigh to the chest. This section includes exercises, which move energy in these areas to energize the liver and gallbladder.

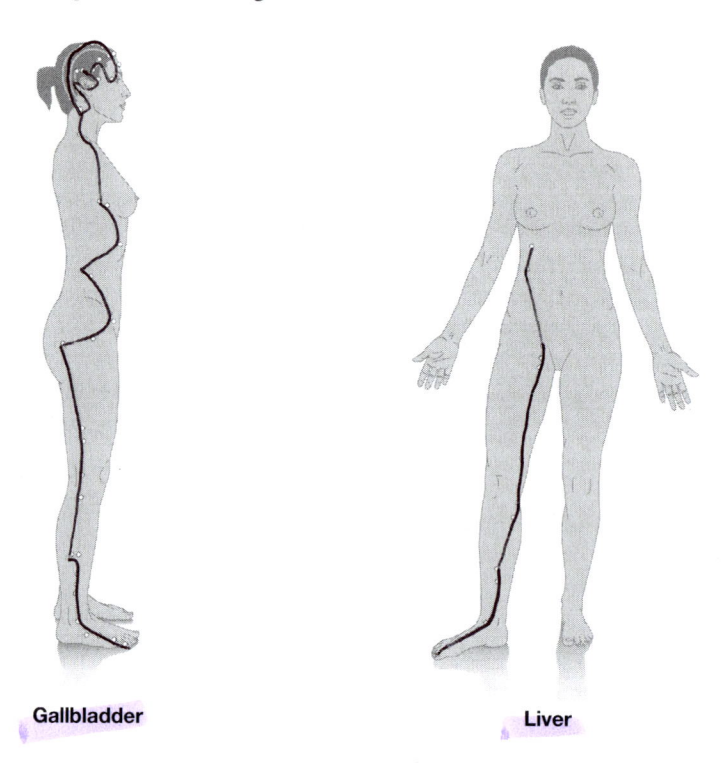

Gallbladder   **Liver**

Exercise for Spring

The Wood element of spring is all about needing to be challenged and stretched into the new season, cleansing and re-oxygenating the body, so physical stretching is vital at this time. It is most important to do lots of side bending and squats in order to open up the energy pathways for the liver and gallbladder.

Ideal types of exercise for spring include:

- Yoga class
- T'ai chi
- Low intensity aerobics
- Body pump
- Squash or tennis
- Any stretch-based classes
- Chi kung (*qigong*)
- Punch bag for home use
- Shadow boxing

Eight Spring Exercise Tips

1. **Start a weight-training regime** or focus on muscles, joints and tendons. Excessively heavy exercise is not recommended, so stick to lighter weights and include a lot of stretching before and after the session.
2. **Include some cardiovascular exercise** as you need to sweat a bit!
3. As the weather starts to get better and the new growth starts, watching the rising energy outdoors motivates us to exercise, so **get out there and feel the fresh air on your skin** in the warmer spring days. Time to get out of the gym and go for a walk, jog or cycle.
4. How do you feel in the mornings? **Take up early morning exercise** as the liver loves it, and you can pick up on nature's rising energy! Try some early morning yoga. (*Look at the spring yoga pages for an ideal sequence*.)
5. **Do something different** or opposite to your usual routine. Is there an area of your body (*or your life*) you are stuck with and not moving? Get a personal trainer to give you a new approach to an exercise routine. Workout with a friend, as it pushes you into a commitment.
6. **Try out shadow boxing**, t'ai chi, martial arts or kick boxing to release pent-up negative energy that you might feel is directed at you.
7. **Take part in competitive sport** at this time of year, and do things that release a little bit of aggression, anger or frustration in a non confrontational way, which if not released can injure the liver. Shouting, dancing or supporting a team relieves any pent up energy. Other ideal exercises are eye to ball sports such as tennis and badminton.
8. It could be a big step for you to start an exercise regime if you have been fairly inactive during the winter. **You need to ease into your spring exercise routine** so if you are at all unsure about your overall health your first step should be to visit your doctor. That is especially important if you have not been active for a long while or if you have not had a recent medical check up. That way, your doctor can identify any potential problems or concerns before you start putting your body through its paces.

Qigong for Spring

Bo (or Collecting) points are located on the chest, abdomen or waist. They are used both for diagnosis and treatment, and are where the energy collects or gathers from each of the relevant organs. These points can become tender either spontaneously or on the application of pressure; in treatments they are used to regulate and balance the energy in their associated organs. The organ meridians are energy pathways that lead to and from a major organ, and pressure points along them are where the energy is particularly accessible from the surface. The initials and numbers refer to the particular acupressure point along an organ meridian. You can gently massage these points using the tips of the thumb, index and middle fingers.

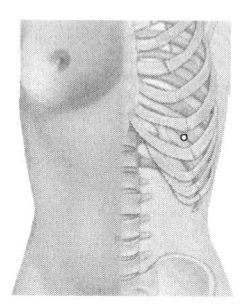

Qimen (Cycle Gate, LR 14) between the sixth and seventh rib below the nipples, used for testing and balancing the function of the liver.

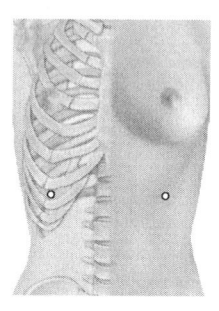

Riyue (Sun and Moon, GB 24) between the seventh and eighth rib below the nipples, used for testing and balancing the function of the gallbladder.

Re-energize the Brain and Detoxify the Liver

Raise your hands above your head with the palms facing forward as you inhale, draw fists down and rotate the wrists so the palms face inwards, pulling down strongly as you exhale through the mouth making a 'SHHH' sound which purges the liver. When the fists reach the level of LR 14 (between the sixth and seventh ribs), turn the hands downwards, shaking the energy strongly out of the tips of the fingers.

Great in the mornings or if hung-over

A Stretch for Opening the Gallbladder Meridian

As you inhale, take a step forward with your left foot in front of the right foot; at the same time, interlace your fingers palms down in front of your navel, sinking down to root into the legs. Inhale and raise your arms over your head, rotating the palms upwards, while rising on to the ball of your right foot, pressing the fourth toe (the end of the Gallbladder meridian) into the ground. Exhale while twisting to the left to look at your right foot over your left shoulder. Inhale to lengthen and exhale to twist still further; this can be repeated up to five more times. Then step back to centre and repeat, stepping across to the left with your right foot. Repeat several times on each side to open and stretch the Gallbladder meridian.

Problems digesting fats? Then give your gallbladder a boost of Qi

A Stretch to Open the Liver Meridian and Increase Your Energy Flows

Stand with your legs as wide apart as possible, keeping the spine straight and with your hands in the groin crease; inhale, and as you exhale, bend your right knee while keeping your left leg straight and the foot pointing forwards and completely flat on the floor. (To increase the stretch, turn your body slightly over the left leg.) Repeat on the other side, bending your left knee.

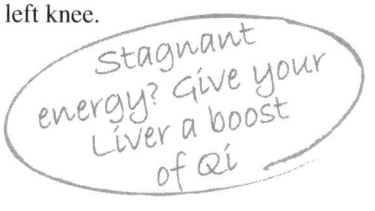

Stagnant energy? Give your Liver a boost of Qi

Embracing the Tiger's Head

This exercise increases flexibility, tones the waist, and massages the digestive organs.

Stand in a wide horse stance with head and spine erect, and keeping the hips and legs still throughout. Have your right arm (*hand fisted*) curved out in front of you at chest level and your left hand (*softly fisted*) slightly out to the side of your left waist. Working from your centre and turning in the waist turn to the left (*without moving the hips and legs*) then turning to the right swing the left fist forward and bring the right fist slightly out to the side of the right waist. Alternate from side to side without tilting as if turning the wheel of a car. Use natural breathing.

Trim the waist and re-charge your digestive system

Activating the Gallbladder

Burn your fat!

Inhale and raise arms above your head, palms facing each other; bend your body as far as you can to the left, pressing firmly down through the right foot and keeping your torso aligned and feeling the stretch down the right side.

Exhale intensely and bring your hands, made into soft fists, level with GB24 (*below the nipples between the seventh and eighth rib*) coming into a stooped position with your knees bent, as if sitting back into a chair. Inhale as you rise up, arms above the head again and repeat stretching to the right. Repeat this eight times on each side.

Stretch to Massage the Organs

Inhale, draw your right hand in an arc over your head, palm down. Put your weight on the right leg, lifting the left heel off the ground without sticking the hip out. Breathe out as you bend over to the left, and hold for one second. Inhale, then as you exhale, stretch a little further (*or pulsing three to six times*). Inhale and return to the upright position and centralise your weight between both feet. Repeat on the other side, raising your left hand over your head.

To increase the power of the stretch you can gaze down to the side of the raised heel.

The Wise Owl Gazes Behind

With your feet facing forwards and about shoulder-width apart, place your hands at your sides with your thumbs level with the indent on the side of the buttocks (GB30). Keep the hips and feet facing forwards, inhale and turn in the waist to the left to look behind, drawing the energy into your eyes as you focus on a point behind you with a glare. Exhale and return to the front, relaxing the eyes and letting them soft focus, repeat to the right. Repeat eight times on both sides.

Tired eyes? Give your eyes a boost

Ten Dragons Run Through the Forest

For the common cold lodged in the head leading to a headache and foggy thinking, or to help with decision-making and improve memory.

Place the fingertips of both hands on the front of the hairline on either side of the midline, with fingers pointing towards the back of the head. Inhale and rub all ten fingers along the scalp from the front of the hairline over the head and down the neck. Once you reach the shoulders, draw your hands out over the shoulders and visualize gathering up the Qi and throwing it away as you exhale through the nose.

Try this to improve your memory and decision-making

Part 1: The Season of Spring   29

Strengthening Your Roots

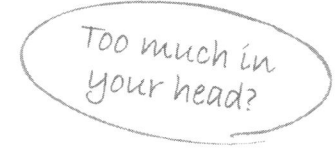

Too much in your head?

Stand with your feet apart in a wide horse stance and place the palms of your hands together. Inhale: bend your right leg and turn at the waist over the extended left leg. Exhale: slide your hands down the side of the left leg and over the toes, and inhale as you draw them up the inside of the leg up to LR 14. Then repeat to the right. Repeat several times on both sides, sinking slightly deeper each time.

Pulling Down the Heavens

Try this to re-balance and re-group

This can be used to end any sequence or close a session.

Begin with your feet hip-width apart and your hands palms up in front of the navel. Inhale and exhale through the nose, using abdominal breathing. Inhale and raise your arms out to the sides with the palms facing downward, absorbing the (Yin) energy from the earth into the body through your palms. At shoulder height, turn them up to absorb the Yang energy from the heavens into the body, as your hands continue to rise overhead. Exhale and begin descending the palms down the front of the body with the fingertips pointing towards each other. The palms face down to direct the Qi flow down the entire body and deep into the abdomen (lower dantian).

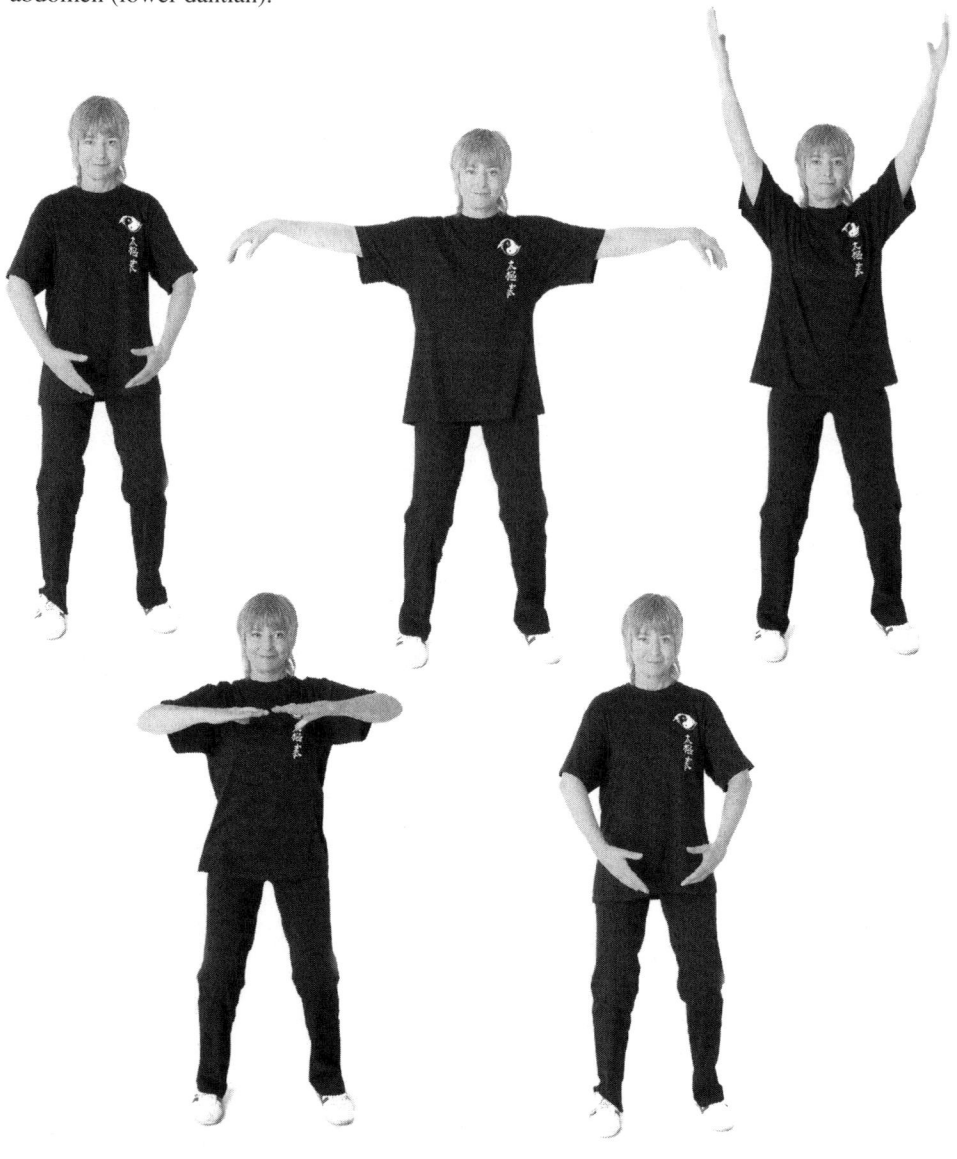

T'ai Chi Moves for Spring

Need to sharpen your wits?

For precision, co-ordination, focus and release of tensions.

Start with feet slightly wider than hip-width apart, hands at your sides (*palms down*). Step out to the left, turning the left foot out ninety degrees. The left arm 'chops' out to the left fully extended with the fingers extending out and the palm down. At the same time fist your right hand, palm up, at your right hip. With your body facing fully to the left, fist the left hand and spiral it back to the left hip, rotating the palm up, while at the same time releasing the right fist forward and spiralling it palm down. Then step the left foot back to the original starting position, drawing your hands down in front of you, palms pushing toward the ground. Repeat several times to the right and to the left, returning to the centre each time.

Now step forward with the left foot, raising the left elbow so the hand comes in front of the face, then turn the palm outwards with the forearm parallel to the ground. At the same time punch the right fist forward in a spiral punch. Then return to centre. Repeat stepping forward with the right foot and raising the right hand and punching with the left, always returning to centre.

Lastly step back on the left leg, raising the right arm and punching with the left. Then having returned to centre, repeat, stepping back on the right leg.

Now repeat the full sequence one after the other, or randomly as a response test. A double punch can be added in the forward and back sections as well, by drawing the raised hand back to a fist at the hip palm up, as the opposite hand punches forwards rotating the fist palm down. Then punching it forwards palm down and drawing the opposite fist back to the hip palm down. This sharpens response and invigorates the qi.

Yoga for Spring

Tips for Enhancing the Wood Element

Spring is a time for new and rising energy. It is the time to work on your foundation within the poses, providing strong roots to grow out of, giving you both stability and strength. Cleansing poses are used at this time of year, to prepare the body for the coming year.

The Language of the Mind

The Sensation
It is one thing to perform the asana, but it is another thing to feel it. Place lots of emphasis on focusing and fixing the eye; if the liver is depressed it is the eye that cannot see the way out.

It is about the smooth flow of energy while getting in and out of the pose. Do not be wooden in the pose, stay soft and strong. Spring is all about moving out of stagnation. It is also very important to focus on challenging yourself a little within the pose.

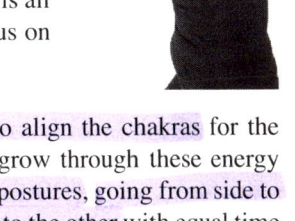

It is important to have a strong trunk to align the chakras for the correct passage of energy, so you can grow through these energy centres. The emphasis is on side-bending postures, going from side to side, and moving from one side of the mat to the other with equal time and energy spent on each side.

Twists are a main focus in the spring, almost like wringing yourself out! It is a good idea to put a twist in after each pose, because after winter the waist is often thicker than at any other time of year. This is because the body makes extra padding, protecting the kidneys from the cold. Therefore our main attention is placed on the belt meridian, which as the name implies, runs around the waist connecting all the main meridians that run through it.

The end result is a much trimmer waist line ... always a welcome sight as the lighter, more revealing clothes of summer emerge.

To start the spring programme, get the foundation and rooting established.

Mountain Pose or Tadasana

This posture brings the feeling of the precise alignment of the pelvis, which provides the correct foundation and root for the spine. Move from standing pelvic tilt position (*navel to spine*) to arch (*sticking the tailbone out*) then adjust the pelvis to find the pelvic centre or neutral spine.

Feel equal foundation through the feet; the big toe and the little toe should have equal pressure. The weight on the pad at the front of the foot should be equal to the heel. The knees are not locked back, but pull up in the front of the thighs, and with navel to spine, lengthen ribs out of hips, keeping the shoulders down, neck long. Perform deep relaxed breathing.

Upward Hand Pose or Urdhva Hastasana

The feeling of rooting into the earth and growing powerfully upward toward the sky. Feeling the energies of earth and heaven with your centre in between.

The Breath

During all yoga and sports practice, the body requires you to breathe. It happens unconsciously, but when you are looking for a certain type of breath to enhance your practice, it becomes strangely difficult! The breath helps fuel the muscles. If you breathe properly you have more energy and feel calmer. A swami, at a weekend workshop of yoga, once told me that if you slow down your breath you lengthen your life, as life is measured in breaths; this made perfect sense to me.

So we breathe in through the nose and out of the nose, and during practice, this also helps to warm the breath. Keep the in-breath the same length as the out-breath. Try to not hold your breath, keep the 'inhale' for the lengthening moves and the 'exhale' for the static part or flexion. As you become more advanced, introduce Ujjayi breathing. Breathe in through the nose, the feeling in the nose is like a passage for the air, not a sniff. The breath comes from the dimples just below the collarbones, which you can feel with your thumb and index finger while we practice. Feel the chest lift slowly, while you hear a breath sound. On the exhale, breathe out from the same area, making a sound similar to Darth Vader (*Star Wars!*). With practice you will feel the calming effect and then work on building this into your yoga practice when you feel able to do so.

Spring—Focus is on the Inner Eye and the Liver and Gallbladder

Focus inward, and think about posture and breath, as well as your foundation, strength and waist awareness.

Tadasana

Wake up the Liver and start the day

1 Stand in Tadasana, feel foundation through feet. **2** Inhale as you reach upwards, pull in the navel to bring centre awareness. **3** Step feet hip-width apart, push down with left foot, inhale and stretch to right side reaching up and pushing down at the same time. Exhale to return to the centre. **4** Change sides pushing into right foot, lengthen toward left side on the inhale. **5** Exhale while returning to centre.

1

2

3. Inhale

4. Inhale

5. Exhale

Firm foundation on the feet

Focus Foundation

6 Bring right heel to the top of the thigh, push in with the foot and back out with the thigh to get a firm hold, concentrate on standing leg, fix gaze ahead, push palms together, relax shoulders down and wide, pull in waist, breathe; hold for three breaths. **7** Repeat other side. **8** Step feet leg length apart. Virabhadrasana 2 (*Warrior 2*) shoulders down arms long. **9** Take left hand and rest on back leg, move hand down inhaling as you stretch through right side.

Vrksasana (Tree Pose)

Stretch yourself out of life's stagnations

6. Fix your eyes ahead on a fixed spot

7. Fix your eyes to balance. Push your foot into your leg, and your leg into your foot

Virabhadrasana 2 (Warrior 2 Pose)

Virasana 2 Pose (Back Lean Pose)

Reverse Warrior

8. Front knee over toe

9. Breathe as you lean back

10 Exhale transition into side angle pose, rest elbow weightlessly on right knee, stretch arm overhead, look up at fingertips. **11** Change sides and repeat as above.

Utthita Parsvakonasana
(Side Angle Pose)

Need to come down to earth?

10. Inhale and lengthen

11. Exhale in transition

Focus on flow — move with ease like the wind bending the trees

→ Exhale in transition →

12. Inhale and stretch back

13. Inhale and reach

14 Start in wide horse stance to build foundation strength. **15** Keep rooted, drop right arm, lift left overhead and stretch to right side from the waist, keeping hips firmly centred, lengthen as you breathe. **16** Change sides, then… **17** Back to wide horse stance. **18** Sink lower into wide horse stance. **19** Then repeat waist stretch, and for a third time sink lower and repeat. **20** Straighten legs and stretch… relief.

→ Exhale in transition →

14. Five breaths

15. Inhale

16. Inhale

17. Five breaths

18. Exhale

19. Repeat three times, breathing in each time you stretch

20

Transition? [handwritten]

21 Turn out left foot, bend knee to soften joints, reach for the foot, floor or ankle. **22** Move away from the foundation into Trikonasana (*Full Triangle Pose*) head level with body and tailbone. **23** Drop right hand on the outside of the left foot, twist the body around lengthening the left hip back, creating more length so rotation can increase. Bend knee if you can not reach, or take hand only to outer thigh. **24** Inhale and come up back into wide horse stance, then to other side, as below. **25** Make sure in the spring that you link poses that open and close the body in flow from one side to the other (*as below*), from Utthita Trikonasana (*Extended Triangle Pose*) to Parivrtta Trikonasana (*Revolved Triangle Pose*).

Utthita Trikonasana
(Extended Triangle Pose)

The morning after detox [handwritten]

21

22

Parivrtta Trikonasana
(Revolved Triangle Pose)

23

24. Five breaths

25. Inhale and exhale as you change sides

26. Inhale as you twist

Trikonasana Sequence

Intermediate flow; these poses are for people who have had some previous class experience.

**Utthita Trikonasana
Extended Triangle Pose**

**Parivrtta Trikonasana
Revolved Triangle Pose**

Parsvakonasana Sequence

**Utthita Parsvakonasana
Extended Side Angle Pose**

**Parivrtta Parsvakonasana
Revolved Side Angle Pose**

Modification for the above right pose

Feeling stuck? Get moving with this daily practice

Parighasana Sequence

1 Keep flowing from the last page. **2** Go onto all fours. **3** Put the left hand on the floor directly under the shoulder, then extend the right foot to the side, pushing the other foot onto the floor. Inhale as you stretch. **4** Back to all fours. **5** Put the right hand down under the shoulder and extend the left leg. Inhale. **6** Exhale back to all fours. **7** Repeat, then **8** adding the extra waist stretch by sliding your hand down the straight leg to get deeply into the liver. Now repeat the sequence on the other side.

42 Seasonal Yoga: A fusion of yoga and tai chi combined with lifestyle tips for every season

Smile whilst you practice even if it's only an inner one!

9. Put your left hand on the floor directly under your left shoulder

10. Flip and do other arm

11. Transition move

12. Rest as long as you need

13. Now on the other side

14. Stretch deeply into your liver

15

16

Go back to (13) and then repeat (14–16) on other side

Konasana Sequence

Feeling tired and lethargic? Re-motivate with these!

1 Keep sitting bones firmly rooted on the floor and the spine as long as possible. **2** As you stretch to the side, push the opposite sitting bone into the floor; this helps anchor the stretch. Breathe in as you stretch while making the effort (2, 3, 4, 5) and breathe out on the relaxation phase (1 and 6) between each stretch and change sides. **7** Do not push this too far.

Janu Sirsasana (Knee Head Pose) Sequence

Intermediate poses for people who have yoga class experience.

1

2. Breathe and lengthen as you rotate

3. Breathe and lengthen

4. Sweep leg around behind

5. Into half pigeon. Lower gently into this pose, being mindful of knee issues

Lost your vision or sense of humour? Gain a new perspective on things!

6. Sweep left leg around over top of right knee, and keep the spine long

Then do the other side.

7. Pull navel in to spine as you extend forward

8. Lengthen spine as you rotate

9. Use the knee to gently help you round

10. Sweep leg around behind

11. Into half pigeon. Be mindful of knee flexibility

12. Sweep right leg over left

Marichyasana (Torso and Leg Stretch) Sequence

Feeling indecisive? Try this!

1 Cross legs, then lift the left leg over the right thigh, inhale as you take right arm and wrap around left leg, rest left fingers on floor, lengthen spine from foundation, look over left shoulder. **2** Take body around in the opposite direction putting both hands on the floor. Lift your hips up, keeping feet where they are as you rotate around in a spiral. **3** Spiral around on both feet. **4** Keep turning. **5** Then finish with opposite leg raised. Have fun and move from side-to-side, increasing your hip flexibility.

Shavasana

Complete with this for a short time after every practice, ideally for ten minutes.

Time to relax

Take a big deep breath in and a long exhale out. Cover yourself with a blanket for shavasana if possible.

Meditations and Contemplations for Spring

In these sections we use the **controlling cycle of the Elements**. Just as one Element supports the next, (the supporting cycle), its energy also has a controlling effect on another. Here we use the Metal element to cut or control the Wood element by using the breath to encourage the muscles to relax.

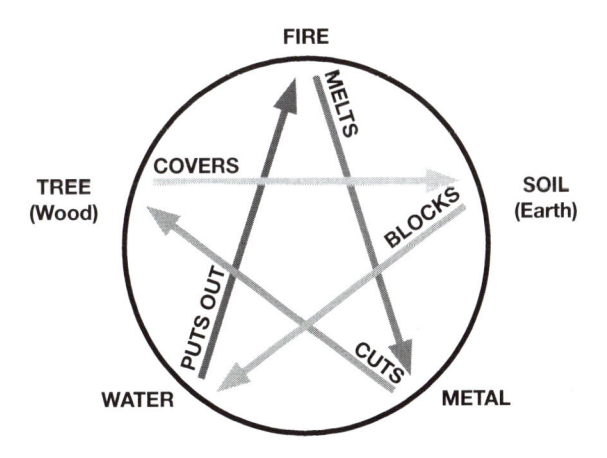

```
                    FIRE
              MELTS
     COVERS
TREE                        SOIL
(Wood)          BLOCKS      (Earth)
        PUTS OUT
                  CUTS
    WATER              METAL
```

Progressive Relaxation Meditation

This is a simple, yet powerful tool, to help you on the journey to a meditative state. It is the perfect way to unwind those tight muscles, the health and maintenance of which is governed by the liver and the gallbladder. We can learn to loosen up so that we are able to feel more clearly where our tension has accumulated. It is best performed lying down at first, and can also be used as a prelude to sleep in cases of insomnia caused by an over-active mind. Once you are familiar with the steps however, you will find it beneficial to use in any position, and throughout the day, whenever you feel unwanted tension accumulating in the body. Persevere with the practice, because each time you perform it you will be starting from a slightly lowered level of tension, so you can optimize your performance, productivity and endurance in either work or play. It is also a good foundation for other meditation methods.

- In a comfortable position close your eyes and take five to ten slow deep breaths in through the nose and out through the mouth.
- Bring your awareness to your right leg, inhale deeply and lift the leg up slightly, tensing the foot and lower leg. Tense a little tighter but avoid clenching so much that the muscles cramp. As you exhale and allow the leg to drop gently and relax completely, roll the foot from side to side.
- Now bring your attention to the right thigh and buttock. Inhale contracting your right buttock and thigh until you reach the end of the breath, then exhale and release. Now roll the entire leg from the hip socket in and out. Pause to feel the difference between the two legs and then repeat on the left side.
- Next lift your pelvic floor muscles, and draw your lower abdomen in and flat, hold for a few seconds and release on the exhalation.
- Raise your focus now to the solar plexus area, between the navel and the breastbone. Inhale, sucking your diaphragm up into the chest. Hold for a few seconds, then exhale and relax the diaphragm completely. (This is done a minimum of three times, but avoid this part if you have high blood pressure or if you have just eaten.)
- Inhale and bring the shoulder-blades together in the back, squeeze tightly then relax and exhale, allowing the upper back to broaden without collapsing the chest.
- Next bring your attention to your right arm, making the hand into a fist. Inhale as you hold the tension, then exhale and relax the arm gently, and roll the arm from side to side. Then do the same with the left arm.
- Inhale and lift both shoulders up to your ears. Hold them up and then exhale and let them drop down. (This is done a minimum of three times.)
- Inhale, and with a slight nod of the head, draw the chin back and inwards slightly to squeeze the throat. Exhale and relax keeping the back of the neck long.
- Inhale, tightening the jaw and facial muscles, squeezing tightly. Exhale and release all the tension, and then roll your head from side to side.

(Each of the above can be repeated several times, if necessary, before moving on to the next area.)

- Now body scan using the conscious awareness of the mind like a miner's lamp mentally scanning the body for any areas of residual tension. Breathe relaxation into any remaining area of tension, feeling the muscles release and soften as you exhale. You can also repeat the part of the above sequence that relates to that particular area. To energize any weak or injured part, visualize drawing healing light into it with the breathe. Continue working with the breath until the whole body is completely relaxed.

* If you find it helpful to verbalize the relaxation, you can do this by saying to yourself: "I am completely and totally relaxed, my feet and legs are relaxed, my thighs and buttocks are relaxed." Then continue throughout the body ending with; " I am totally and completely relaxed."
* Remain in this calm and relaxed state for 5–10 minutes.

Cool Down and Meditation for Spring

(handwritten note: Depressed or lost your get up and go? Try this)

Colour meditation to clean the Liver meridian and re-charge the liver

This powerful meditation makes use of the energetic attributes of colour. As mentioned previously, the five-element theory assigns a colour to each organ system; the colour strengthens deficiency in the organ it targets. Green is the colour associated with the Liver and Gallbladder. So you can **use this in cases of depression or if there is a lack of get up and go**:

* Stand in Wuji posture (feet hip-width apart); alternatively you can sit in a chair. Breathe deeply, relax your whole body and quieten your mind. Visualise any tension or tiredness melting into the ground. Place the tip of your tongue in the roof of your mouth.
* Place your right hand on the liver located on the right side of the body under the lowest part of the rib cage, and place your left hand on top. Massage with circular rotations twelve times clockwise and anti-clockwise.
* Visualise an orb of colour green in front of you or being in a forest or among trees. Inhale the clear green light, or feel the energy of the green trees flowing down into your liver on the lower right side of the rib cage. As you exhale, visualise any dark or pathogenic Qi (chi) leaving the Liver via the mouth. Repeat this until the Liver retains more and more clean green Qi.
* To create more focus, concentrate the mind under your hands, as you inhale and exhale through the nose. Exhale while pressing or squeezing the liver with your hands. Inhale and lift the hands away from the liver as you visualise the green light flowing into the organ like bellows. Repeat for twelve inhalations and exhalations.
* **This meditation can be used to benefit any of the organs by changing to the colour of the season and the position of the hands.**

A Mental Contemplation for Spring

On the screen of your mind visualize a tree to symbolize your life:
- What type of tree would it be?
- What does it represent to you?
- What is the condition of the tree and what shape is it in?
- What is the environment surrounding it, is it alone or in a forest or city? Is its environment beneficial? What is the weather condition like?

Move your attention to its roots; these represent foundation, stability and nourishment:
- What/who is the support system in your life, and what gives you a sense of stability?
- What are your foundations, what is important to you, what do you value, do you need to re-evaluate or change your belief patterns to support your life?
- Are there any positive affirmations you can meditate on, so they can take root in your life and stabilise you in these changing times?
- What do you do that nourishes you? Do you need to change your eating habits or educate yourself about nutrition?

Now focus on the trunk through which the sap (life force) rises:
- What do you draw on to give you power?
- Do you need to take a break or have a change of scenery to re-charge your batteries?
- Is there anything/or anyone sapping your strength or controlling your growth?
- Is there something you can do or take up to increase your vitality?

Lastly the branches represent your talents, gifts and opportunities:
- Is there a new area or direction you need to nurture or want to grow in?
- Is there a problem that seems to weigh you down, that you could turn into an opportunity for new growth?
- Are you overloaded or are there any old branches (attitudes or habits) that are dead and that you need to prune to improve the look of the tree?
- Are there new areas of growth you need to nuture and encourage?

Revisit the tree of life regularly to monitor its growth and development and help to maintain its structure and beauty.

Home and Lifestyle Section

Eight Home and Lifestyle Tips

1. At home, **spring clean** half the house; do not give yourself an overwhelming project. **Open the windows** and let the fresh new oxygenated air in, do one room at a time, or maybe one a week for the spring period. As you go through your spring-cleaning, add spring items to the room. Put **yellow or green** items in the room such as fresh flowers in a new vase, picture frames or cushions which can be bought inexpensively these days to create an instant fresh spring look. **Burn cleansing and invigorating** oils at this time such as grapefruit, chamomile and lavender.
2. **Eye stuff** is important, not just in spring but throughout the year. Television and computer screens make our eyes lazy so make the following a habit, just like cleaning your teeth.
   - To clean your eyes, stare at your nose for two minutes without blinking.
   - Stare at one object with one eye closed for two minutes, then repeat on the other eye.
   - Rapidly focus on one object after the other, alternating between distant and near objects for up to five minutes.
   - Inhale and roll your eyes eight to ten times in one direction, exhale and roll them in the other direction.
   - Now, as mentioned previously in this section, rub your hands and stimulate their electromagnetic field and hold them over your eyes.
3. **Scrape your tongue**; many Eastern cultures scrape their tongues in the morning — they believe this reduces the amount of germs and infections we carry, because eighty per cent of bacteria is found on the tongue, gums and cheeks. So either scrape your tongue with your toothbrush after brushing your teeth, or invest in a tongue scraper. (*Yes there is such a thing! They now have them on the back of a toothbrush, available from your local chemist or supermarket.*)
4. If you are **angry**, work out what it is and face it head-on. Write it down then take whatever action is necessary.
5. Try on last year's summer wardrobe and **throw out** anything you haven't worn in the last year.
6. **Set three new goals**, things that will enhance your life this year. Then think of two things you can do to move you in the direction of each of your desired goals, and do them immediately!
7. **Start something new** this month. A new project/hobby/fitness regime/friendship or simply commit to becoming tidier.
8. Start a **new business or marketing campaign** for an existing business; it is the right time of year to do it because you have nature behind you!

In your lifestyle, avoid:

- **Becoming obsessive** about time or too fanatical about exercise.
- **A stagnant, monotonous or pressurized lifestyle**, which leaves little possibility for creativity, innovation and humour.
- **Over-eating** or eating late at night.
- **Being overbearing** or controlling.
- **Exposing yourself to too many chemicals** at work or at home.

Spring Summary

- ☑ Do you have more humour in your approach to life?
- ☑ Do you have a clear sense of direction but still enjoy living in the moment?
- ☑ Are you finding it much easier to make decisions in life?
- ☑ Have you planned your year ahead and thought about what you want to have achieved by the end of this year?
- ☑ Did you spring clean and sort out all of the messy corners and cupboards in your home?
- ☑ Are you less irritable than you were at the beginning of the season, or suffer less muscular tension as a result of stress?
- ☑ Are you more relaxed about needing things done immediately? Can you be more patient and go with the flow without the need to control every circumstance?
- ☑ Have you managed to effectively transform any anger into motivation or more zest for life?
- ☑ Do your eyes feel more rested, are the whites looking brighter, and can you see things a bit more clearly than before?
- ☑ Are you feeling clear headed and cleansed on the inside resulting from the detox programmes you have done, or at least, as a result of the moderation of toxins?
- ☑ Is your complexion more radiant and your energy more evenly distributed throughout the day?
- ☑ Have you gained from the early morning exercise or improved your flexibility with a stretching routine?
- ☑ Has your diet improved and become lighter with less saturated fats?

The season of early summer

21 May

The Space Element

The subject at this time of year is all about connection - Early Summer is the element of space connecting with and living with the atmosphere bringing all the elements together, just like the skin (the largest piece of connective tissue in the body) holds the body together.

space

Energy resides, and can be felt in space which is why space in the body created in the yoga and Chi Kung practices are vital for the optimum flow of Prana/Chi and nourishment of all the internal organs and systems.

Energy is present in space

The Early Summer is the secondary part of the fire element, which comes before summer as a warm up, energetically less extreme, considered to be more preparation for the full potential of summer.

The warm up in the human body will affect the connective tissue/facia, the component that binds us together and where you feel the result of movement or stretch in the body. Comparing this to Grand Prix racing in the essential pre race laps, where connecting rubber to the road to warm up the tyres for optimum performance and the driver for optimum focus.

Early Summer starts around 21st of May where the spring has finished its growth time but the summer has not yet started.

If Summer is the time of maximum potential, and we are part of the nature that surrounds us, we can see how nature combines the growth of spring with the expansion of Early Summer in order to reach its fullness. Like warming up before a strong workout nature has Early Summer, and then late summer is considered to be the cool down stage.

The Feeling of Early Summer

A time of inner and outer abundance so we share love unconditionally, give and receive warmth, respond appropriately to meet the tasks at hand, yet know when and with whom to be open or when we need to be more protective.

Part Two

Connection - the key word

That word has so many meanings and modern day connotations.
Heart connection, social connection, connective tissue in the body binding us together, and the obvious do you have a connection? This applies to the internet that has taken over as the most used variation of it!

Years ago the word would have meant to touch or reach out or attach to someone or something. Now it means to be connected to the invisible lines of communication that in turn are causing us to be totally disconnected from who we actually are!

Connecting to the world via these lines are disconnecting us from our true selves.
Who are we? So we become victims of our social profile!

If you are in a heightened state of social media addiction, you start to lose connection with what is you and who you are? Perform the practices or movements in this book to re-establish this link.

Connecting with self is the key. As a student of yoga or even a teacher of it, unless there is a connection with your internal intelligence, there will be no ability to react to your imbalances and rebalance them. A balanced life is about constantly correcting your imbalances, learning how to listen to them and then knowing how to deal with them - cerebral communication!

If Early Summer was a person

Their nature would be someone who is an agent for happiness, who is calm, confident and communicative and knows how to relate to people, family and friends appropriately. They are connecters, great networkers who are self assured, happy in their own skin, helpful and learns from experience. Generous and emotionally stable, they allow life to flow through them, and are not afraid to talk about their emotions and how they feel. They can be great at helping people to work together as a team, to orchestrating events and galvanizing others into action. They like to have everything in its proper place, but can be over re-active or hyper sensitive if over worked or stressed.

So it makes sense to develop the positive qualities and watch out for the negative at this time of year to match the energy of the Early Summer season.

If you feel out of balance at the moment, these are the issues that might come up in Early Summer to be dealt with:

- [ ] If you are tired do you become over sensitive to what people say or be easily offended?
- [ ] Do you have issues around rejection or feeling left out?
- [ ] Do you suffer allergic reactions regularly? ?
- [ ] Do you suffer from hyper mobility or excessive tension and is there a healthy balance between your flexibility and strength
- [ ] In social situations do you ever feel, shy, vulnerable or become over protective?
- [ ] How is your body's temperature control and thermostat?
- [ ] Do you always feel responsible for the happiness/mood of others?
- [ ] Do you feel that your body easily takes the shape of your negative thoughts so you feel rigid, defensive or withdrawn
- [ ] How is your immune system, is it working intelligently or does it attack you?
- [ ] How is your internal body clock? This schedules your sleep, eating and other bodily functions to happen at the right time.
- [ ] Do you have a stiff red tongue or suffer tension in the chest? This can indicate heat in the heart of pericardium.
- [ ] Is there a big difference in the weight distribution between the upper and lower body or visually a difference between the upper, middle and lower portions of the face?
- [ ] Do you allow life to flow easily and effortlessly?
- [ ] Do you have a healthy relationship with social media?
- [ ] Do you having difficulty in choosing the appropriate way to respond in certain situations?
- [ ] Are you permanently on line ?

Eight Priorities for Early Summer

1. **Cultivate positive emotional state especially before sleep**. This is because according to our bodies biological clock, the pericardium, (the sac protecting the heart and the organ of Early Summer) is at its most influential around the hours of 7 pm and 9 pm. Too much negative emotional stimulation can have an impact on the heart being able to rest and can create tension in the fascia (triple burner). Our body, it is said, takes the shape of our thought and feelings.

2. **Communicate your needs**, ideas and feelings so others can understand and respond to how you feel. So that you don't close off or become a martyr.

3. **Balance your exercise regimes** working on your health on all the 5 levels. Body, including diet, energy levels by including rest and down time, emotions by being positive, mind by observing the quality of your thoughts, and spiritual taking time out to nurture your higher self.

4. **Practice increasing flexibility** or practice the Dao-yin of the Dragon daily Dao-yin of the Dragon is an ancient Taoist practice, which energetically strengthens and detoxifies the internal systems of the body, through a deep internal massage. Practiced daily it re-aligns the spine and strengthens the nervous system, increases lung capacity, stimulates metabolism, regulates the endocrine system encourages lymphatic drainage, keeps the body flexible, supple and trim. The form is an excellent warm up for Yoga, T'ai Chi and Pilates practitioners. (see later in the Chapter)

5. **To support the immune system** learn to work on the relationship with yourself. Do not attack your self or put yourself down as this has a direct effect on our immune cells, which follow the commands of the mind. It also has a deep impact on all your other reltionships.

6. **Work on your non-verbal cues** because in the first 7 seconds non-verbal cues determine how others see and respond to you. Or whether they are drawn to you or not. Are you confident, comfortable and glad to be there? Be the kind of person who radiates pleasure and geniality, so in your presence others feel good.

7. **Convey the right messages** when it comes to hearing or seeing. According to communication expert Sonya Hamlin, we remember 85 percent of what we see and 15 percent of what we hear. Facial expressions can take attention away from what you are trying to say. Whether you are aware of it or not, you convey a message by the expression on your face, so make sure it is communicating the right message!

8. **Make speaking positive affirmations** to yourself and others a daily requirement! You will be amazed at how good your body begins to feel when you stop think negative thoughts to yourself and others all day long. How can you ever expect to feel well if you think all day?

Eight Things to Avoid for Early Summer

1. **Becoming addicted to certain types of food** because by eating them all the time you may become intolerant to them. This is why seasonal eating is so important.
2. **Looking to social media for your sense of self worth and validation.**
3. **Thinking communication is merely about the words you say** rather than body language, facial expression and all the other senses. Otherwise you will have a hard time connecting with others.
4. **Too much mental and emotional stimulation before sleep** as this can disrupt it and you will not get the depth of sleep you need.
5. **Avoid creating disorder within yourself,** as you have little control over what happens in the outer world but within yourself you do!
6. **Participating in extreme sports without warming up first** and cooling down afterwards.
7. **Reacting to things too quickly** and not allowing the thinking mind to work out how to respond appropriately.
8. **Getting into relationships that do not give you the level of affection you need** ADD (Affective Deprivation Disorder) this can give you the same symptoms as SAD (Seasonal Affective Disorder) things such as ME, sleeping and eating disorders, fatigue. PTSD (Post Traumatic Stress Syndrome), low self esteem, feelings of guilt, low immunity.

The Ideal Day in Early Summer

Morning
Get up as it is getting light, for a re-charge of energy work with hours of light, getting up with light and go to sleep when it gets dark. Warm up for the day with a practice of Yoga or Qigong ending with a seated or standing meditation this is like putting on an emotional safety belt. Eat a light breakfast perhaps with a savory composition to it.

Midday
Make sure you schedule in some down time, take a break, or move and stretch regularly, especially if working on the computer. Remember the body takes the shape of your thoughts/feelings, so stressful emails or telephone conversations can create a stress response and tensions in the body's fabric. Get away from work to have lunch so you allow the body to go into the rest and digest mode.

Afternoon
A short Yoga Nidra is an excellent way to take a pause and centre yourself in the afternoon. Your energy level is naturally slowing down, so learn to work with the natural fluctuations, and not against them.

Evening
A short Yoga or Tai Chi practice on your return home to put down the stress of the day and unwind is an ideal habit to get into all the year round. It changes your state like taking the lid off a pan to prevent it boiling over.

Before sleep
If the day has been very stressful or demanding take time to review the days events. In observing your own actions and re-actions in daily life you can learn and process the day so you are clear and ready for the next one.

Eight Daily Habits for Early Summer

1. **Live at the calm and still bottom of your ocean** – as His Holiness the Dali Lama says, our default position should be in parasympathetic mode. Sometimes it is necessary to rise to the surface and come into the strong waves and currents of life but then we should go back down. This way we preserve our energy levels and do not wear ourselves out needlessly by over reacting.
2. **Work on calmness, integration and empathy** they will hold us in good stead at this time of year
3. **Practice asking yourself** not just what you think about a given situation but how do you feel about it.
4. **Learn to practice reading faces and body language,** it can give some great insights and help to cultivate rapport with people.
5. **Work on opening and closing postures and cross patterning exercises** to move and integrate the flow of energy along the fascia.
6. **Walk a healthy line between over protection and under protection,** try not to internalize your fight and flight responses.
7. **Any exercise that brings you joy is good for you** in both the secondary (Early Summer) and full summer. It's about finding the balance between passion and peace. The key to this element is moderation.
8. **Manage your energy wisely at this time of year,** work on balancing, sharing and conserving one of the principles of Yang and Yin

Early Summer is the season to work on your connection with your self!

Early Summer energy balancing - in conscious contact
Move your attention to the inner body instead of external stimulation. Emotions will surface - dig deep get past the agitation the body needs attention.
Awareness- if you are not in your body emotions stay high in your consciousness. Work on the aspects of health needed to bring you back into present.

The five essential energy evolves!

It's such a short season Early Summer - so you can totally go to town on making a commitment to energy balance - just for a few weeks
The five aspect which need attention together ARE
1. **Alkaline diet** – see chart and explanation later in this section.

2. Filtered or Alkaline water.

   It has a higher PH and some people believe it neutralises the acid in your body, giving benefits for people with high blood pressure, diabetes, high cholesterol and it's said to help with anti ageing. These claims are being researched but there is no scientific evidence that fully verifies the claims. A few studies, however, have found that it may be helpful for certain conditions.

3. Exercise (of course) but be nice to yourself with exercise that feels easy in your body and finds space within it.
4. Meditation & pranayama to improve your head space
5. High quality super nutrients and minerals

But of course there is always the things you need to **not** do also

Five essential energy enemies - so do less of these just for a few weeks

6. No social media - it's an outside identity (or less if you can't go cold turkey)
7. Less acid foods - see the acid alkaline list later in the book
8. Less acid activities - see acid alkaline activates later in the book
9. Gossiping or harming by being cruel and non inclusive
10. Avoid exhaustion - try less rigorous routines - just for few weeks !

What is our constitutional energy and where do we get our energy type from?
The concept of vital energy

The Chinese hold the concept that we acquire our Chi or Energy from two sources:

The Original Chi originating from our parents and grandparents and dependent upon their physical, emotional and mental health as well as the country they lived in. Also what was happening in our mothers lives from the time we spent in the womb prior to birth. This they see as a deposit account of energy, our inheritance that influences our cycles of ageing and maturation. This is the energy we are born with and is often referred to as our essence or in western terminology our constitution. This is the energy we can personally do little about, although practicing Chi Kung (and yoga) is said to have a strong influence on this energy and can literally re-charge the batteries of our body, and also influences the quality of the energy that will be passed on to our children. All disciplines and practices that work on an energetic level, and in particular ones which focus on the meridians, chakras and parasympathetic nervous system can benefit our Original Chi.

The second source of energy is our current bank account energy, which, from the moment we are born, we learn to manage ourselves. It is acquired from the air we breath, the exercise we take, our environment, social interaction and the food we eat.

Both these serving to make our True Chi. our personal fundamental energy. If we manage our current account of energy wisely, this includes the energy of the mind and the emotions, and put in more than enough to cover what we are drawing out, we will live a long and healthy life. Alternatively, if we do not manage the current account wisely and run it down, we will then draw more on our inheritance or deposit account. This speeds up the cycle of ageing running our life batteries down, unlocking within it illnesses from previous generations.

Diagram 1: The 2 sources of energy / inputs to form our true energy (chi)

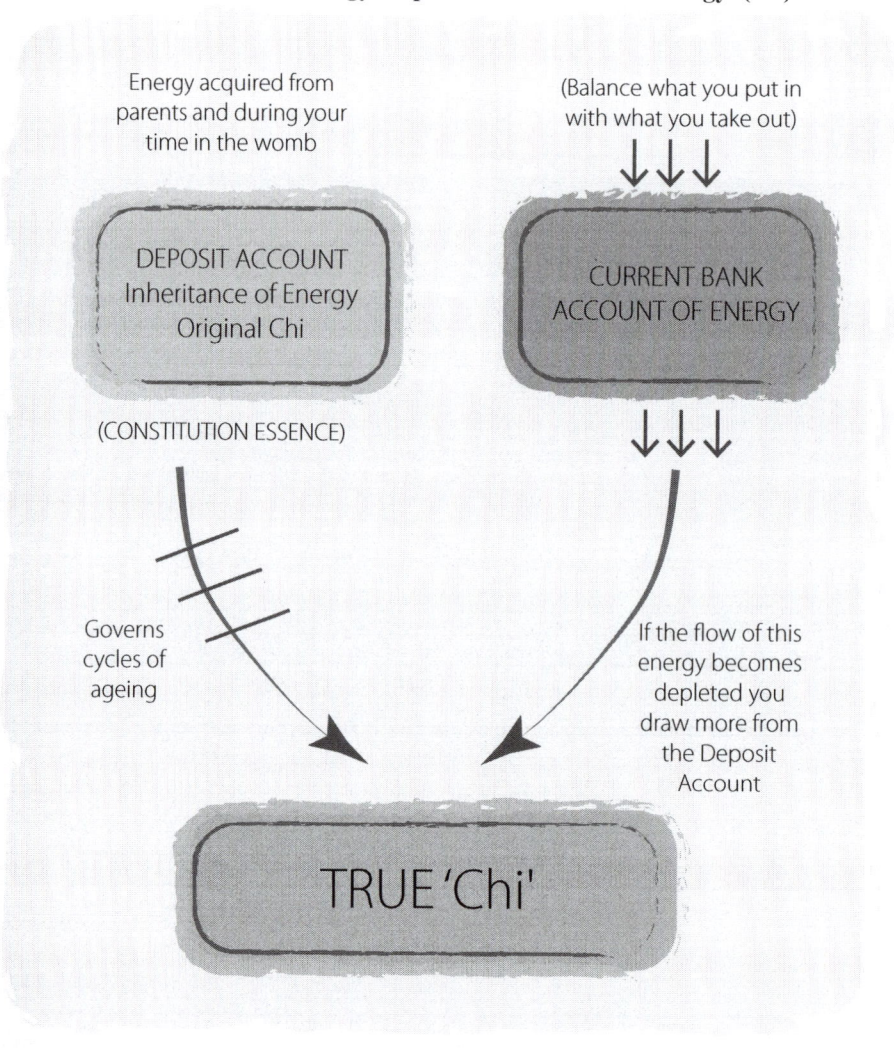

Energy acquired from parents and during your time in the womb

(Balance what you put in with what you take out)

↓↓↓

DEPOSIT ACCOUNT
Inheritance of Energy
Original Chi

CURRENT BANK ACCOUNT OF ENERGY

(CONSTITUTION ESSENCE)

↓↓↓

Governs cycles of ageing

If the flow of this energy becomes depleted you draw more from the Deposit Account

TRUE 'Chi'

Energy output and how it manifests in the body
Our True Chi or energy takes on two forms in the body: Yin and Yang.
The Yin energy nourishes the organs, particularly via the blood, the air and food we take in, and via parasympathetic nervous system allows the body to rest and digest.
The Yang serves as a protective force, protecting the body from external negative influences and is linked to the immune and sympathetic nervous system.

Diagram 2: How true chi outputs / manifests in our bodies

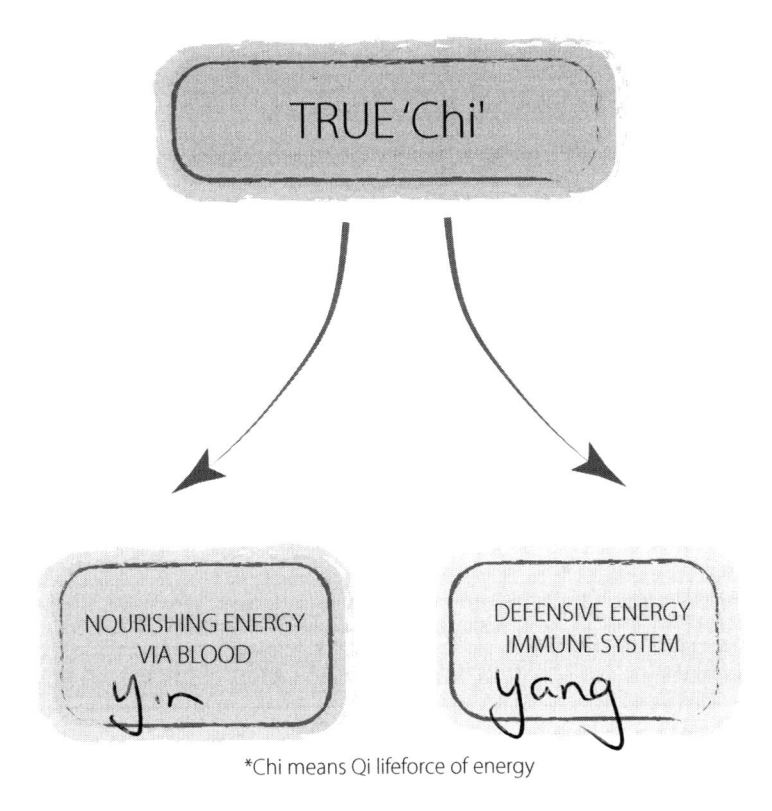

```
                    TRUE 'Chi'
                   /          \
                  ↓            ↓
         NOURISHING ENERGY    DEFENSIVE ENERGY
            VIA BLOOD          IMMUNE SYSTEM
              yin                  yang
```

*Chi means Qi lifeforce of energy

If our energy is depleted it considers the internal ying Chi or energy to be of more importance. This can causes the Yang Chi (energy) or defensive energy to become reduced therefore weakening our ability to resist 'dis-ease' or external pernicious influences.

Food Section

Early Summer - A bridge between Spring and Summer

In Early Summer we are starting to see the abundance of seasonal colourful foods coming back onto our market shelves from local areas. There is no shortage of availability of healthy colourful vegetables at this time. The diet is lightening from spring onward, Early Summer is when we should be more inclined toward lightening our heavy food load.

In Early Summer we need a combination of sour and bitter foods like sourdough, tangerines, tomatoes, rice vinegar and apple cider vinegar.

Sprouting can be started in spring time, and continued through to late summer/autumn. These are great for enzymes and a tasty way to get concentrated vitamins and minerals into our body.

The key word for Early Summer is alkalinity - to do this we need to reduce the amount of animal protein substantially - keep it below 10% of total calories. Salads, lighter soups, stir fries, seasonal fruits, seasonal vegetables, less fats and oils. Lighter cooking methods, cooking for less time, don't over heat. Like juicing add in raw food gradually, they are necessary but very stimulatory. Be mindful of how your body is feeling, if you are aware of inflammation in the body then raw food could be beneficial for cooling down the system.
Karen Scobie (nutritional therapist) & part of the Seasonal Yoga specialist team

Guide to an alkaline diet

Firstly, its good to see where you are - test your alkalinity!
PH test strips are cheap (around £ 10) and easily available on the internet, they let you test your Alkalinity, they give an instant result with one quick dip of urine or saliva.

The PH type of diet has come under attack for many reasons over the last few years. According to some research it is difficult if not impossible to change your stomach acid which is always around 3.5 PH or below, (it needs to be acid to digest food), the blood PH is between 7.35 - 7.45, again scientific opinion is that it cannot be changed by this diet either. However, there is some evidence that lowering acid conditions in the body's main organs helps in preventing or lessening the chance of calcification in the areas prone to collection of this sandy type substance.

Examples of the conditions are Gall stones, Kidney stones, type 2 diabetes, lower blood pressure and cholesterol so less acid diet is a plus for heart health.
A PH of 0 is total acidic while a PH of 14 is completely alkaline.

"I can report that my own body has a little arthritis as my father did before me. I usually avoid the high acid foods and if I do that stay fairly pain free. So, through trial and error, I can confirm that I do feel the difference if I watch what I eat and keep my diet towards alkaline and away from high acid foods." - Julie Hanson

This type of eating in truth is giving the same messages, as we hear all the time how fruit & vegetables are good for us while cakes bread and pastries are not! (this news come as no surprise !) It's not complicated any more as we all know this.
Hydration is the key, good quality filtered water frequently or fresh herb teas, fresh ginger or mint tea are also great to encourage an internal alkaline environment.

This type of eating at this time of year will definitely give you a boost of energy.
The acid/alkaline charts give you a little more information on just how acid your favourite foods are. Trying this approach in the Early Summer season seems right, listening to your body and it's attitude to eating. It is always good to try out different ways to eat at different times of year, you will know if its working for you by going on a voyage of inner discovery (just what the season is about) and seeing if you do have more energy than usual.

Health and longevity

We have made a simple acid/ alkaline chart so you can overview your likes and dislikes.
Try for a couple of weeks in this season to avoid an overly acidic diet, which strips the body of minerals. The proven research of this is the life span of the Eskimo (meat based, high acid low in vegetable diet) compared to the diet of the people who live in Okinawa - world famous for a large population of 100 year olds who live longer than anywhere else in the world. While rice, soy, seafood and meat (highly acidic foods) are squarely in the diet, but so are a vast range of different vegetables and fruits, which are rich in anti-oxidants, as well as minerals that counteract acidity.

Acid / Alkaline chart

HIGHLY ACIDIC - AVOID!
Alcohol, Artificial Sweetener, Coffee, Fruit Juice, Honey, Jam, Mushroom, Mustard, Soya Sauce, Sugar, Syrup, Vinegar, Yeast Beef, Chicken, Cow's Milk & Cheese, Eggs, Farmed Fish, Pork,

MODERATELY ACIDIC - UP TO 30% OF DIET
Apple, Apricot, Banana, Blackberry, Blueberry, Cranberry, Fresh Natural Juice and Smoothies, Grapes, Guava, Mango, Mangosteen, Orange, Peach, Papaya, Pineapple, Strawberry.
Goat's Cheese, Vegan Cheese, Rye Bread, Wheat, Wholemeal Bread, Wild Rice, Wholemeal Pasta, Ocean Fish

MILD TO MODERATELY ALKALINE - 70% OF DIET
Asparagus, Artichoke, Aubergine, Beetroot, Brussels Sprouts, Chili, Celery, Cauliflower, Carrot, Cucumber, Courgette, Cabbage, Dark Leafy Greens, Endive, Green beans, Lettuces, Peas, Pumpkin, Runner Beans, Snow peas, Squashes, Sweet Potato
Avocado, Citrus Fruits, Coconut, Pomegranate, Rhubarb, Tomato
Almond Milk, Amaranth, Buckwheat, Quinoa, Tahini, Tofu
Avocado Oil, Coconut Oil, Flax Oil, Olive Oil

HIGHLY ALKALINE - EAT FREELY!
Broccoli, Cucumber, Grass, Kale, Kelp, Parsley, Spinach, Sprouts.

NEUTRAL - UP TO 30% OF DIET
Cantaloupe, Cherry, Fresh Dates, Nectarine, Plum, Watermelon
Brown Rice, Buckwheat, Cous Cous, Millet, Oats, Pasta, Rice, Spelt
Almond Milk, Black Beans, Brazil Nuts, Chickpeas, Kidney Beans, Freshwater Fish, Hazel Nuts, Hemp, Lentils, Lima Beans, Mung Beans, Pinto Beans, Red Beans, Seitan, Soya Beans, Soya Milk, White Beans, Grapeseed Oil, Sunflower Oil

Avoid totally

Toxic additives create an acid environment

Sweeteners
Aspartame
Sucralose & Saccharin
High fructose corn syrup

Fats
Palm oil
Partially hydrogenated oil

Artificial Flavour enhancers & colours
MSG (Monosodium glutamate)
Yellow, blue, green or red dyes
Diacetyl

Preservatives
Hydroxytoluene
Sodium Benzoate
Potassium Bromate …and many more
If you can't pronounce it - don't eat it!

So what do I eat in Early Summer?

Have a salad of green leaves with bitter flavours - the stuff you have to chew
Regular radishes - Mooli also counts
Use avocado as your spread of choice, lemon juice and pepper added on top.
Fresh Lemon juice on Veg and salads
Pepper on everything
Green juice once a day - ideally breakfast time (see below for an easy juice)
Endive, parsley, kale, asparagus, broccoli
Grow and eat your own fresh sprouts
Apple cider vinegar rather than Balsamic
Ginger tea instead of caffeinated drinks
Berries, cantaloupe melon, tangerines

Simple green juice

(Use a cold pressed juicer if possible)
1 Cucumber
2 Sticks of Celery
1 Handful of Spinach
1/4 Lettuce or Kale
1 Apple
1 Pear (optional)
1 thumb size piece of fresh Ginger
Gradually add the leafy greens in between the other ingredients

Hydration:

Fluid movement around the body is high on the subject matter of this season, so it only makes sense that good quality and frequent hydration are a key to balance at this time. As you will read in the following sections the triple Heater is responsible (according to Traditional Chinese Medicine) for controlling the pathway of water between the organs, so water and keeping hydrated will be crucial to this functionality.

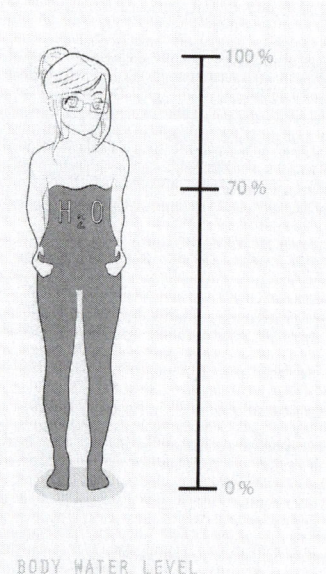

Our body consist of 55 - 70% water, the brain 75%, which is why hydration is crucially important. De-hydration can cause many malfunctions in the body some more serious than others. It is a natural purifier - it helps to bring oxygen into the blood stream; helps to balance blood pressure; lubricates joints; improves productivity keeping you alert and refreshed; the list is endless. We have both been filtering our water for many years and are certain it is one of the important contributions of anti ageing. A very good book to read on the subject is

"Your Body's Many Cries for Water" by Fereydoon Batmanghelidj, M.D.

BODY WATER LEVEL

Exercise and Movement Section

Organs

We can enhance our own health and vitality by understanding how to work with the special features of this Early Summer stage. Through this awareness we can help to support and build up the Fire energy, circulate and disperse it, and also regulate any extremes within us. The organs of Early Summer are the Pericardium, the sac of connective tissue that surrounds, protects and keeps the heart in place, and the Triple Heater, which is in charge of circulation of Chi and protecting Chi by means of the fascia and connective tissue.

The Pericardium

This is the more straightforward of the two as it is recognised in western medicine. It is the sac of connective tissue around the heart protecting it by providing lubrication to prevent friction during its activity, anchoring it in place and preventing it from over filling. In eastern medicine it is seen as the emperor's bodyguard, protecting the heart from over stimulation and emotional disruptions. It's job is to create pleasure for the heart, it's governor. When the Heart's protector is overburdened it can cause anxiety, palpitations and erratic commitment to others, with a tendency to over trust or distrust.

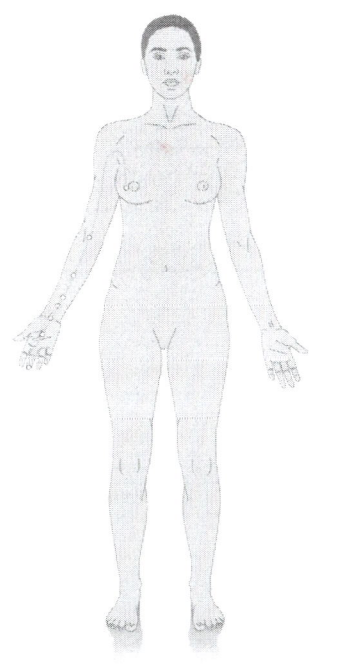

The Pericardium 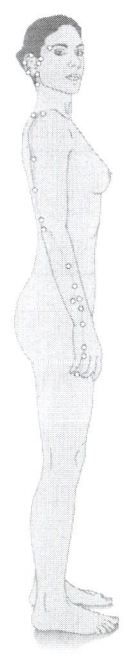   The Triple heater

The Triple Heater

This organ is the sixth yang organ in the body, it has no form yet gives form, it separates yet integrates and is responsible for moving the fluid, information and energy around the body.

As part of Chinese medicine it has caused centuries of dispute, because according to conventional medicine it is invisible. But now, with so many new instruments and discoveries, things are changing. If you read the section further down about the Interstitium this may start to make sense. Traditional medicine studied the living body, where as early scientific medical research had to be carried out on cadavers or corpses, because of the lack of technology. Now, however, we are seeing the body as a living entity and have discovered fluid trapped in between our connective tissue. This pathway of communication between the organs allows "a functional relationship between organs" says Ted J Kaptchuk in his book Chinese Medicine. "The triple heater makes a pathway between the other organs to make a complete system, regulating the water and energy between all the organs. In the Yellow Emperor's classic text the Triple Heater is called "The Irrigation official" mediating between the elements of fire and water, helping to distribute and disperse water and fluids in the body.

The Triple Heater is so called because it divides the body into three sections:

The upper burner: is everything from the thoracic diaphragm upwards including the lungs, heart, ribs, throat and skin. The moisture taken in by the lungs is called "the mist".

The middle burner: comprises the area between the navel including the spleen, pancreas and stomach. The fluids from digestion is called "the foam". Metabolism in this burner involves churning food and water into a digestible, souplike consistency. Digestive disorders are often described as middle burner imbalances.

The Lower burner: comprises the organs below the navel: the intestines, kidneys and bladder. It is considered a "swamp separating pure and impure fluids since it is the sewage system of the body excreting waste.

It's job is also to create heat to allow for transformations, create change and move energy around the body.

Try this: rub up and down the outer side of the arms along the Triple Heater Meridians

Connective tissue

Just by its name you should now realise why it is being featured in Early Summer connecting our mind to our inner body, intuition, sixth sense, our window into how we are actually feeling.

Teaching yoga in the Early Summer sometimes is called opening the web. The web being the network of connective tissues that wrap around every nerve, blood vessel, organ, bone and muscle connecting all the individual parts so energy flows.

Chinese medicine respects fascia, a type of connective tissue, yet it is the most overlooked substance (organ) of western medicine. Not withstanding this, every good surgeon values fascia. Every nerve, muscle, blood vessel, organ, bone and tendon is covered in it. It tells a surgeon, and more importantly the body, where things should be and what they should be doing. If surgeons follow the plane of the fascia they will cause minimal damage in surgery, and Langer's lines tell them how the collagen in the skin is arranged, and where to cut along them to minimise scarring.

Fascia defines and encapsulates organs and we know that it is difficult for biological things to pass across fascia, but relatively easy to pass along it. This is true of fluid, hormones, blood, air and even electricity. So fascia allows for connection, integration and communication, the essence of the fire element. It is the most abundant type of tissue in the body and therefore is now considered to be an organ, a living elastic web.

Fascia and connective tissue are the means by which energy is conducted to and from every cell, along the surface and why the balance of strength (collagen) and flexibility (elastin) of the connective tissue, is so vital for the health and intrinsic wisdom of the body. Because Chi/Prana is not just vitality but has its own innate intelligence.

The Triple Heater is also seen as linked to allergic reactions, marshalling the organs and immune system to react to what it sees as a threat. Being on the opposite side of the body clock to the spleen, the more depleted or inactive the spleen becomes, the more over active the triple heater.

This under activity of the spleen comes about by such things as the over use of antibiotics or eating food containing them, low self-esteem, excess sugar and, especially in children, an environment that is too clean

The other very important point is that this tissue can hold memory, the body can literally take the shapes of our thoughts. Emotional feelings, even trauma, can surface when working with the deep tissue within this complex web. As a teacher or as a practitioner feeling emotional or being aware that you are feeling different can be your brain trying to release long forgotten thoughts or emotions, bringing them to the surface to dispense with their restrictive qualities as we explore the movement.

It is always rewarding as a teacher when a student reports a mysterious rising need to eat a better diet or learn to meditate because they are starting to feel more centred and peaceful.

We live in a fast moving period of existence with rising anxiety present in most walks of life, the relief that these eastern philosophies and practices bring is becoming increasingly important.

Interstitium

Years ago before we had the sophisticated scanning technology we now have, the only way scientist could examine a body was when it was a corpse. Working on cadavers where the life energy chi and fluids were not present it would have been impossible to see the small pockets of fluid trapped between the connective tissue. This is currently surfacing as relevant to the communication within the body, a fluid filled highway.

Information is passing between and around the whole body via the interstitium. Scientific research is looking at it as a way that cancerous cells can spread around the human body and also how communication between the organs happens, also why acupuncture works. This fluid drains into the lymphatic system for filtering and supporting immunity.

Total fluid volume of the interstitium in a healthy person is about 20% of body weight, Microscopic technology which once looked on areas as dehydrated stacks between tissue is now seen as fluid filled spaces in a connected network of cells thanks to modern expertise.

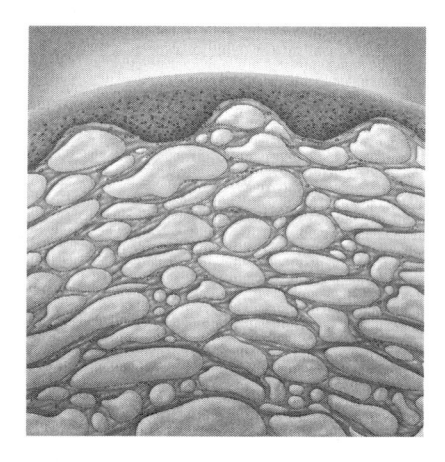

Picture: *Interstitial pockets - our bodies natural shock absorber*

The question is how do we keep it in prime functionality?

Could it be that keeping this highway of fluid working is the way to help communication between the organs in the human body? If they gather and pool, becoming stagnant like a puddle, this fluid in the body becomes a breeding ground of potential Dis - ease.

Sitting for long periods of time, poor posture and lack of fluid movement in the fascia becomes compressed and therefore thins and dehydrates allowing the surrounding cells to get starved of the nutrients present in the **Interstitial** fluid.

Organs support each other according to TCM (Traditional Chinese Medicine) but if this communication doesn't have a clear path they cant help each other. Is this why we present symptoms of dis - ease?

It seems the message is loud and clear: Movement, quality hydration, massage, regular stimulation of the lymphatic system (e.g. dry skin body brushing etc.), a healthy diet, less stress, and the feeling that life is flowing will help keep this interstitial fluid healthy, flowing and communicating.

Energy maintenance Tips

Try the exercises below and notice any changes in energy:

1. **An exercise to understand the influence of the mind and emotions:** This exercise helps you to understand the influence your mind and emotions has on your energy or chi. Have a friend hold their hands out in front of them toward you at chest level, with wrists crossed and their dominant hand underneath. Test their strength by asking them to hold this position as you press down on their hands to test life force. Then ask them to think of something they dislike about themselves or feel a negative emotion and test again by pressing down on their hands. Then repeat the exercise but with them thinking of something positive.

2. **Understanding postural alignment:** This exercise helps you to understand how proper postural alignment influences life force. Ask your friend to take up an asana or posture correctly and test their ability to hold the position against light pressure trying to push them off balance. Then ask them to lift their shoulders, or take their knee out of alignment or push chin forwards and test the difference.

3. **Understanding how locked joints affect the flow of energy:** Both people stand left foot forwards and right foot back. Person A extends their right arm with a locked elbow and right knee and pushes their fist in to the open hand of Person B who feels their force. Person A now pushes their fist into the palm of Person B keeping the elbow and back knee slightly open and not locked and pushing from the back foot through to the fist. Person B now feels the power of the force.

4. **Understanding how external tension affects core strength:** External tension means a week core. Both people stand in a wide horse stance, with soft fists and tensed core. Then they try to tense the core of the body with tightened fists and notice the difference in the core.

5. **Understanding how posture influences emotions:** Ask your partner to take a position as if they have a feeling of low self-worth. Then adjust them into an upright aligned position and ask them how they feel. Note the differences in how they feel between the first and second position.

6. **How energy can be strengthened and directed by the mind:** Have your partner stand with feet hip width apart and look at an object on the ceiling with shoulders raised up to ears, then test their rootedness by gently pushing them. Then get them to think of roots growing down into the floor from their feet, relaxing the shoulders and dropping their tailbone down two inches so that the energy releases down into the legs and relax and test again. Feel how the body becomes a conductor of energy as it relaxes under the direction/intention of the mind.

The Body Clock

Now more than ever, we need to look at the importance of the body clock as it is such a vital health maintenance tool. Both from the conventional medicine point of view in terms of it's anatomical influences and how it can manifest in good health or disease/illness. Also from traditional medicine's view point which for hundred of years had known about the body clock in relation to meridians and organs and the flow of energy relating to the circadian rhythm.

The Western view of the Body Clock anatomical composition

According to Wikipedia a great deal of research on biological clocks was undertaken in the latter half of the 20th century. It is now known that the molecular circadian clock can function within a single cell, i.e. it is cell-autonomous. At the same time, different cells may communicate with each other resulting in a synchronized output of electrical signalling.

These may interface with endocrine glands in the brain to result in a periodic release of hormones. The receptors for these hormones may be located far across the body and synchronize the peripheral clocks of various organs. Thus, the information of the time of the day as relayed by the eyes travels to the clock in the brain, and through that, clocks in the rest of the body may be synchronized. This is how the timing of, for example, sleep/wake, body temperature, thirst and appetite are coordinated and controlled by the biological clock.

The influence of the circadian rhythm is present in the sleeping and feeding patterns of animals, including human beings. There are also clear patterns of core body temperature, brain wave activity, hormone production, cell regeneration and other biological activities. The root of most disease is caused by things not happening in the correct amount, in the right way or at the appropriate time.

The Traditional view of the Body Clock in relation to energy flow

The Eastern school of thought and study of the Body Clock:

Reservoir meridians to balance our supply of energy: there are eight specific meridians, in addition to the organ meridians, which act as reservoirs in order to balance supply in case of deficiency or excess.

Yin and Yang meridians: meridians are classified as either Yin or Yang on the basis of the direction they flow and the basic nature of the organ and it's function. When you look at the clock (below) you will see a Yin organ time is opposite the time for a Yang organ, and vice versa.

A constant unimpeded energy flow that is vital to maintain good health: The organ meridians are actually unbroken energy flows, which flow from one meridian to another in a well-determined order. Since there is no beginning or end it is just a continual ebbing and flowing cycle, just like the tides of the sea or as day transforms into night. However if an organ is overloaded or stressed it can block the energy in that meridian and cause a breakdown in health.

The importance of the Body Clock and how to use it as a tool for optimum health

The earth's daily rhythms, time zones and seasonal changes affect the flow of energy in our meridians and their associated organs. Just as tides go though their daily cycle, each of our meridians has its own 24 hour cycle - a time when it's energy flow is at it's strongest and a time of rest. Therefore, having an understanding of how we can re-set the body's clock is an essential tool to restore congruity and unity as well as helping to maximise our energy. This is especially useful after illness, trauma, travel, long periods of stress or medication and other energy interference.

The effects of unrestricted or blocked energy flows will manifest in the body as follows:

Unrestricted energy provides optimised function: when the energy flow is unrestricted the body harmonises to optimise body function and healing, ensuring less need for external intervention from drugs or surgery.

Blocked energy flows cause a breakdown in function: when constant stress occurs, it overloads the energetic circuit, which causes various imbalances and disease in the body's systems and organs. Regular use of the Body Clock Sequence can be used to re-balance and flush the system. This may be one of the reasons why the sun and moon salutations are viewed as the mainstay of Yoga practice.

12.

7 PM – 11 PM TRIPLE HEATER PERICARDIUM

7 AM – 11 AM STOMACH & SLPEEN

RESET YOUR

BODY CLOCK

11 PM – 3 AM LIVER & GALL BLADDER

11 AM – 3 PM HEART & SMALL INTESTINE

3 AM – 7 AM LUNG & LARGE INTESTINE

3 PM – 7 PM KIDNEYS & BLADDER

How to use the Body Clock Sequence to resolve stress overload and restore optimum health

When using the Body Clock Sequence always begin and end with a meridian flush this can be done in one of the following ways:

- **Performing sun or moon salutations**
- **Performing cat and cow by flexing and extending the spine**
- **Tracing up the midlines (governing vessel and conception vessel) or the front and back of the body.**

The approach for the Body Clock Sequence can then be tailored as required:

- Note the time of day of weakness: If you or your client are regularly exhausted at a specific time of day note which organ might be involved. The time indicated on the clock is when the flow of energy through that organ meridian is at it's strongest and therefore when any energy distortion is most obvious. You can focus on the moves/stretches that open up and enhance the flow in the preceding meridian and then support the power flow of the meridian in that time zone. Alternatively, massage the Bo points of the corresponding organ (refer to the chi Kung and energy sections in the book)

- Match the time of day with the high tide shown on the meridian wheel (see following section): For example, if you loose vitality between 17.00 (5pm) and 19.00 (7pm) this time relates to the kidneys. Therefore start with the kidney meridian sequence and go around the flow ending with the kidneys.

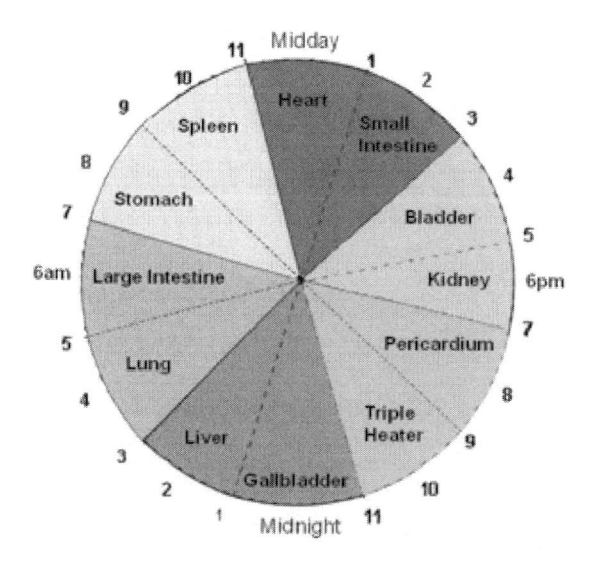

Diagram 1: *Meridian Wheel showing times of day for each organ (Eastern/Chinese view of the Body Clock).*

- If you want to enhance the flow even more start with the preceding organ time, which in this example is the Bladder, whose time is 15.00 (3pm) to 17.00 (5pm) and then proceed round the clock and end with the Kidneys again.

- Alternative to start with the weakest time: Alternatively you can start at the weakest time and trace the entire clock. Using the Lao gong points in the palm of your hands, a few inches off the body, trace all the way round the meridians on the clock and then repeat by tracing the weakest one again

- For general balancing: Match the time of day with the meridian and begin and end with a yoga flow or tracing with the meridian (each day if possible) in the body clock sequence. For a quick boost, trace the meridian for that time of day this boosts your energy and prevents future illness by strengthening the vulnerable systems of your body

- For a more prescriptive effect: you can target particular organs on a daily basis for a week or so.

- If the person is very depleted: advise that they rest during the depleted period so the energy is available to restore the energy in the organ concerned.

- For Jet lag: Trace the clock starting with CV and GV (up the front and back midlines of the body) then, do the corresponding yoga flow for the time you are in before you leave, ending with the flush of CV and GV. When you arrive at your destination, do the same matching to the new time zone and the corresponding organ. Alternatively, after starting with CV and GV, trace the entire organ meridian system beginning and ending with the organ of the corresponding time before you leave and when you arrive at your destination.

- In case of heightened or imbalanced energy: for example if a depleted/imbalanced Liver is waking you up between 1 to 3am you can trace the meridian the opposite way to its direction of flow a few times, followed by one in the right direction, and then working on strengthening the flow in the meridian on the opposite side of the clock, which is the small intestine. In the case of allergies, try tracing the triple heater in the wrong direction and then work on strengthening the spleen.

- A note of precaution on blood pressure: In cases of imbalanced blood pressure keep your arms below shoulder level and your head above the heart. If you are menstruating, avoid the inversions and do not perform the practice if you are feeling light-headed / dizzy or immediately after a heavy meal.

Conclusion

The Body Clock balance (and imbalance) is recognised by both the Western (anatomical) and Eastern (meridian and energy flow) schools of study.

Using the technique of the Body Clock Sequence within your teaching and personal practice will provide a useful tool to re-balance the body's rhythm and flow of energy following times of illness, trauma or following any period of stress on the body

Dao-yin of the Dragon

An ancient Daoist exercise for health

To energetically strengthen and detoxify the internal systems of the body through a deep internal massage. Practiced daily it re-aligns the spine and strengthens the nervous system, increases lung capacity, stimulates metabolism, regulates the endocrine system, encourages lymphatic drainage, keeps the body flexible, supple and trim and improves brain function. It forms an excellent warm up for Yoga, T'ai Chi and Pilates practitioners.

The Chinese Dragon

Dragons are deeply rooted in Chinese culture, nobody knows where the dragon comes from but they are described visually as a composite of nine animals and so were credited with having great powers. Amongst their powers are to be the governors of the rain falls, to make rain and control floods and they are also credited with the transportation of humans to celestial realms after death.

They are symbols of the natural world, adaptability and transformation. When two dragons are placed together but turned away they symbolize the famous Yin and Yang. They also represent living in total harmony with the five elements or transformations in nature; Wood - the capacity to fly high into the sky (rising energy of Yang); Fire - breathing it!; Earth - to live in caves; Metal - eating minerals; Water - to dive under the oceans in the winter (cooling Yin). People showed great respect for the dragon, it is depicted in pictures and carvings dating as far back as the 16th to the 11th century BC and many powerful exercises for health and longevity have been named after them.

In China and Asia the dragon is a symbol of good luck appearing on the second day of the second month of the Chinese calendar bringing thunder *(the power of change)* the trigram of the east, to water, nourish and fertilize the soil. In Feng Shui the dragon is one of the four heavenly animals and is a symbol for energy, strength and prosperity. It stands for the east, the place of sunrise, and therefore is placed to the left of the door of property. It represents spring, creation and new beginnings, and is widely used on gates, roofs, royal flags, clothing and many objects used in daily life. A dragon talisman is often carried for attracting luck and perseverance. For the placement of houses the environment is explored to find the dragons crest which is the most favourable site for the house for the optimal flow of chi. In Chinese mythology images of the dragon were often used to represent the action of the internal bodily energy so the dance of the dragon is about having the optimal flow of chi in the body, and because it symbolizes the East the movements start to the left.

Dao-Yin means to 'induce or guide' and is one of the oldest methods of energy work on record in China. Dao-Yin exercises were prescribed to spread Chi throughout the body and used to target specific organs or ailments with the rhythmic rise and fall of the breath. Performed slowly and deliberately while keeping the whole body relaxed so as not impede the free flow of chi. Throughout the exercises the mind must remain calm, quiet and clear with the attention focused on the attuning of body and breath and the flow of internal energy.

The health of the organs depends on the balance and flow of chi in the organs and their corresponding meridian pathways.

The Dao-yin of the Dragon

- Improves and maintains health.
- Cultivates, circulates and stores the chi *(vital life force)*.
- Improves muscle tone and enhances the flexibility of the joints.
- Improves posture and strengthens the spine.
- Sends energy to the vital organs and deeply massages the entire body.
- Strengthens the immune system and the body's resistance to disease.
- Increases circulation and blood flow.
- Improves the metabolism and encourages weight loss.

Focusing and training the mind

Start with your palms on Qihai (two finger widths below the navel). Men place their left hand underneath the right, women place the right hand underneath the left - this balances the chi and helps focus the mind on the body. Take five long slow breaths, filling the abdomen. On the in-breath draw the mind back in from the busy world outside, through the Yintang point between the eyebrows over the bridge of the nose (the third eye). On the out-breath send your attention down to your hands, slightly drawing your navel back towards your spine and lifting the pelvic floor (Hui-yin).

Stretching your spine and massaging your organs

Inhale: stretching your abdomen to lift your arms above your head, raising your gaze to follow your hands, and drawing your navel in.

Exhale: lowering your tailbone to stretch the spine then lowering your gaze and hands, bringing your ribs down to compress the organs - giving them a deep massage, returning the heel of the hands to touch Qihai.
Repeat 6 - 12 times

Stage 2: Raise and lower the heels to activate the channels in the legs especially the Yin channels Liver, Spleen and Kidneys.

Massage and strengthen your neck and upper part of your Trapezius muscle

Inhale: lift your hands to the side of your left ear, turning your head to the right and looking up to the sky.

Exhale: lower your hands slowly down to the centre of your breast bone. Repeat on the other side and continue, doing 6 each side.

Massage your heart and lungs and the entire thoracic cavity

Inhale: pressing your palms together, move your arms out to the left side, moving your left ribs in and stretching out the right, drawing the breath into the right lung, looking above your arms.

Exhale: return back to the centre, repeat on the other side and continue for 6 - 12 times on each side.
NB Feel both the pushing and pulling action of yin and yang.

Harmonize your chi of upper body

Inhale: as you combine the moves of 3 and 4 circle your arms to the left and above your head to Baihui (the point between your ears on the top of the head). Visualize the chi filling the left side.

Exhale: as you circle down to the right, visualize the chi washing down the right side. Repeat the other way. Continue with 6 - 12 repetitions.

Let the power of the waist counterbalance the movement in the shoulders like a dragon swishing it's tail and kidneys.

Massaging your shoulders, ribs, lower trapezius, rhomboid muscles and your digestive organs

Inhale: as you lift your left elbow up to the left and lower your right, hands in prayer position and your knees go to the right. You should be looking down at your knees.

Exhale: as you lower the elbow keep your hands at the centre of your chest.

For a deep abdominal massage

Inhale: as above and turn in the waist.

Exhale: bring your right elbow to left knee.

Inhale: draw the breath into the abdomen and up through the spine as you come up.

Exhale: return to centre 6 - 12 reps.

Strengthening and lifting all of the internal organs and diaphragm, particularly supporting the spleen, also encourages thoracic rotation

Place your palms together in prayer position fingers pointing forwards with the heel of your hands touching your waist.

Inhale: swivel your hands so the right is over the left, lift the toes and internally apply the three locks: draw up the pelvic floor, suck navel towards spine to lift your diaphragm and bring your chin slightly down and in towards the throat. The gaze is down towards the navel. Draw the heels of your hands around your waist to the left as far as you can and lift your toes. Visualize drawing the breath up the central channel and the new chi through the stomach and spleen and left kidney. Hold for the count of 6.

Exhale: as you draw your hands back to the centre, fingers pointing forwards.
Repeat the opposite way focusing on the gall bladder, liver and right kidney.
Repeat 6-12 times in both directions

Massage and energise the kidneys, bladder intestines and reproductive organs also strengthens the spine and lower back

Place your palms together in prayer position, fingers pointing forwards, with the heels of your hands touching your left waist.

Inhale: draw up internally, lengthening through the spine, and drawing your breath into your kidneys.

Energize and re-align the spine

Exhale: rotating the waist and hands to the left, bend your knees as if sitting back into a chair. Bring your arms by your ears, flatten the back and draw a wide circle in front of you to the right. Strong exhalation as if breathing fire.

Inhale: as you come to the vertical position, lengthening through the spine and breathing into the kidneys again.
Repeat exhaling and circling to the right. Repeat 6 - 12 times.

Massaging the hips and waist and intestines

Inhale: sweep the hands to the left, finger tips pointing down, knees to the right and the gaze is to the knees, drawing your navel inwards and upward.

Exhale: draw the hands back to the midline.
As your heels and thighs are squeezed together it encourages secretions of the internal organs and glandular hormones.

A deep massage for the intestines, reproductive organs and bladder, and exercise to strengthen the knees and legs

If you cannot reach the floor this is not important just bend the knees as far as you can and visualize the chi nourishing and flowing through the joints.

Exhale: bend the knees and squat towards the floor taking your finger tips to your left heel, visualize chi going deep into the ground as you open the areas at the base of the skull, base of the shoulder blades and on the spine below the waist known as the three doors.

Inhale: draw up internally, imagining the yin chi rising through the legs and up the front of the spine (through the thrusting channel) as you straighten and lift your hands up to the heart. Repeat on the other side

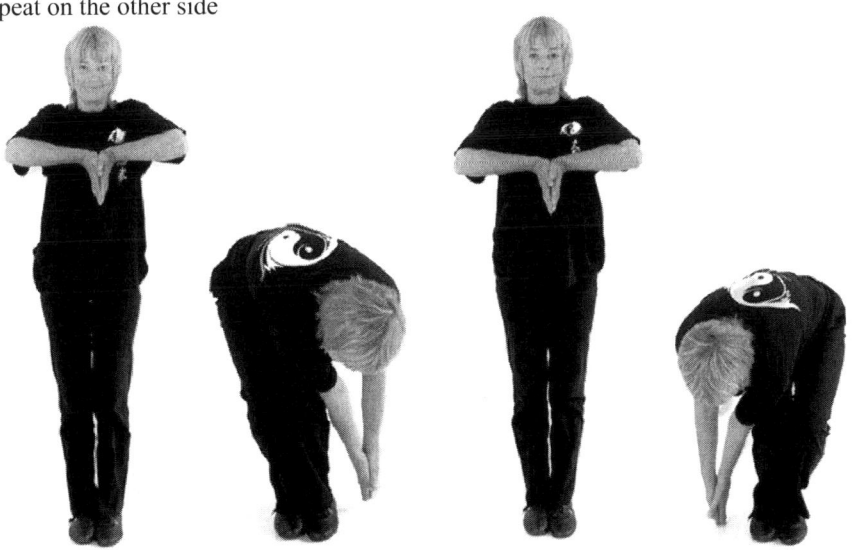

Opens leg channels and gives a deep pelvic massage

Inhale: imagine filling the right leg with energy and step out to the left..

Exhale: Sink into a deep squat.

Inhale: imagine filling the left leg with energy and step out to the right, turn waist.

Exhale: stretch down the side of the right leg to the ankle (Yang Chi).
Inhale: as you come up visualizing (Yin Chi) flowing up the inside of the leg.
Exhale: as you centralise your weight and sink back into a deeper squat and repeat on the other side.
Repeat 2 more times on each side.

Energize and re-align the spine

Inhale: lift and lengthen the arms overhead.

Exhale: Draw navel to spine as you fold forwards releasing neck.

Inhale: Sit into tail bone and uncurl spine one bone at a time keeping chin to chest until shoulders are aligned over hips.

Exhale: and draw shoulders down. Repeat 5 more times.

Energize and re-align the spine

88 Seasonal Yoga: A fusion of yoga and tai chi combined with lifestyle tips for every season

Swimming Dragon Sequence

Full body massage and exercise to strengthen spinal column and increase breathing capacity.

Inhale: As per figure 5 in the sequence, circling hands to left and over the head to the right, then place right hand over left and draw them across to left under your chin slightly sinking your body.

Exhale: Continue taking the hands to the left knees to the right (look right). Then turn your left hand on top of the right thumbs pointing forward and sweep to the right level with the solar plexus, knees to the left making an S shape with the spine (look left).
Turn the right hand over the left and lower your centre of gravity and sweep down with the back of the left hand past the groin sinking as low as you can possibly go.

Inhale: Left hand over right sweep back up to right knees and hips to left (look left), right hand over left under the chin, past your left ear as you look up to the right. Arms come up above your head to Baihui and rise on to balls of feet and hold for a few seconds
Exhale: Lower hands back down the mid-line till your return your hands below the chin as you lower your heels. Repeat up to 20 times

Points to note

- The Dao-yin of the Dragon is about having the optimal flow of chi around the body.
- In Feng Shui it symbolizes the East so the movements start on the left first.
- Use the breath to guide the movements as indicated and keep movement and breath synchronized.
- Keep the feet together and knees and hands pressing against one another all the way through.
- Keep your weight evenly distributed over Kd1 (Bubbling Spring) in centre just behind ball of foot, massaging this point is beneficial to the whole body.
- Use the gaze of the eyes, this helps to focus the mind and develop inner concentration.
- You can use any of these exercises on their own or as part of the whole sequence.
- Practice twice a day for true benefit.
- Let your head float up so the spine can relax and the weight of the body sink down naturally.

Energize and re-align the spine

Early Summer practice in a circle

Early Summer is all about connection so to practice from the front to the back of the mat is a very important part of Early Summer energy. It balances the sun and moon energy and the ideas of moving energy from the centre to the periphery and back.

Connecting with others then disconnecting.
Facing the inner circle then facing outer circle.

The flows in this section all work from this aspect. It also teaches class members (if you are a teacher) to work on their own ability to remember the flow without relying on you to give visual instructions and also the participants to enter more into the feeling mode! As a practitioner it's great to use the space on your mat to roam around opening the body, finding space in the connective tissue.

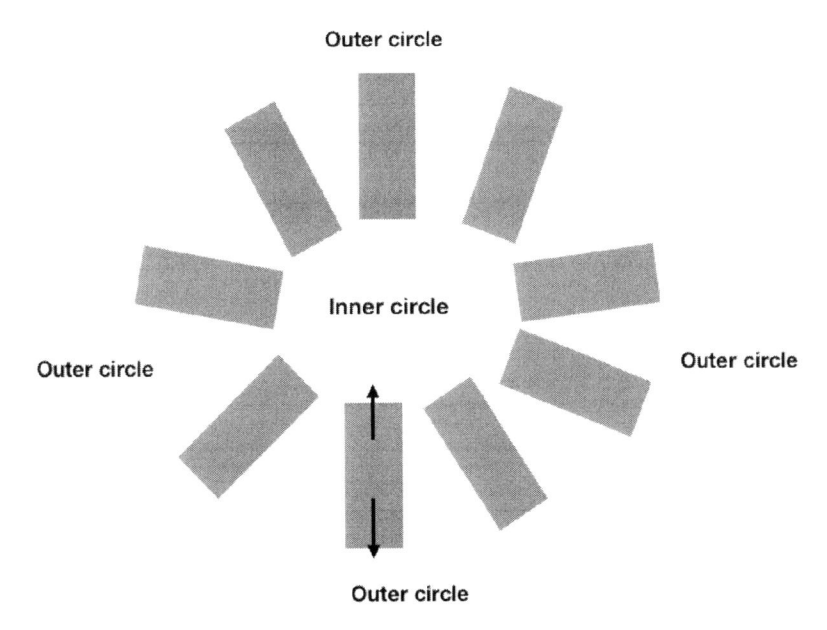

The mat plan of an Early Summer class

Ball rolling for Connective tissue and Facia flexibility

The later part of this section features ball rolling techniques which are using an inflatable ball ideal size 5" circumference. These balls are ideal to create space and flexibility in the back and shoulders either as a warm up or as a relaxation. They are available on the internet for either personal use or as a class technique. These balls are also ideal for travel (placed behind the back, very deflated) or to sit on for meditation sessions. You can also place them behind the head in the occiput area and move the head in circles for a relaxing neck mobility exercise.

Dancing warrior A - all facing inner circle

One breath per move

Inner circle

outer circle   outer circle

Part 2: The Season of Early Summer   93

Dancing warrior B - all facing inner circle

One breath per move

Inner circle

Early Summer garudasana flow-

Using the front and back of the mat, circle formation, connect with others then disconnect

1. Inhale reach up, face inner circle

3. Eagle twist - Garudasana, engage bandhas and stay for 5 breaths, face inner circle

4. OPEN OUT, big Step back & open up to face the outer circle in Warrior 2.

5. Back lean warrior 2 Virabhadrasana 2 facing outer circle

6. Side angle pose, high Utthita Parsvakonasana facing outer circle

7 Swoop into high lunge, Ashwa Sanchalasana

8. step back foot into pyramid pose, Parsvottanasana stay for 5 breaths

Inner circle

Early Summer Ball rolling - small soft ball needed 5 - 7 " diameter

Place soft ball on the sacrum (just below waist - triangle of bone) then roll side to side, massage the ball into the back

Circle ball clock wise then anti clock wise, then repeat on other leg!

Ball rolling for Early Summer connective tissue release

Still on the the sacrum Pelvic tilt then arch

Inner circle

Now place ball under heel and roll leg forwards and back - lean into bent leg so hip is off the floor - it opens hips!

Now draw circles around the sacrum, with feet wider than hip width, move around the pelvis - now lie flat and see how you feel ?

Roll up and down the ball, making sure you support your head with your hands, bringing chin onto chest supporting the weight of the head

Place the ball between the shoulder blades, deflate slightly if uncomfortable

Lie on ball spread the arms wide and breathe for 5 breaths, roll to side and take the ball out - see how you feel ?

Ball rolling for shoulder and thoracic spine mobility

1. Place ball under wrist and keep arm straight as you roll wrist forward and backward

2. Rest head on bottom arm and bend the knees at a right angle to give a stable foundation

3. Reach as far forward as you can keeping arm straight so you roll torso towards the floor

Helping thoracic spine and all the complex muscles around the shoulder area have free and fluid movement

4. Hold ball in open palm and prepare to draw circles around the upper body as if drawing circles in the sand

5. Inhale as the ball reaches over the head

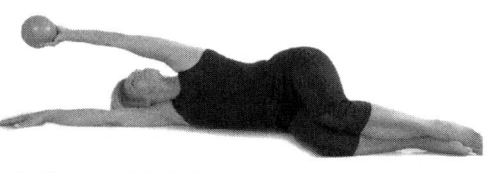

6. Keep stable in lower part of the body by keeping a knees bent foundation

7. Try to keep the ball on the floor especially in the difficult parts

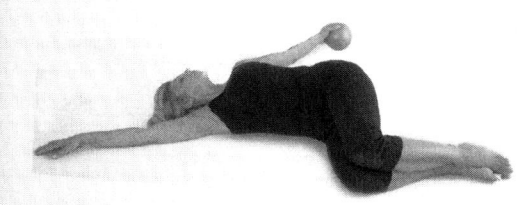

8 Move at your own speed, the slower the better

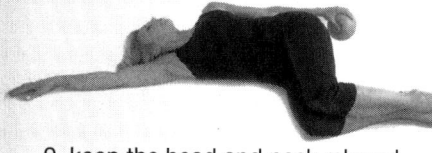

9. keep the head and neck relaxed

10. The only time the ball should leave the floor is as it jumps over the legs!

11. After a few rounds change direction

Part 2: The Season of Early Summer   97

Arm and shoulder mobility

Mobilising the complex muscles of the rotator cuff is essential if you want to put your arms in the difficult positions required to open and stretch the muscle groups in this area, this can be used as a warm up or cool down

1. With arms extended and shoulders down move the fingers, wrists, elbows and arms first upward and backward

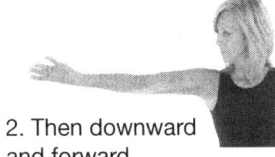

2. Then downward and forward

3. repeating the movement several times

4. To make the more complex arm stretches easier to perform

5. Change sides, after stretching the arms wide

6. Change to reverse prayer pose

7 Forward fold to child's pose then extend the arms upward and forward in a stretch

8. Relax arms and hold the elbows

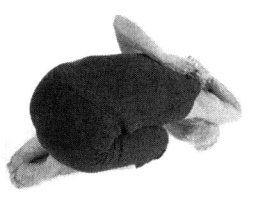

9. Fold one arm back and the other bend to the side at the head to meet at the back, then change sides

10. Finish in Childs pose

Mental contemplations for Early Summer

Yoga Nidra (conscious sleep)

In our fast paced modern society, with it's high expectations and demands and dependence on technology, people of all ages are turning to such things as alcohol, excess food, drugs, television and computers as relaxation tools to try and find equilibrium

Yoga Nidra is a method that offers the body and mind an alternative to the above, practicing it for 20 minutes a day, it is a way to re-charge the systems and train the unconscious mind.

An added bonus is that when we are extremely relaxed and the conscious mind is less dominant, we can implant information into the unconscious mind and use suggestions on purpose, to improve ourselves and re-direct our life in a more positive direction.

Taking the participant through particular imagery, including sensations, visualisation and other practices the unconscious can be released of tension on the different levels listed below, and also the senses are enhanced. Nidra means sleep, but by maintaining consciousness through the various stages of the sleep process deeper states of consciousness and awareness can be reached.

The four stages of sleep which are recognised in the east and west are:

Beta wakefulness and normal conscious functioning, then moving towards Alpha as the brain waves slow down and relax.

REM dream states

Deep sleep without dreams the Theta waves

Delta where the body freezes and you do not move during delta waves

During the night your sleep follows a predictable pattern, moving back and forth between restorative sleep (deep sleep) and more alert stages and dreaming REM sleep. Together the stages of sleep lasts about 90 minutes and repeats four to six times over the course of the night

The amount of time you spend in each stage of sleep changes as the night progresses. For example most deep sleep occurs in the first half of the night, where as the restorative process is mainly working on the physical level and the body. Later in the night your REM sleep stages become longer where you are mainly working on the mental levels. Both stages are very important to your wellbeing and why doing without 8 hours of sleep, the mental level is not so well revived.

The yoga Nidra can help us to pass through and discard any unnecessary stress from the different Koshas (sheaths) or levels of our being.

Annamayakosha: By using rotation of consciousness and awareness of sensations in the physical body we can help improve the mind and body connection.

Pranamayakosha: To work on the energy level we can use awareness of the breath and energy by directing energy into areas, pressure points or along meridians (energy pathways) so your mind becomes attuned to the breath and life force in the body.

Manomayakosa: The astral/sensory mind body, also known as the emotional body, we can train the senses and encourage emotional awareness and learn how to change emotional states.

Vijnanamayakosa: The mental body, abstract/superior mind is the layer of the superior consciousness, forming the discriminating consciousness that crosses the illusory and influences thought so we can learn to view thought patterns and train the mind.

Anandamayakosa: The cosmic/causal level never changes as it is above time and belongs to the ultimate Self, so at this level is the passing from ego to the Self (the observer of the other levels).

The physical effects of this form of deep relaxation include:
- Movement from the sympathetic (flight and flight) into the parasympathetic (rest and digest) mode
- Reduction of stress and its impacts on the systems of the body such a digestion, elimination, sleep, concentration and memory
- Improved immune system functioning through deep relaxation
- Improved mental balance
- All the benefits of the sleep (I hour of Nidra equals 4 hours sleep)
- Problem solving as the answer to our most pressing questions are hidden in our

unconscious, so yoga Nidra gives the means to deliver them to the conscious.
- Improved memory, so we can absorb teachings better.
- It can be used to support those suffering from trauma and addictions. It can calm and refresh those who have problems with relaxing or sleeping.
- Enhances creativity, as some of the greatest works of art have been attributed to the unconscious mind. Yoga Nidra allows us to tap into that creative centre and pull it into the conscious
- Enhanced self awareness and understanding

You can record the seasonal yoga Nidra below and listen to the recording whenever you feel like it, to recharge your energy or as precursor to sleep.

Here is the Seasonal yoga Early Summer script

You can record it with your own voice and listen form you mobile device or find a comfortable sitting position and read to others.

Early Summer Seasonal Yoga Nidra

Get ready you are going to practice Seasonal Yoga Nidra, which will bring you into a light altered state of consciousness. Here you will experience deep relaxation and rejuvenation, which will prepare you to reach the deeper state of meditation. At the end of the practice you will emerge wide-awake with a clear alert mind and a body full of energy. (If you are using the Nidra as a precursor to sleep then miss out the previous sentence)

Lie down in on your back in Savasana, with your legs slightly apart and your arms comfortably extended a little at the sides of your body, palms upwards.

Become aware where you are right now and the time of year and time of day. Then close you eyes and keep them closed till the end of the practice. Make sure that you don't move your body any more, no more physical movements, so throughout this practice the body will lie in one position, absolutely still.

I am aware, I am awake and I am going to practice Seasonal Yoga Nidra.

Make a resolution to yourself... I will not sleep... I will remain awake throughout the practice. When the body is still and the mind is in a mood to relax you are not trying to concentrate, so make no effort to control the mind... you are practicing Seasonal Yoga Nidra.

Take a deep breath and as you breathe out feel the cares and concerns of the day flow out of you.

First become aware of the sounds outside the room, focus on the sounds outside the room.

Now bring your awareness to any sounds inside the room.

Now become aware of the whole body lying on the floor, awareness of the whole body lying on the floor, feel the weight of your body on the floor.

Now concentrate on the contact between the body and floor, one plane of contact between the body and the floor from the heels to the head. One unified horizontal plane of contact between the body and the floor.

Feel the whole body, you are at one with your body, awareness of the whole body.... the whole body, the whole body,
Every part of your body is part of this experience.

Become aware of the breathing process... the body is breathing and you are experiencing it. Follow the breathing process without interfering and not controlling your breath... merely experiencing this breath awareness as part of the normal breathing process. You don't have to think about it just watch your breath.... don't change it... let it be... just follow the normal flow of breath.

Now comes the time for the resolution or Sankalpa. This is a sincere desire or resolution, framed as a short mental statement, stated silently 3 times, in positive language and in the present tense. It is like sowing the seeds of change in the mind, which, without a doubt, will manifest in your life, in fact it is already happening.

It is a resolve, to reshape your personality, or direct you in positive line so you become the creator of your destiny.

Pause for them/you to make the statements......

Rotation of consciousness

Now we will begin the rotation of consciousness and awareness, by taking a trip through the different parts of the body

Right: become aware the right-hand thumb, second finger, third finger, fourth finger, fifth finger, the palm of the hand, the back of the hand, the whole hand, the wrist, lower arm, the elbow, the upper arm, the shoulder, the armpit, the right waist, the right hip the right thigh, the kneecap, calf muscle, ankle, the sole of the right foot, the top of the right foot, the big toe, second toe, third toe, fourth toe, fifth toe

Left: Become aware of the left-hand thumb, second finger, third finger, fourth finger and fifth finger. Palm of the hand, the back of the hand, the whole hand, the wrist, the lower arm, the elbow, the upper arm, the shoulder, the armpit, left waist, the left hip the left thigh, the kneecap, the calf muscle, ankle, the sole of the left foot, the top of the left foot the big toe second toe, third toe, fourth toe, fifth toe.

Back: now move to the back, become aware of the back of the head and the neck, the right shoulder blade, the left shoulder blade, the right side of the back, the left side of the back, the whole of the spine, the right buttock, the left buttock, the whole of the back together, the back of the right leg and the heel, the back of the left leg and the heel.

Front: now go to the top of the head, the right side of the head, the left side of the head, the forehead, the right eyebrow, the left eyebrow, the space between the eyebrows, the right eye, the left eye, the right cheek, the left cheek, the nose, the upper lip, the lower lip, the right jaw, the left jaw, the chin, the throat, the right side of the chest, the left-side of the chest, the middle of the chest, the upper abdomen, the navel, the lower abdomen, the right side of the abdomen, the left side of the abdomen, the whole right leg, the whole left leg, both legs together, the whole right arm, the whole left arm, both arms together, the whole of the back the whole of the front, the whole of the head, the whole of the head and the body together, the whole body on the floor become aware of your whole body on lying on the floor.

The whole of the body, awareness of the entire body
I am awake, I am flexible and strong and I am practicing Seasonal Yoga Nidra

Now I invite you to visualise yourself in a place from nature that relaxes you.
Engage all the five senses: seeing the beauty, hearing the sounds, feeling the feelings and even smelling and tasting. As you are relaxing the mind the body will start to release any stress, feel a sense of connection with yourself and nature.

Picture how the scene would look in winter…in spring… in the Early Summer,…..full summer….. then late summer….. autumn…… and winter.
Notice the difference and changes of energy around you.

Now once again picture the scene in spring and then Early Summer how does it feel, how is nature manifesting itself at this Early Summer time of year?

I am aware, I am flexible and strong and I am practicing Seasonal Yoga Nidra

Now return to your breath…. experience every breath as the quality of the seasons moving in your body

As you breathe in feel the rising quality of spring beginning in the abdomen.
The spreading of Early Summer as the breath rises into the chest.
Then breath moves up to the collarbones as the full potential of summer.
Now feel that moment of change as the breath leaves the upper chest, as returning of late summer.
As the ribs descend in and down, the letting go of the breath from the chest as autumn.
Now feel the descending and sinking of winter, as the abdomen flattens.

Feel the breath and the quality of the seasons in every breath.
Feel the breath and the quality of the seasons in the energy moving in the body.

I am conscious, I am flexible and strong and I am practicing Seasonal Yoga Nidra

Now experience how still your body is now, it has been still for sometime and it is not making any sounds…. feel the stillness and how it is increasing when you are experiencing it.
When you become still you are aware the body is alive, feel the life in your body, the body is being still… but you feel the life in your body.

Now feel the energy pathway running from a point just to the side of the left nipple, and feel it running down the middle of the left arm into the centre of your palm to the tip of your middle finger. Feel the warmth in the centre of your palm, feel the energy here, stay there and let it build.

Now feel the energy running from the back of your left fourth/ring finger up the back of your left arm and along the top of your left shoulder blade then up behind your left ear, close around the back of the ear to come to the outer end of your left eye brow.

Now feel the energy pathway running from a point just to the side of the right nipple, and feel it running down the middle of your right arm into the centre of your palm to the tip of your middle finger. Feel the warmth in the centre of your palm, feel the energy here, stay there and let it build.

Now feel the energy running from the back of your right fourth/ring finger up the back of your right arm and along the top of your right shoulder blade then up behind your right ear, close around the back of the ear to come to the outer end of your right eye brow.

Now see if you can feel both sides at once
Now feel both the energy pathways running from the points just to the outer sides of the nipples, feel the energy running down the middle of your arms into the enter of your palms to the tip of your middle fingers. Feel the warmth in the centre of your palms, feel the energy here, stay there and let it build.

Now feel the energy running from the back of your fourth/ring fingers up the backs of your arms and along the tops of your shoulder blades then up behind your ears, close around the back of the ears to come to the outer ends of your eye brows.

I am conscious, I am aware, I am flexible and I am strong, I am practicing Seasonal Yoga Nidra

Now experience the feelings of calmness, connection, protection and adaptability.
Feel the whole body is calm, connected and secure, feeling a release of any tension or armouring.
The mind is calm, the emotions are calm, the body is calm, experience the feelings of calmness, connection, protection and adaptability, feeling how this feels throughout the whole body, the whole body

How does it feel to be calm, connected, protected and adaptable to any situation……….

I am conscious, I am flexible and strong and I am practicing Seasonal Yoga Nidra

Now I invite you to visualise the symbol of infinity, a sideways figure of eight filling the head, with the cross over in the middle of the mind, behind the third eye point.
Feeling the symbol of infinity filling and connecting the right and left sides of the brain, crossing over in the middle of the mind.

Trace the symbol with your eyes and your awareness feel it connecting the right and left sides of the brain crossing over in the middle of the mind.

Then without stopping and to change direction, draw half a circle and trace the symbol with your eyes and awareness the opposite way.
Then rest in stillness, rest in the middle of the mind. Feel the infinite healing energy filling, clearing and balancing the mind

I am aware, I am awake, I am a field of infinite possibilities and I am practicing Seasonal Yoga Nidra

Now I invite you to place the infinity symbol in the chest cavity, a sideways figure of eight with the heart at the centre.

Feeling the symbol of infinity filling and connecting the right and left sides of the chest. Trace the symbol with your eyes and your awareness. Feel it connecting the right and left sides of the chest crossing over in the point behind the middle of the breastbone.

Then without stopping and to change direction of the energy, draw half a circle and trace the symbol with your awareness the opposite way.

Then rest in stillness in the middle of the chest. Feel the infinite healing energy filling, nourishing the heart and lungs and balancing your emotional energy.

I am aware, I am awake, I am a field of infinite possibilities and I am practicing Seasonal Yoga Nidra.

Now I invite you to visualise the symbol of infinity, a sideways figure of eight, filling the abdomen with the cross over in the area of the navel.

Feeling the symbol of infinity filling the abdomen. Trace the symbol with your awareness, feel it connecting the right and left sides of the abdomen and above and below the navel crossing over in the middle behind the area of the navel.

Then without stopping and to change direction of the energy, draw half a circle and trace the symbol with your awareness the opposite way.

Then rest in stillness in the middle of the abdomen. Feel the infinite healing energy filling, nourishing and balancing the function of all the internal organs there.

I am aware, I am awake, I am a field of infinite possibilities and I am practicing Seasonal Yoga Nidra.

Now get ready to end the practice ….
Return to the breath, feel your body on the floor and yourself in the room….

Remember your Sankalpa (resolution) you made at the start of the practice, repeat it mentally three times.

(Miss out the following sentence, if using as a precursor to sleep).
Become aware of the external environment and return to normal awareness, open your eyes and slowly sit up, wide-awake with a clear alert mind and a body full of energy.

Home and Lifestyle section

- Connect with the people you feel an attachment to. It is also a time to be social and re- connect with those you have lost connection with.

- Look at places in your home which you dislike or lack energy and change things around. Early Summer is time to be adaptable and open to change.

- Create space for the new to come in, not only in the body but in your life and your home too.

- Make your home a place that you would be really confident about asking people back to. Make sure your inner home expectations are matching you external standards.

- Dress from the inside out and make sure your foundation garments make you feel good, well dressed and good about yourself. As your grandmother used to say "dress for the unexpected" especially at this time of year, as Early Summer is about being adventurous and trying out new things but from an inner confidence.

- Find your spirit of adventure and apply it to any area of your life which lacks spice!

- Start to use your connective tissue like your personal Guru. Notice what makes you tense, have an awareness of who, why and where tension arrived in life. Use your connective tissue to be your personal adviser, observe your armouring or tensions.

- Maintaining a fluid flow in connecting the rooms of the house, energetically. Open your eyes to seeing your home as someone else would. Try this exercise: Close your eyes as you step into your home open them as if you were entering for the first time look for areas that are stagnant or needing attention and clear them. Also try this in your garden, balcony or any outside area.

- Your home should be a collage of your life. But get rid of anything in your house you are feeling obliged to keep but you have always disliked (Granny's furniture etc ..) or brings with it a negative feeling or memory. Break connection with the obligation. Remember that your loss is the local charity shops gain! Let it go.

- External and internal communication: your home and environment are reflecting things back to you that need addressing in life. For example a leaking tap can mean address any leaking taps in life! Spending money on subscriptions that you don't use i.e. health clubs, T.V subscription etc .. Anything that is draining resources or causing a leak in the energy of your finances.

Oils: Ylang Ylang (nourishes skin and lifts mood, increases blood flow and relieves inflammation, regulates heart beat and energy boost)

Geranium (eases tension and promotes connection to inner life)

Frankincense (high spiritual frequency)

Avoid
Being too open or being over protective yourself.

Final questionnaire:

- ☑ Are you feeling less sensitive and less over reactive?
- ☑ Are you feeling more connected with friends and colleagues?
- ☑ Is your allergy situation getting better, do you feel your immunity has improved?
- ☑ Have you been getting more structure back into your body and noticing that your joints were locked or overextended?
- ☑ Is your body feeling less tense and is there a healthy balance between your flexibility and strength?
- ☑ In social situations are you less shy, vulnerable or over protective?
- ☑ Has your body temperature control improved?
- ☑ Do you feel less responsible for the happiness/mood of others?
- ☑ Have your become less negative and withdrawn in your thoughts?
- ☑ Are your body and mind working intelligently and does it attack you less?
- ☑ Has your internal body clock improved ? Sleeping, eating and other bodily functions are now all happening at the right time.
- ☑ Check your tongue again - remember red stiff tongue can indicate heat in the heart and pericardium or do you feel less tension in the your chest?
- ☑ How is the weight distribution between the upper and lower body or visually is a difference between the upper, middle and lower portions of the face. - has that improved?
- ☑ Do you have a more healthy relationship with social media?
- ☑ Have you improved finding a more appropriate way to respond in certain situations?
- ☑ Do you appreciate time alone to re-connect with yourself?
- ☑ Have you included a daily practice into your life, seeing it as important as cleaning your teeth?

The season of summer

The summer and fire energy is more warm, active, physical and passionate than any other season. The days are long and light with very few hours of darkness. Nature's energy is at its peak, so try to match it with yours!

The Fire element is all about heat and energy; a time to live life to the full, stay up later and get up earlier. A chance to soak up energy from the sun, and absorb oxygen and perfumes from the outdoors while everything is in full bloom. This is the time to create energy and power which will carry us into the harvesting of the late summer and then the storing of your resources in the autumn for the long winter ahead.

Traditionally, summer was the time of year when we all worked outdoors for long hours spending time in the healthy sun and then, after work, it was the time to; dance, sing and party, have fun, be in love, with plenty of laughter — the food of the soul, providing the extra momentum when needed and the feeling of internal joy and happiness! It delights in the richness of the moment.

The colour associated with the season is red, which has the ability to stimulate the pulse and heart rate. Hence the saying to 'paint the town red', inferring to celebrate and go out partying.

The Feeling of Summer

This is to balance calm with being adaptable, friendly, outgoing, warm, peaceful, charming, spontaneous, vibrant, expressive and joyful!

If summer was a person, their nature would be someone who loves to enjoy rather than strive. They move and operate from the heart, which makes them open but sometimes vulnerable. Their strength is that they are warm, empathetic, joyful and exuberant. They can perform with passion and are able to draw out the positive and the hopeful in others and be extremely persuasive. They focus outwards, can be extremely charming, and love to communicate and elicit people's co-operation. In the extreme they can manipulate. They have charisma and tend to easily grasp the whole picture and can ignite the actions of others with compassion and clarity. They can be the catalyst in helping others to believe in themselves and have more confidence to move forward into the future. They hate dullness and love to be inspired by things outside of themselves such as art, music or beautiful places. They like nothing more than to make people happy, but have a tendency to burn out if they have difficulty with discernment, set up expectations they cannot meet, or over commit.

> So it makes sense to develop the positive qualities and watch out for the negative at this time of year to match the energy of the season. If you feel out of balance at the moment, these are the issues that might come up in summer to be dealt with:
>
> - Are you tense when meeting new people?
> - Do you have circulatory problems?
> - Do you suffer from insomnia or have an overactive mind?
> - Do you have times of emotional unease?
> - Are you absent-minded or confused regularly?
> - Are you always needing to be busy and have difficulty slowing down?
> - Do you suffer from tension in your neck and shoulders?
> - Do you do what it takes to be liked and try to make everyone happy, sometimes at the expense of yourself?
> - Do you have a ruddy complexion or does your face flush a lot?
> - Are you prone to stammering or have difficulties with communication?
> - Are you easily wounded, rejected or offended?
> - Do you laugh continuously or at inappropriate times?
> - Do you respond to issues by clowning, performing or being over cheerful?
> - Do you constantly need a source of fuel to keep yourself stimulated, amused or entertained?

Eight Priorities for Summer

1. **Try your best to stay at peace and to be compassionate;** remember the expression 'seeing red'? It immediately conjures up the feeling of anger or aggression and involves some amount of passion. Learn to use passion positively!
2. **Try to balance** the intensity of living in the moment with an awareness of what follows. Only take on what you can handle and learn to say "no". **Re-establish some order** so that you have more calm and rhythm in your life.
3. **Develop ways find contentment** through learning to love yourself and believing you are lovable. If you do not know where to start, meditate on, or think about the things that you are good at and the things that you have done to make people happy. If you can not think of any... go out and do something to make someone happy today. It can be as simple as a phone call to an elderly relative or telling someone you love them.
4. **Take control** of your levels of openness with others; stop yourself from saying too much; discriminate between the different contexts. Know what you want from others and what they want from you.
5. **Learn to let go, forgive and move on**; try not to take things too personally. Act and speak from the heart... with feeling.
6. **Find different ways to express yourself** such as art, playing an instrument or just sit and listen to your favourite music turned up loud, and sing along. Voice and speech have a strong connection to the heart.
7. **Exercise; yoga builds stamina and heat** in the body. Try a sun salute or three... every morning for a week; see if you feel any different! If yoga isn't your thing then go outdoors for a brisk walk every day, even for just ten minutes!
8. **Communication; spend time with others**, such as family and friends *(with the phone off)*. Get in touch with some old friends and arrange to meet once a month in the local pub or café. Find different ways to communicate with people who you have difficulty in getting on with; see what makes them tick!

Eight Things to Avoid for Summer

1. **Burning out** and being chaotic in your work and private life, or losing control.
2. Avoid **extremes** of any kind, in behaviour, environment or food.
3. Being **isolated** or alone, and staying in bed too long!
4. **Constipation**. Keep the system moving; fibre in vegetables and fruit should do the trick.
5. Becoming excessively **self-indulgent** or obsessed with your appearance.
6. Avoid **caffeine** after midday or late at night and avoid developing addictive habits.
7. Getting **stuck in the same** old routine. Instead try changing it, even if it is just going to a different place for lunch.
8. Becoming inhibited, disillusioned, autocratic or **obsessed with detail**.

The Ideal Day in Summer

Morning
Get up early and do some outdoor cardiovascular exercise such as cycling or running, perhaps to work? Eat a light, cooling breakfast.

Midday
A good time to sell something, be creative and be communicative. *(Do some aerobic exercise in your lunch break if you didn't get out in the morning.)* Have a light, cool lunch in summer or hot weather and avoid sugar and caffeine to prevent an afternoon energy crash.

Afternoon
This is the time to come back to your centre, slow down and think things through. If your eyelids get heavy, take deep breaths to oxygenate the brain. Have a siesta if possible or even a ten-minute meditation to give your energy a boost for the longer days.

Evening
Let go of your day, enjoy an evening out, dinner in the garden or socialise. Avoid a heavy carbohydrate meal at night. Keep it light; maybe enjoy a barbecue, which you can marinade.

Night
Go for a late night walk because less sleep is needed in summer.

Eight Daily Habits for Summer

1. Make time to **experience emotions** and watch their quality!
2. **Give from the heart and bring** a bit of sunshine into your or someone else's life every day. Just a small thing will do it.
3. **The joyful heart:** find out what really makes you happy. Make a list, meditate on it, re-evaluate, put the list somewhere you can see it every day, and then do one of those things every day in the summer! It can be as simple as spending a few minutes admiring your flowering hanging baskets, or managing a nightly run in the park.
4. **The open heart:** get your arms in the air! Open the armpits as it opens your Heart meridian and increases lung capacity, which in turn supports the heart function.
5. **The sharing heart:** communicate with everyone around you. Do not detach yourself; it is not good for the heart.
6. **The key to self-development for summer, and the fire season** is meditation, as a healthy fire will have both high flames and then burning embers. So sit for ten minutes every day, whenever you can. Arrive ten minutes early for a meeting or the school run; sit in the car and breathe your vitality, so that you conserve your vitality and do not run on a flat battery!
7. **The heart of the matter** is your food and diet. Have a diet that keeps you cool, light and active; water-based foods, fresh foods and plenty of filtered water.
8. **The physical heart:** it is very important at this time of year to get some exercise every day. Include exercise for the upper body and chest, and team sports as these involve being with others.

Food Section

Getting Slender in Summer

Summer is the BEST time to diet. However, if you are truly living in the season and eating the fresh seasonal food, there should be no need to diet, as the foods you are taking in are enough to make you lighter and more energetic. Exercise will be easier and feel like the natural thing to do, encouraging weight loss without you even noticing it.

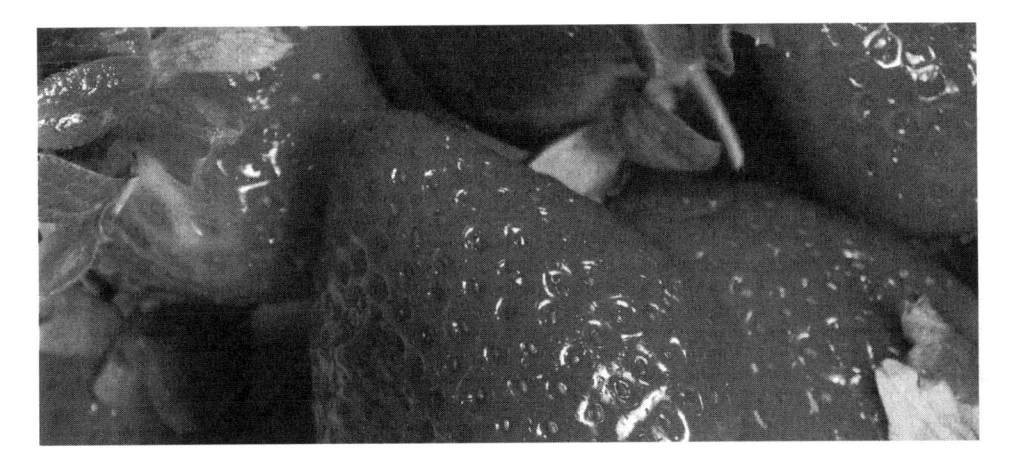

Clean Light Diet

Summer's colour is red, and the element is Fire, so it is time to be active and the foods you eat should fuel you for this purpose. Food colours reflect the colour of the season, so this means that lots of red and purple foods are great for fire energy, i.e. strawberries, raspberries, blackberries, blueberries, tomatoes, red peppers and beetroot. Keep your diet real, clean and light, full of fresh summer foods, and try not to buy processed or pre-prepared foods, including cut up salads. Buy foods as near to the way it was grown as possible, as every process it goes through takes a little more of its vital life-force. Aim for forty to sixty per cent of your diet to be made up of fruit and vegetables, such as pea pods, baby leaf spinach, broad beans, pak-choi cabbage, and asparagus and have lots of raw foods to help your body reach a balance with the heat outside. A way of effortlessly feeding yourself nutritiously in the summer is with freshly made fruit juices. If you do not own a juicer, it is a good time of year to buy one.

The Clean Energetic Approach to Eating

- **Remember** to eat food grown in season, locally and organically if possible. Genetically modified foods have a weaker energetic effect and are harder for the body to break down, so are best avoided.
- **Avoid pesticides**, insecticides, chemicals, pre-prepared food and microwaving.
- **Buy glass containers** rather than plastic to avoid wrapping or storing in plastic, and unwrap food bought in plastic as soon as you get it home, before storage.
- **Eat food as near to the way it was grown,** or as close to its natural state, as possible; every additional process it goes through draws more energy out. Even pre-chopped vegetables have half the original energy!
- **Drink filtered water, not water that has been lying dormant in a plastic bottle.**
- **Chew** your food properly.
- Make sure in the heat of the summer that your **sodium (*salt*) levels** are kept balanced, as they can become imbalanced by drinking too much water. Eating natural salt products, such as Wakame and Nori seaweeds, help keep your minerals up.
- **Buy food in proportion**: make forty to sixty per cent of your diet fruit and vegetables; grains thirty to forty per cent; beans, dairy, meat and nuts ten to twenty per cent.

Diet—the Right Fuel

In Japan, the body is thought of as a fire mass and can only continue to exist if the appropriate fuel is added from time to time: this fuel we call food and drink. We also need oxygen to make the transformation of food into energy complete.

1. We can choose a quick burning or slow burning fuel. If you consume a slow burning fuel, such as meat, then you need to eat less often.
2. Certain foods like vegetables are eaten in larger quantities, whereas other foods such as fats are eaten in smaller quantities, to give the same amount of energy.
3. Some foods are cleaner burning fuels, other highly refined foods give off fumes, which cloud our perception, fog our minds and stop clear thinking.
4. Some foods can be stored, whereas others decay or rot easily. So if certain foods are allowed to remain in the intestines, they can cause stagnation and fermentation. An example of this is eating fruit after a large meal, which causes it to ferment, so it is best to eat fruit between meals and not on a full stomach.
5. By drinking too much at mealtimes or eating too much cold or raw food, we can literally put out the digestive fire or over-dilute our digestive juices.
6. The fire of our digestive process also needs oxygen to revive it. Breathing is the quickest way to restore energy and health. You can live without food for up three weeks, water for three days but without oxygen for only three minutes.

Food for the Summer Energy

As previously mentioned, you must watch out for some red foods. Fiery in nature, foods such as red meat can overheat organs, especially the liver and lungs. This is caused by the heat of the stomach and liver rising into the lungs resulting in excessively red cheeks, or red in the whites of the eyes.

Heat Reducing Foods

Asparagus	Cucumber	Mung beans	Watermelon
Aubergine	Elderflower	Peppermint	Wheat
Bamboo shoots	Grapefruit	Potato	White of a
Banana	Kale	Seaweed	chicken's egg
Celery	Lemon	Salt	
Clams	Lettuce	Tofu	
Cranberry	Millet	Watercress	

Foods to Assist Blood Circulation

Aubergine
Cayenne pepper (*a very important spice for the Fire element; used in moderation, it helps strengthen the heart and blood vessels*)
Chestnut
Chilli pepper
Chive
Crab
Mustard leaf (*great with shaved parmesan and olive oil*)
Onion
Peach
Scallion/spring onion
Sturgeon
Vinegar

If you have a tendency to retain fluid, including the following in your diet may help:

Aduki beans	Broad bean	Grapes	Mackerel
Alfalfa	Celery	Kelp	Sardine
Anchovy	Clams	Lettuce	Seaweed
Barley			

Fish oils are great for the heart and the body. Omega 3 is also in linseed oil, vital for optimum brain function. Include two portions a week of fish that have teeth, e.g. salmon and mackerel.

Bitter is the flavour of the season, so this is the taste to promote as bitter foods stimulate digestion. They can also help the respiratory system — handy for this time of year when one is supposed to be doing more cardiovascular exercise (*any exercise which makes you breathe faster!*).

Grains are great, so enjoy rye, wheat-germ, and corn.

Vegetables

Alfalfa sprouts	Avocado	Chicory	Watercress
Artichoke	Broccoli	Kale	Cucumber and
Asparagus	Celery	Lettuce	seaweeds for their cooling qualities

Fruits

Rhubarb and papaya for a bitter flavour. For cooling, pick melon, mango, pear, blackcurrant, banana, and cranberry.

A word of warning: if you have a history of high acid, arthritic joints, a possibility of kidney stones, gout or you know that you are high in uric acid, avoid red foods as they encourage the production of uric acid.

Ideal cooking methods for the summer are boiling or steaming, as these methods are cooling or neutral. Funnily enough barbecued food is the most heating, so avoid it if you are overheated. This is indicated by a red face or tongue, or a tendency for high blood pressure, so instead include more raw foods.

Seven Food and Nutrition Tips

1. Eat more **light foods** as they make you feel, and be more active!
2. Summer is the time when you can afford to **eat little and often** because it is kinder to the small intestine.
3. Eat **more of the cooling** water-based foods like salads, cucumber and celery with dips and fruits such as melon, pear and mango.
4. Eat **more seeds** and nuts as they give you the valuable omega oils, and eat fish with teeth (*e.g. mackerel, salmon, herring and tuna*) at least twice a week.
5. **Buy a juicer** and start to juice fresh summer fruits and vegetables. For weight loss, make the focus more on vegetable juices rather than the fruits.
6. Eat food that is colourful and has **plenty of variety**, because it will lift your mood and be reflected in your personality!
7. Eating locally grown food will **balance your internal climate** with the climate outside.

What to avoid:

1. **Too much spice**: These are helpful to stimulate your liver out of stagnancy and add variety to meals, but too much of them can aggravate it, leading to too much fuel being put on the fire!
2. **Red meat and animal fats** as they raise blood cholesterol. Eggs, dairy products and sugar also do this and should be avoided if your cholesterol is high.
3. **Nightshade vegetables** are best used in moderation; these are peppers, aubergines, tomatoes and potatoes. Avoid them if you have arthritis.
4. **Cakes and biscuits** are best avoided at this time, and cut down on sugars and refined foods.

5. **If the weather is damp**, keep the consumption of fruit under control as these can cause aching joints.
6. **'Red herrings'**: These are foods/additives that deceive, such as artificial sweeteners, low fat foods or man-made products. Keep your food real!

Quick Fix Guide for Summer

Have you left it too late to lose a little weight for a holiday or special occasion? Follow and act on the nine points below for a two-week simple food and exercise plan which is ideal pre-holiday or to prepare you for a special event!

1. **What goes in the mouth?** Keep it light so eat little, and more often, to keep the metabolism going.
2. **Eat half of what you can normally eat.** Stay off dairy products and wheat for two weeks. Replace wheat with oatcakes and if you feel like eating cheese, have goat's or sheep's cheese. Replace cow's milk with goat's, soya or rice milk.
3. **Avoid carbohydrates after 6pm.**
4. **Eat seeds**, using them in salad dressings, because they are full of omega 3 oils and are good for the skin.
5. **Eat a mixture of blueberries, raspberries, blackberries and strawberries in the morning**. Ideal this time of year to juice for breakfast or a 'between meals' snack, or for quality nourishment on the run!
6. **Eat light, cool foods for lunch,** e.g. salad leaves, rocket, spinach with added nuts, plus chicken or fish to make it a bit more filling. Use a good quality olive oil *(or flax seed)* as a salad dressing along with some freshly squeezed lime.
7. **Think Mediterranean food for your evening meal**, and again, keep it light, similar to lunch. High-energy sprouting beans, great at this time of year, mixed with a handful of fresh prawns with some goats' yoghurt and fresh lemon squeezed over the top.
8. **For snacks**, try hummus with raw vegetable dips, seeds and olives. For a sweet snack, try banana on oatcake, dried fruit, nuts, and dates.
9. **Drink plenty of water** and fresh mint or jasmine tea at night.

Important tip
Avoid sugar, biscuits, etc. for two weeks; once sugar is out of your diet, you do not crave it.

Exercise and Movement Section

This section will show you various ways to stimulate the energy lines for this time of year. As you have read earlier, each time of the year has a pair of organs, which are complementary and associated with it.

The organs for the summer are the heart and small intestine. So, what do they do? The heart pumps blood around the body delivering essential nourishment to the organs and clearing away waste; it is essential to life. The small intestine acts on the quality of blood by controlling nourishment via the digestive system. It produces enzymes, which breakdown the food and absorb the nutrients into the blood, so the heart can transport them to where they are needed. If it does not work properly, the whole system slows down and becomes less efficient.

Because the function of both of these organs is circulation, you can see why the heart needs exercise to make it beat faster in order to do its job more efficiently delivering energy and nourishment to every cell. Our blood depends on the quality of our food we eat. Also it is seen, in traditional Chinese medicine, as housing the mind. If inadequately nourished by the blood, the mind floats, giving rise to restlessness and anxiety, particularly noticeable before or during sleep. 'Abundant blood' *(a term used in traditional Chinese medicine or TCM)* allows you to feel well nourished, have vitality and stamina, a strong immune system, and bright complexion, then the mind can withdraw inwards allowing sleep to bring renewal. The following sections will include exercises, which move energy in these areas and therefore energize the l

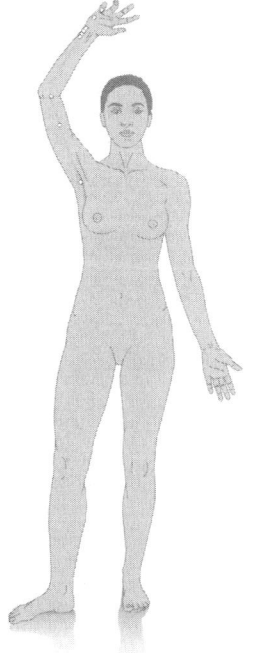

The Heart 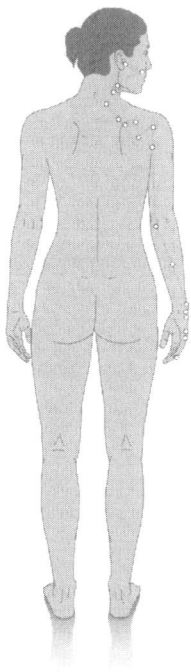 **The Small Intestine**

The Quick Exercise Guide for Summer

Get the heart beating, burn the fat and work with the body and mind at the same time:

1. **Take a brisk walk** in the morning and in the evening, checking your posture as you walk. Feel for length between the bottom of your ribs and the start of your hips, grow an inch taller, stride out, and use the arms. Get a friend to do it with you to make it more fun.
2. **Start cycling everywhere!** Riding a bike is a fantastic fat burning exercise.
3. If you have never practiced **yoga**, now is the time to start. Perform three Sun Salutation A and three Sun Salutation B poses, every morning except Sundays. Keep it simple and reap the benefits, for just ten minutes a day, to trim the arms and the abdominal muscles, which is essential for summer clothes.
4. **No time to 'waist'!** Tie a bit of rope around your middle, stand normally and tighten it so that you can feel it on the waist. Now pull the whole waist in feeling the rope becoming loose, taking care to keep your shoulders down so that they do not get tense. Wear it at least three times a day for half an hour.
5. **Skin.** Exfoliate twice a week and rub almond oil mixed with some rosemary aromatherapy oil every morning. This is good for promoting circulation, so rub vigorously and thoroughly all over the body in the direction of the heart.
6. **Clear your mind**: Start going through the pile of paperwork: pay off all your bills so that you can be carefree when you start your holiday. Do a bit at a time, making a list and crossing off, so that you can see progress.
7. **Meditation.** Yes, fit it in, because you will feel the benefit. Prepare yourself by sitting or lying for ten minutes every day, whenever you manage to find space *(both time and room!)*. With the earth energy supporting you, think of something you love and feel the energy of it expanding through the heart out to the periphery of the body and re-energizing every cell.
8. **Above all... Keep it fun!** Try to talk a friend into doing it with you so that you can motivate each other and compare notes. Make it fun and laugh about it!

Exercise for Summer

Nature is now in full bloom, the season of passion, abundance and high energies, and the time of the year when we should flourish physically, mentally and emotionally; a time to work vigorously and energetically and, if desired, to concentrate on a weight loss programme. The heart and circulatory system is functioning with optimum energy, therefore **cardiovascular exercise** is most beneficial, along with a full energy **yoga** practice such as Ashtanga, power yoga or Vinyasa flow as an ideal balance.

A **cardiovascular exercise programme** of thirty minutes per day if possible, will burn fat, speed up your metabolism and improve your endurance and appearance. The choice of **outdoor exercise** is vast in the summer; e.g. power walking, cycling, rowing, tennis and running; plus all that fresh air and a few beneficial rays of sunshine to give you an extra healthy glow.

Eight Summer Exercise Tips

1. Work on the body's **circulation**, keeping lots of cardiovascular exercise in your routine.
2. Your summer **yoga** practice should reflect the same cardiovascular qualities — Ashtanga power yoga or Vinyasa flow.
3. **Balance** a more strenuous practice and exercise with a long period of meditation to train the mind.
4. Hi/lo aerobics or a martial art — **make your heart pump**!
5. Discover your favourite routine or exercise and do it for the month of July to **keep happy** and bring you **enjoyment**.
6. Take part in a dance or salsa class, which has **rhythmic music** and is great fun!
7. **Circuit training** or fun classes, which are done as part of a team or a group.
8. **Include both warm-ups and cool-downs** from the Qigong section as these can be done out of doors every morning to warm you up for the day!

Qigong for Summer

Bo points or collecting points are located on the chest, abdomen or waist and are used both for diagnosis and treatment. These are where the energy collects or gathers from each of the relevant organs. They can become tender either spontaneously or on the application of pressure. In treatments they are used to regulate and balance the energy in their associated organs. The ones for the Heart and Small Intestine are shown below. The initials and numbers in the brackets refer to the particular acupressure point along an organ meridian, which is an energy pathway that leads to and from a major organ. These points are where the energy is particularly accessible from the surface.

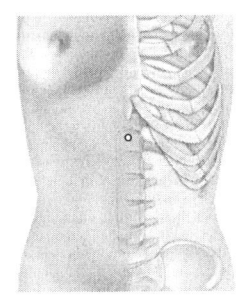

Juque (Great Palace, Con 14) at the end of the breastbone, four cun (about a hand's width) above the umbilicus. It is used for testing and balancing the function of the heart.

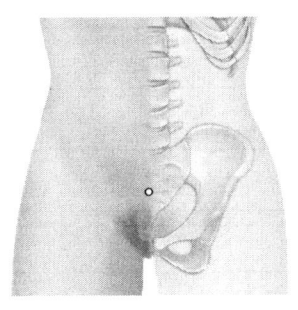

Guanyuan (Gate to the Original, Con 4) four cun (about a hands' width) below the umbilicus. It is used for testing and balancing the function of the small intestine.

Pressing the Ball Under the Water

This is great exercise to pacify the fire energy of the heart, which you can use to compose and centre between all of the exercises, reduce high blood pressure or calm the emotions.

Stand with your feet in horse stance slightly wider than hip-width apart. Inhale while raising the arms out to the sides of the body *(palms down)*, then at shoulder height rotate your palms up and draw both hands in toward the midline with your fingertips pointed towards each other. Whilst exhaling, press down as if pushing a ball under the water until your hands are level with your navel, and feel the crown of the head float upwards. Repeat the movement several times, feeling that when you press down toward the navel, you are pressing down on a strong spring, drawing your shoulder-blades down the back to make the movement.

Are you under pressure? This will calm things down

Daily Warm-up Exercises for Summer

Balance the body by stretching the muscles, loosening the joints and vertebrae, releasing physical tensions, whilst stimulating the circulation, activating the endocrine system and opening up the energy meridians. This establishes a strong foundation for health and for your t'ai chi, chi-gung *(qigong)* and yoga practice.

Spinal Twists for Summer to Find Your Natural Rhythm

This is a tonic for the digestive system (especially the liver and stomach) and it also benefits the spleen and kidneys, while loosening the spine.

Stand with feet slightly wider than hip-width apart, shoulders relaxed and arms hanging loosely at your sides with your knees unlocked. Start turning slowly from left to right and back again, using the power of the thighs to promote the movement and letting the waist and torso naturally turn from side to side as one unit. Let your hands wrap around the waist. Then move the arms up, slapping the upper body *(chest and top of shoulders)* with open palm of the upper hand and back of the hand with the lower one *(at waist level)*. Gradually increasing the power and speed of the twist, and change the speed and rhythm from fast to slow and back again, until you find your own preferred and comfortable rhythm.

Now raise one hand up above the head bending the elbow to take the hand back to slap the top of the spine and the base of the neck, letting the palm of the hand cover the knobble at the base of the neck *(C7)*. The lower hand slaps the side of the ribs. Then change hands. This stimulates the thyroid, frees tension in the neck, stimulates the end of the Spleen meridian and opens the chest and the Heart and Small Intestine meridians.

Are you out of sync? Get back into life's rhythm

Rotate Each Ankle

This is especially indicated for swollen ankles and heart problems.

Stand with your weight on one leg, and keeping the other leg straight and with the foot just off the ground, rotate the foot four times in a clockwise and then in an anti-clockwise direction. Inhale and flex the foot up towards the leg, then exhale and point it, repeating this several times. Next point the toes and draw the arch upwards and inwards, then downwards and outwards. Lastly rotate the foot four times clockwise and then anti-clockwise. Repeat several times on each leg.

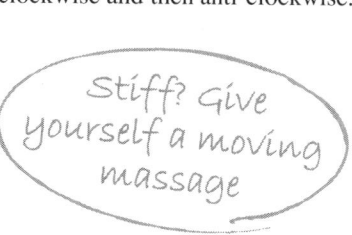

Stiff? Give yourself a moving massage

Knee Rotations

Place your feet and knees together, and then rub your palms to create friction and heat. Now place them over the knees, gripping the kneecaps with the tips of your fingers. Bend and straighten your knees several times, as if sitting back into a chair. Now rotate them to the left, down towards centre and then to the right and return to centre. Do this several times one way, and then reverse the circle. Then bend and straighten the knees several times, as if to sit back on a low stool.

Turning at the Waist and Massage the Intestines

Place your hands on your hips and tilt the pubic bone forward and then backward several times. Then move it from side to side several times keeping the upper body as still as you can. Then rotate the hips in a circle taking the upper body and shoulders in the opposite direction.

Free Up the Chest and Shoulders

Stand with your feet shoulder-width apart, extend your left arm forward and the right arm straight out behind you palms down. Swing the arms from the back to the front, allowing them to drop at your sides as you swing. Keep the hips facing forward allowing the arms to come to shoulder level, swinging them quite fast, so that you can feel the movement in the centre of your chest.

Now let the arms swing higher until they come up above the head, with the elbows slightly bent, so that you feel the movement in the shoulder-blades. Then lower them to swing back and forth at chest level again. Keep the hips still all the time so the rotation is in the waist, thoracic spine and neck.

Shoulder and neck tension? Perform these daily

Neck Rotations

Maintain the bridge on your brain

Look over your left shoulder, and now the right. Roll the chin down along your right collar bone then towards the left, and then make a full circle over to the right. Do this several times and then reverse the circle. Draw a circle with the chin to massage the throat and the thyroid rather than taking the head back as you rotate it.

Cool the Head and Warm the Heart

This keeps you cool headed but warm-hearted! It helps to peel away the emotional and mental armour we build up around us and allows us to remain open hearted.

Inhale and then as you exhale, bend down, taking your hips backwards and bringing your chest down toward your thighs, while crossing your arms over in front of your knees. Inhale, rising up and drawing your crossed arms up over your head as if you are pulling a sweater over your head, to draw the new energy up through the body and clear away any cloudy or negative thinking. Exhale as you uncross your arms and lower them down to your sides, bending down and taking the hips backward. Lower your chest down again toward your thighs, to cross your arms again in front of your knees. Release the head and neck, and energy tensions from the mind. Repeat eight times.

Are you working too hard? Clear the head and warm the heart

Balancing the Flow of the Heart and Small Intestine Meridians

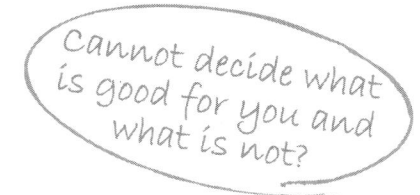

Cannot decide what is good for you and what is not?

Inhale drawing a circle over your head with your right hand. Turn the palm outwards, by rotating the little finger, as your right hand passes in front of the face. Exhale as you bring the right hand back and down to the right side with the palm down. Repeat this seven more times.

Inhale as you raise your right arm in front of you and stepping the left foot forward to rest the left heel on the ground, the weight staying on the right leg. Place your left hand behind your back just below the waist, resting the back of the hand on the sacrum.

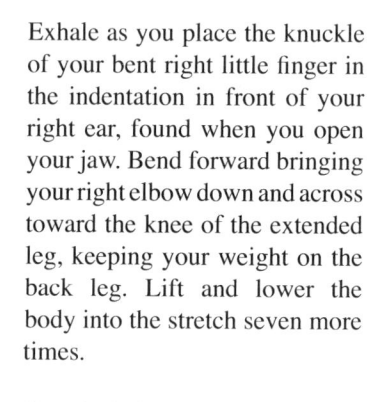

Exhale as you place the knuckle of your bent right little finger in the indentation in front of your right ear, found when you open your jaw. Bend forward bringing your right elbow down and across toward the knee of the extended leg, keeping your weight on the back leg. Lift and lower the body into the stretch seven more times.

Step the left foot back and repeat by bringing the left arm around the head and stepping the right foot forward.

Supporting the Sky With Both Hands

Slouched and tired? Try this!

The aim of this exercise is to regulate all the internal organs from the heart and lungs to the kidneys and intestines. It also relieves fatigue and corrects the posture of the upper body.

Start in a relaxed position, feet shoulder-width apart, shoulders relaxed and arms by your side. Bring your fingertips in towards each other and inhale to slowly raise your arms up in front of you, keeping your shoulder-blades down. As your hands reach chest height, turn your palms upward to the sky and bring them to the crown of your head. Feel the stretch in the wrists as the fingers, slightly open, point toward each other, keeping your palms flat.

Exhale and press your palms to the sky while pressing your feet firmly into the ground, stretching the spine and neck without adding any tension. Do not lock your elbows, keep your shoulders relaxed and extend the arms to open the joints. The rotation of the palms is a continuous flowing movement. Lift the Yintang point, in the third eye area between the eyebrows, to face the sky.

Inhale as the hands return to the crown of the head, keeping the palms facing the sky but the gaze now looks forwards. Repeat, pressing the sky with the palms several times. Then lower the arms out and down to the sides.

Advanced level

1. As you press up with the hands, slowly rise up on your toes completing the stretch and balance. For this exercise, gaze is kept looking forwards, and the head aligned to the spine.

2. **Reverse breathing**: Pulling the abdomen in flat as you inhale, and relaxing the abdomen as you exhale. (Avoid if you have high blood pressure or asthma.) As for the above, the gaze looks forwards, feel as if your hands are pulling up an internal invisible thread, and releasing it on the exhalation.

3. **Stepping out into a wide horse stance**: With feet slightly turned out and knees over toes. Inhale and push your hands up to the sky, while sinking down into a wide squat and bending in the legs, stretching the entire spinal column. Exhale as you lower the arms circling them out to the sides, and rising up in the legs.

T'ai Chi Moves for Summer

Movements in the form should focus on:

- Speeding up responses, or slowing down movement. Working to re-establish rhythm.
- Breathing to support the heart function.
- Holding poses to build power and heat.
- Martial applications are used to burn through tensions and release the impure 'bin chi' (bad energy).
- Emphasis can be made between hard and soft moves during training.

For the Heart and Small Intestine: The cleansing quality of fire burns through stagnation and tension, whilst at the same time balancing extremes to maintain a sense of inner calm. This means that we can act with the appropriate responses to all of life's challenges. Keeping the heart area open ensures free circulation is maintained, both in the body and in the emotions. The relaxation phase between the moves helps us to relax and come back to centre.

Fair Lady Weaves the Shuttles

Start by holding a circle, left hand on top and with your weight on the left leg. Exhale and step forward onto the right foot, raising the right hand in front of your face, palm inwards. As it passes the face, turn the palm outwards, *(rotating the little finger)* and pushing out into a block. At the same time, push the left hand forward and slightly up from the centre of the chest. Rotate the waist, rather than allowing the left hand to cross the midline, as you push slightly to the right side.

Inhale and return to the start position, by stepping the right foot back and holding the circle with the right hand on top. Then feel relaxed and prepared, ready to step forward on the left foot.

The above exercise can be done in pairs or as a partner exercise. As your partner steps forwards on the right leg to punch with the right arm, you step forwards on your right leg to their right side, lifting your right arm, as fair lady weaves the shuttles, to left up underneath their right upper arm, and push their body with your left hand.

Up tight? Regain your calm and come back to centre

Yoga for Summer

The Fire Element and Yoga

Just like a true fire, the element of fire requires tending. It needs to be controlled and have regular attention, as occasionally the flames need to be fanned and yet at other times allowed to quietly sustain their own energy in the burning embers state. The secret of fire is to know when and which is appropriate. Fire or heat creates change; in yoga, this is called *tapas*. So it is reasonable to say that summer is the time to make changes within the body. This can only be done, in yogic terms, by regular and frequent practice.

The mistake many people make with this knowledge is to overcomplicate it. To practice something on a regular basis without getting overwhelmed means keeping it simple and accessible, the following information is the key to this. When the energy is high, life can be busy, so spending only 10–20 minutes a day on your yoga practice can make a huge difference to how you feel ... even you can manage that!

Surya Namaskara A (Sun Salutation A)

This standard and most well-known sequence in yoga is perfect; it opens the heart, lifts the heart rate, improves circulation, and sends energy/prana/chi around the entire body. All you need to do is repeat this 3–5 times every morning and feel the difference!

A perfect warm up for the day and any Yoga flow!

6. Keep shoulder-blades in neutral and neck long

Surya Namaskara A (Sun Salutation A)

Start your yoga experience with this sequence. Breathe your way through it

7. Make it easy when you start, drop your knees

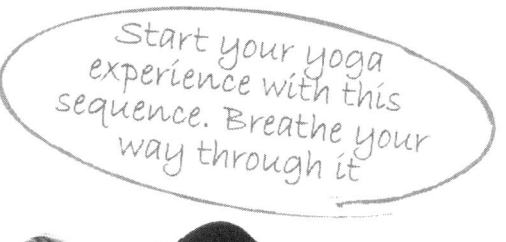

8. Keep the shoulder-blades in neutral, the neck long and the elbows pulled into the side of the ribs. Slowly lower yourself down to the floor

9. Drop the hips to the floor, keep the arms directly under the shoulders, take a long breath in as you bring the head up last, stretching the neck back

10. Work on spreading the fingers and the toes wide. Push down to create a good foundation

11. Step onto the front of the mat

12. Inhale and look up then exhale to stand

13. Inhale as you look up

Surya Namaskara B (Sun Salutation B)

After a while you might want to add on something a little more difficult, so start to practice Surya Namaskara B, Sun Salutation B.

Feeling flat and lost your zest for life? Create heat, energy and joy with this sequence

1. Inhale

2. Exhale

3. Inhale

4. Exhale

5.

6. Still... exhaling

7. Inhale

Part 3: The Season of Summer 135

Balance extremes of life with this flow

8. Exhale

9. Inhale

10. Exhale

11. Still... exhaling

12. Inhale

13. Exhale

14. Inhale

For beginners or easy flow start with three sun salutations, then build to five. Take a breath with each move.

15. Exhale

16. Still... exhaling

17. Inhale

18. Downward dog, five breaths

19. Inhale

20. Exhale

21. Finish

Heart Opening Flow

Fire is about action and expression and using the upper body and arms. Balance the practice by introducing cooling poses. Experience joy in the poses, focus on the mind and circulation. Release the neck and shoulders and flow with the movement between poses. Create the space to move within the body. Opening the armpits helps to open the heart.

Feeling miserable and depressed? Try this

Inhale, open armpits, keep shoulders down, five breaths

Inhale as you stretch up, open armpits and lengthen fingertips

Exhale, cross right foot over left, toes facing in to foot about six inches away from other foot. Bend back knee slightly, secure your foundation by connecting back shin with front calf

1. Reach for your spine, creep your fingers down as far as you can

2. Stretch and rotate the left arm

3. Continue full rotation, then bend elbow to meet other hand

4. Reach fingers and then grip

5. Stay for five breaths

If you can not reach, use a belt or tie to help

6. Open and stretch arms

7. Stay again for five breaths

Then repeat on the other side to open the Heart meridians.

Part 3: The Season of Summer 139

Add these on after a couple of weeks but keep your arms down if you become dizzy, light-headed or have blood pressure issues.

1. Breathe for five counts

2. Big inhale

3. The foot six inches from the heel, the toes turned in and push the back leg with the calf

Follow teaching points from page 76.

4. Grab left wrist with right hand, inhale and stretch to the side, opening armpits. Inhale

5. Grip opposite wrist and stretch the other way, slowly

6. Open out and stretch

After a couple of weeks progress to this

7. Exhale and tip forward from hips making sure both knees are slightly bent

8. Lace fingers together, bring arms overhead, maintaining breath

Then repeat on the other side

Part 3: The Season of Summer 141

Practice these moves for peace and contentment

9. Move hips around to face front. Stretch out back leg, pushing the heel to floor, bend through front leg and bring hands into the heart

10. Inhale as you stretch your arms up, keeping shoulders down, neck long and shoulder-blades down. Open through the armpits, hold for five breaths

11. Pull up with navel and move ribs down the front shin, bending the front knee slightly to soften pose. Come up and repeat on the other side

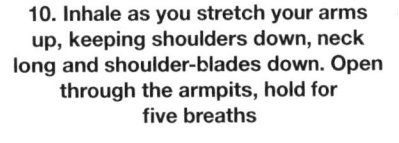

Move hands behind back, keep shoulders down, squeeze palms together

Threading the Needle

This sequence is beneficial to open both the Small and Large Intestine meridians and is about transformation and processing.

1

2. Reach the left arm under the body as far as possible. Stretch the back of the shoulders, push on the right hand rotating the spine... hold for three breaths then back to all fours

3

4. Then same on the other side

5. Back to all fours

Re-establish some order, calm, and rhythm in your life with these moves

6. Same as move 1 but extend the leg and rotate, staying on toes of the right leg. Hold for three breaths, and stabilise with the right hand

7. Then ... lift the right arm up to the ceiling rotate the arm so that the palm faces back, drop hand behind the back, increasing rotation. Try to keep the shoulder down, the neck and spine long, breathe

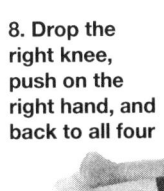

8. Drop the right knee, push on the right hand, and back to all four

Repeat on the other side

9

10. Slide the right arm under the left armpit, push on the left hand, look up to create further rotation in the neck and top end (thoracic) spine... breathe and hold for three breaths

11. Extend the left leg, and rest on the left toes

12. Lift the left arm to the ceiling and rotate as on the other side

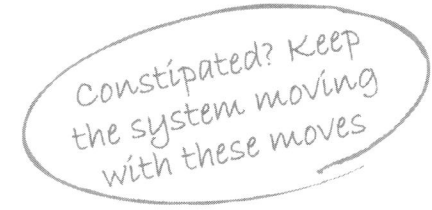

Constipated? Keep the system moving with these moves

13. Back to all fours

14. Stretch up the right arm on an inhale, open the armpit, back to all fours and then repeat on the other side

15

16

Anahatasana Sequence

For opening the heart, and great for stiff shoulders; also good for people who work leaning forward all day long (desk posture!).

Do this to feel more in harmony with yourself

1. Start on all fours

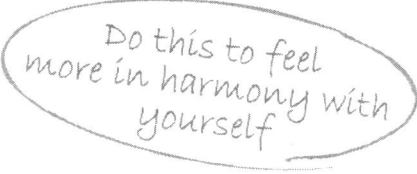

2. Bend elbows, arch back and start to lift head lengthening the front of the neck. Then slide your arms away from the body along the floor

3. Open armpits as you breathe in, try to get chin and chest on the floor (this may take a bit of practise) and stay for 3–5 breaths. All the time feel a lengthening through the front of the body and armpits. Keep stretching arms straight out so your fingers reach as far as possible

4

5. Sit on your heels, putting hands into reverse prayer position. To get this position, put your arms behind your back with the backs of the hands together and then turn hands so palms face each other. If you can not manage any of that, just fold your arms behind your back to hold your elbows

6. Then stretch forward into Child's pose, keeping your arms in the same position for a few breaths. Then drop them to either side of body and rest

7. Try this pose as an alternative to anahatasana, open armpits and breathe

Meditations and Contemplations for Summer

In these sections we use the controlling cycle of the five elements. Just as one element supports the next (the supporting cycle), its energy also has a controlling effect on another. Here we use the Water element to control Fire by slowing down the energy and calming the ever-distracted mind and rooting it in the body. Allowing time to reflect, refuel and experience joy.

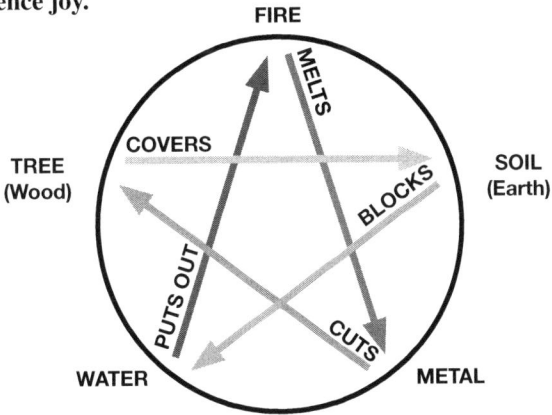

Walking Meditation

Some people find that there comes a moment, after sitting meditation and much concentration, that their head feels as if it is about to explode, as the nervous system releases certain stresses. In these cases, t'ai chi walking is excellent, as it can be used to direct excess energy down to the arms and the legs so that balance can be restored.

There are many differing styles of walking meditation. This form of T'ai Chi (Taiji) walking is a slow rhythmic walking, which integrates the principles of Chi Gung (Qigong) and T'ai Chi, and includes specific foot placement. It is both a spiritual and physical practice. It aims to unite and improve mind and body, whilst enhancing posture and balance, creating a smooth, even gait, which particularly encourages the use of the postural and leg muscles. It aims to stimulate the flow of Chi (life force) around the body, by drawing in the terrestrial energy from the ground in through Yongquan, the kidney point in the ball of the foot. It then stores this energy in reservoirs called the *eight extraordinary vessels/meridians*, which are intimately connected to our immune systems and from which the twelve organ meridians can draw energy if needed.

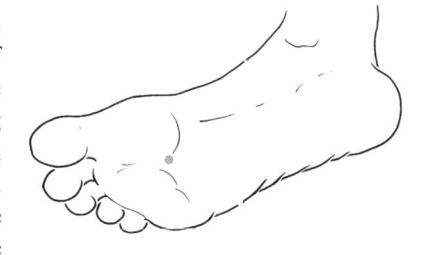

Yongquan

It is a suitable exercise for people of all ages and levels of physical ability. As you become more conscious of your body and the way you walk, you become more sensitive and attuned to the world, both inside and around you. It is an excellent antidote to stress and the fast pace of modern life.

Some of the founders of tai chi ch'uan were monks who were seeking knowledge of the Self, so meditation formed an important part of their daily practice and spiritual routine. The word 'meditation' comes from the Latin root of 'media', meaning centre. So this specific and exact discipline is the act of turning consciousness towards its own centre, so that it perceives and acquires knowledge of itself and brings about a state of self-realisation or enlightenment. Whether doing active or stationary meditation, one should be aware of certain prerequisites:

- The spine should be held straight and vertical on the pelvis, allowing the natural energy system in and around the spinal column to move freely up and down the body. It also allows the body to act as an antenna, making it alert and ready to pick up any energy vibrations.
- The mind is brought back into the body, which is relaxed and quietened, so that both are relieved of any anxiety and agitation.
- Breathing must be slow and rhythmic; this allows oxygen to the brain and all the major organs.
- The hands or fingers are arranged in one of several possible postures, so the positive and negative poles of the body are connected and the electro-magnetic energy of the body is equalized and balanced.

Any system of meditation, regardless of its philosophical affiliation, is comprised of three basic stages:

1. **Concentration**: The mind can be viewed as a nervous bundle of thoughts and ideas; always wandering, easily distracted and jumping from one thing to the next. Often under the control of the senses but rarely under the control of its owner, this is why the Chinese often refer to it as the 'monkey mind'. So we must first seek to gain control over the mind's restless state so that it can be directed and harnessed.

This first stage is the ability to direct the mind onto one subject and hold it there, and unless this stage is mastered, it is pointless to talk about further stages. For the purpose of this training, we have chosen t'ai chi walking, as the student can apply the same progressions as when learning any form or series of movements or postures:

- First the concentration is on learning the moves or posture.
- Then the focus is on perfecting them.
- Next, concentration is on the breathing, which can be co-ordinated with the moves.
- Then comes the focus on circulating the Chi (life force) around the body and through the meridians (energy pathways).

2. **Contemplation**: Once the student has learned the art of concentration and is able to hold their mind intently on a chosen subject, they will naturally pass into the second stage of contemplation. This is when they become so absorbed in the object of concentration that they lose awareness of themselves as the concentrator.

3. **Meditation**: This is the state of union where the concentrator and the object of concentration merge into one, transcending the duality of Yin and Yang. So that in the case of practicing the art of walking or the practice of T'ai Chi, one eventually merges the Chi within oneself to the Universal Chi. The ultimate aim of the study of a form is to attain formlessness, and reach the Tao. (This term dates back over 5000 years and refers to the concept of living in harmony with laws of life.)

The purpose of this exercise of walking is to:

- Increase receptivity to Chi energy through the relationship between your feet and the earth (or water), while at the same time bringing the energy down out of the head. (It can be performed in water as well as on land.)
- Feel the space before the foot touches the ground so that you become aware of the energy within this space.
- Relaxation, so that we can drop anxieties and trust and blend with universal forces greater than ourselves.
- Experience the concept of emptiness and fullness on every level of being.
- Maintain slowness and evenness in order to perfect our manner of living, while developing patience and forbearance.
- To develop rootedness for security and foundation for our life and practice.

Variations:

- Practice in water.
- With eyes closed.
- Walking in a circle.
- One person blindfolded, the other holding their arm.

Walking Forwards

Too much thinking and head explaning? Try this

Place your hands behind your back, one hand holding the wrist of the other, resting on your sacrum (just above the upper end of your buttock crease).

Start with your feet together, then sink your weight down into your left foot and lift the right foot to hover above the ground next to the left ankle

Extend the right leg forwards, and hover the foot above the ground, and then gently lower it to touch the ground, keeping the weight in your left leg

Without shifting your weight and to challenge the balance, lift the right foot slightly off the ground

Now sink the weight into the right foot, placing the sole down slowly, evenly and flat (not heel and then toe)

Shift the weight forwards into the right foot and then back into the left leg feeling the sensation of the body weight emptying and filling in the legs

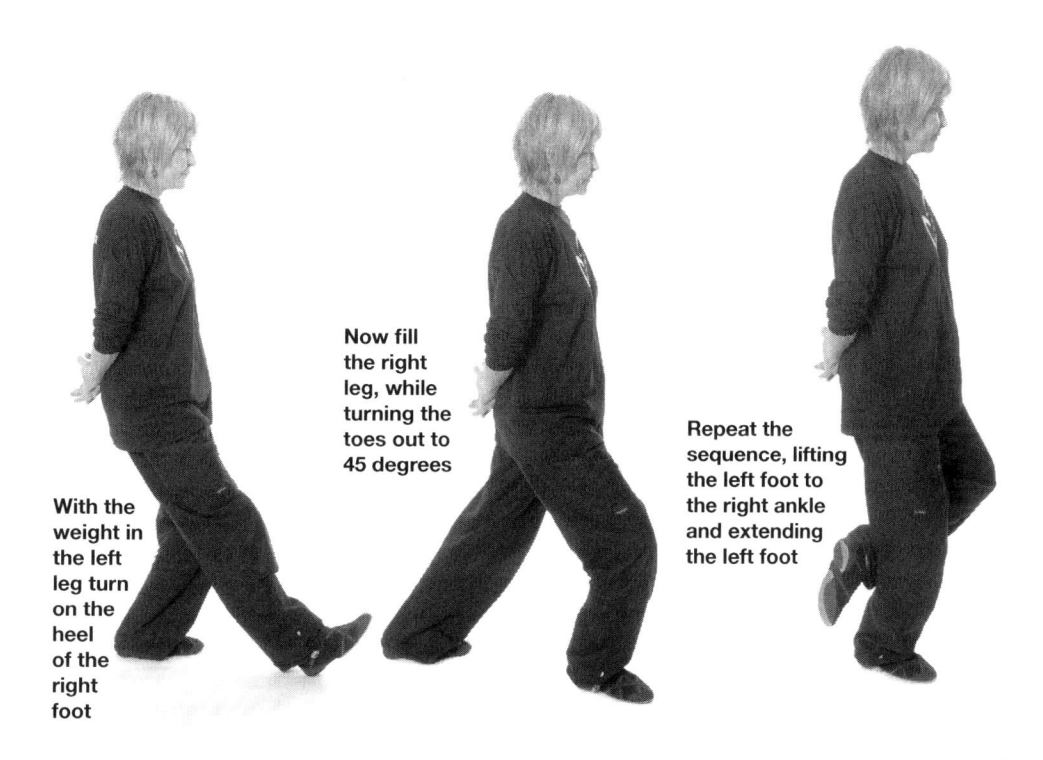

With the weight in the left leg turn on the heel of the right foot

Now fill the right leg, while turning the toes out to 45 degrees

Repeat the sequence, lifting the left foot to the right ankle and extending the left foot

Walking Backwards

- Place your hands, palms inwards, so that they are resting just below the navel (men with the left hand under the right, and ladies right under the left).
- Having ended with the right foot ready to step forwards and lifted by the left ankle, step back (toes preceding the heel) with the right toes pointing slightly outwards to 45 degrees, hip distance apart from the left foot, as if walking on tram lines.
- Sink the weight back onto the right foot as you rotate the left toes from pointing out at 45 degrees to pointing straight forwards.
- Slowly lift the left foot and bring it back to the side of the right ankle to hover above the ground. Then repeat, stepping back on the left foot, toes out to 45 degrees, and as you move your weight back, spiral the right toes to point forwards.

(To challenge the backward walking you can lift and lower the extended front foot, before bringing back to the side of the ankle.) Make sure your tailbone is drawn down, as if you are sitting into the back leg, and so that the upper body does not sway backwards.

Improves balance, mental focus, body awareness and co-ordination.

Microcosmic Orbit—Fire Cycle

This exercise calms and roots the mind as it fuses the body's main yin and yang reservoirs of energy. The yin reservoir is called the Ren meridian or Conception vessel which runs on the midline of the front of the body, and the yang or Du meridian or Governing vessel running along the midline of the back.

The Small circulation of qi allows you to sense the warm glow of qi moving in and around the body. It enhances a feeling of balance, trains the mind, and distributes energy evenly throughout the mind and body by keeping the energetic reservoirs full. During this exercise, the Governing and Conception vessels (two of the eight extraordinary meridians) are filled to overflowing with qi. Use your mind to lead the qi by imagining your qi as a golden thread, as a ball of golden light passing along a tunnel or as flowing water with electric powers. Keep the mind focused and concentrated so that there is no mental or physical tension and the abdomen remains relaxed.

- Stand in Wuji *(feet shoulder-width apart, ankle and knee joints open, sitting down slightly into the legs, arms and shoulders relaxed and head held up as if by a string from the crown of the head).* You can also sit in a chair to do this. Relax the body and quieten the mind with the hands held in front of, or crossed over the lower abdomen.
- Place the tongue in the roof of the mouth behind the upper teeth, which will connect the Ren and Du meridians mentioned above.
- Visualize the Qi *(energy)* as a red neon light rising up the back, along the spine and over the head to the mouth, and then down the midline of the front of the body past the abdomen to the perineum and then to the back where it will ascend again. *(In the case of high blood pressure it is better to visualize the colour pink).*
- As you inhale feel the energy rise up the back, and as you exhale feel it descend down the front. Lift in Huiyin point in the centre of the pelvic floor at the end of the exhalation. Continue for at least 5–15 minutes a day.
- To balance and calm your energy, you can also place the right hand just below the navel and the left hand on the centre of the chest. The right hand will move forward with inhalation and backward with the exhalation while the left hand remains relatively still. Feel the abdomen expanding on the inhalation and contracting on the exhalation without force.

Benefits

This will aid the discharge of toxic emotions from the body and allow better access to the Yuan Shen *(Original Spirit)* via these two primal meridians. It is as if you are re-setting and flushing out your entire energetic and emotional systems.

Hanging on to toxic thoughts and emotions? Flush them out with this

Mental Contemplations for Summer

The most important places to keep clean and tidy are my mind and heart

The Heart Mind: The Fire Element rules the Heart and Small Intestine, but in the oriental tradition, the Heart not only includes the organ itself but also the concept, shared by many Western people, that it also is a mental and emotional centre. This is reflected in such phrases as: "let's have a heart to heart," or "I have to learn it by heart". It is not only seen as regulating the blood and circulatory system but controls consciousness, the spirit (referred to as the Shen), sleep, and memory whilst also housing the mind. In acupuncture, to needle the Heart meridian is seen to not only affect the Heart but also someone's state of mind, just as for certain emotions strongly experienced. (Refer to the Meditation section in the Winter chapter.)

Joy is seen as being the major emotion connected to the well being of the heart. As the heart in traditional Chinese medicine is often referred to as the emperor, when the emperor (heart) is happy, so are all his subjects (the other organs). In our modern culture, there are more and more breakthroughs in science on understanding the world of electromagnetic phenomena, and also dramatic insights into the unconscious mind and emotional dynamics.

Good health, both mental and physical, does not just rely on good nutrition, diet and exercise, but also relies upon how we think and feel. How we feel emotionally hugely effects how we feel physically, and how fit we feel physically impacts upon how fit we are mentally. **Studies by the British Medial Association have shown that as much as eighty per cent of disease is caused by negative mental attitudes**. The fact that chemicals can create moods is not new, as many of these drugs can be found in nature while others are manufactured. Recent findings, by people such as Dr. Candace Pert in the field of psycho neuro-immunology, have discovered that other chemicals are actually produced by the body itself. She found that when hormones, called *endorphins*, are produced by the human body, they reduce tension, allowing the body to absorb the vitality of nature and the universe. As well as reducing stress, they enhance the immune system and prevent cardiovascular problems.

Research conducted at Chicago University showed that laughter produced high endorphin surges. The highest sustained flow however, was not from those who laughed the most raucously, but from those who had a consistent smile and twinkle in their eye.

This gives us an insight into the valued health-giving properties of yoga, taiji and qigong. The harder styles of these practices and qigong can create a toned and vital body, but do not necessarily encourage internal endorphins to flow. The softer styles however, induce an emotional state of happiness, pleasure and well being, which encourages the release of endorphins, making the body more flexible while opening the arteries and tissues, which is essential for enduring health and longevity. When the body tissue is tense or armoured, the production of endorphins is blocked and the flow significantly reduced.

This following exercise is a basic skill we all should endeavour to possess, as it gives us a powerful tool to look after ourselves and is a gateway to trigger endorphins, or at least turn up the volume on their production. How people respond to external events is very much a matter of perception; there is a mental and emotional filter at work here which judges what is liked and disliked. If it is liked, it triggers endorphins, but if perceived to be threatening, it triggers adrenalin, so it depends on the psychology and state of the individual. Different people have different moments when they are moved by different things, so try and notice an activity, event, person or thing that brings you joy or pleasure. This can be a smile on your face, in your eyes, or just a feeling of warming and opening of the heart. Make the following a habit:

- Make a list of things that bring you enjoyment.
- Make a habit of noticing some activity, event, person, place or thing that is giving you pleasure and add it to your list.
- Give yourself permission to do what you enjoy.
- Surround yourself with images and objects that remind you of what you love.
- Keep the list up-to-date and be willing to change it.

The unconscious mind cannot tell the difference between what is real and what is imagined so people can actively choose to use this mental and imaginative ability to change the biochemistry of their body. **Cultivating the inner smile** is a Neidan practice of the Chinese internal alchemy (a way of cultivating life).

Sit comfortably in a straight backed chair or on the floor. Take a couple of deep, slow breaths, noticing how your abdomen rises with each inhalation, and then relaxes back towards your spine with each exhalation. Release any thoughts of the past or future and rest the tip of your tongue behind your teeth on the roof of your mouth. Now think of the thing, activity, event or place you really love or which gives you pleasure to recall. Allow an inner smile of joy, wisdom and compassion to form behind the eyes then direct it towards the heart or any area of the body that needs healing or to release tension. Stay there until it feels complete and then return the focus to the abdomen.

Home and Lifestyle Section

- Read any **books that inspire you** or **develop your spirituality**.
- **List the things that open your heart**, stimulate and impress you and develop appreciation. Take time in order to have time. The heart suffers worst from time pressure so schedule in enjoyment time.
- **Bring the outside in**: Try to make the indoor merge with the out, lots of fresh flowers inside and hanging baskets and tubs outside.
- Develop a warm, comfortable and unconventional style and do the same with your living space; **dare to be different**!
- **Wear bright colours to reflect your personality**. Bring reds and bright colours into the house with scatter cushions, etc.
- **Become aware of your personal concerns**, what you reflect upon, agonize over and dream about. Remember the small things in life are just as important as the big ones, and the hidden just as significant as the obvious.
- **Make life more simple and harmonious**. Work on your relationships and make them the same.
- Speech and communication is particularly associated with the Fire element so **keep a check on what you are talking about and the words you use**: do they bring confidence or fear, hope or discouragement, joy or sadness, love or bitterness?
- **Oils for the Fire element**; put them in an oil burner and place around the house, in your bath or daily after shower use as a massage oil *(a few drops in almond oil or a similar carrier oil)*.

Rose is anti-depressive, anti-inflammatory, balancing, calming, traditionally used as the herb of love, and as a sexual and general tonic.

Rosemary is a tonic that helps prevent hypertension and was used in the 1500s for bathing to make you lively, lusty and joyful! It promotes the circulation of Qi and Blood. It strengthens the heart beat and encourages the flow of arterial blood. It alleviates cardiac fatigue, e.g. palpitations, low blood pressure and cold hands and feet. Avoid if pregnant or breast-feeding.

Ylang Ylang has a calming effect on the heart and works to clear heat. It harmonizes the Shen *(spirit)* allowing it to express and experience joy. It relieves nervous tension, promotes sleep, relieves agitation, and helps re-unite the emotional and sensual natures.

- Avoid... Having no time for yourself or feeling dreary or aloof.

Summer Summary

- ☑ Are you more relaxed when meeting people and more light-hearted in general? Have you noticed that your communication skills have improved?

- ☑ Has your circulation improved, or your heart rate stabilized to an acceptable level?

- ☑ Do you have improved mental clarity and seem to be less forgetful?

- ☑ Are you enjoying a good laugh more regularly? It's a great tonic!

- ☑ Are you noticing that your speech has slowed down a little and that you are speaking more quietly with a sense of calmness?

- ☑ Has your pace of life slowed a little and are you noticing that your energy reserves seem to be enhanced?

- ☑ Are you making time and space for meditation?

- ☑ Are your neck and shoulders more relaxed with less tension or headaches?

- ☑ Are you doing more to make yourself happy rather than putting the happiness of everyone else first?

- ☑ Now that you have been taking the summer advice, are you on a more even keel emotionally, at peace with yourself, and having lots of fun with frequent feelings of joyfulness?

- ☑ Has your sparkle come back and are you finding you have more resilience to those who want to put it out?

- ☑ Constantly check throughout the summer that you are not having or needing constant stimulation from other sorts of fuel, e.g. caffeine, refined sugar or alcohol, rather than drawing on natural energy and from being out-of-doors more.

The season of late summer

The smell of late summer is the aroma of damp earth, ripened blackberries, sun-warmed dry grasses, and home grown tomatoes. There is a feeling of heaviness about nature, a sense of peacefully slowing down. You have no need to mow the lawn every week as the growing season is coming to an end. Plants are large and bushy. The wheat is harvested and there are beautiful landscapes of colour on our rolling hillsides, which will gradually change over the next month or so to yellow, gold, orange and brown.

The temperature is erratic too. Nights are cool and getting more so, and the weather is becoming damper waiting for the drier crispness of autumn to arrive.

The Feeling of Late Summer

Life should be peachy! Late summer is a season that we do not have as one of our established seasons in the west; spring, summer, autumn and winter are all we have! However, late summer is a very important transitional season, which comes between summer and autumn; a time for preparation, to create comfort, stability and balance in preparation for the coming autumn and winter. Nature does this in its own time, some years it is quicker than others. We need to match this with what we are doing with our lives. How we feel, eat, treat ourselves, think and spend our time is very important at this time of year.

If late summer was a person, their nature would have a strong sense of centre and self, one who seeks balance and stability. They can assimilate change so they hold steady, and this gives them the capacity to be supportive of others, while at the same time nurturing any changes happening around them. They bring compassion and confidence in times of transition, so people feel safe with them. They love to be involved and at the centre of things which can lead to them becoming overloaded or taking on too much. Their skill is to help others to integrate their own experiences but in their desire to protect and support they may start to worry or become overprotective of those they are trying to help.

So it makes sense to develop the positive qualities and watch out for the negative at this time of year in order to match the energy of the season. If you are out of balance at the moment, these are the issues that might come up in late summer to be dealt with:

- Do you worry a lot?
- Are you never satisfied? This can be applied to your work, life or food.
- Is the level of exercise you achieve out of balance with the amount or type of food you consume?
- Do you tend to accumulate excess weight around your stomach and thighs?
- Do you regularly suffer from a feeling of weakness or heaviness in your legs?
- Do you crave food, often with a high liquid content?
- Do you suffer from food sensitivities, digestive problems or have an eating disorder?
- Do you suffer from a prolapsed organ, hernia or varicose veins?
- Do you have a tendency to over think or analyse?
- Do you often feel knocked off your centre or out of balance?
- Does your life feel empty or unfulfilled?
- Do you regularly have bouts of self-doubt or self-pity?
- Do you have issues around self-sacrifice or being needed?
- Do you suffer from an inability to concentrate, or muzzy headedness?

Eight Priorities for Late Summer

1. **Regularly examine the quality of your food, thoughts and relationships**; are they nourishing and supporting you, doing you good and giving you good energy? Or just draining you?
2. **Chew** your food well and avoid heated discussions or arguments during meal times; do not eat on the run!
3. **Nourish yourself** on every level. Strengthen yourself from the inside out, returning to centre to gather your power and stability.
4. Try to **remove worry** from your life. Worrying wastes energy. Learn to concentrate the mind and free it from worry, doubt and guilt, especially about food.
5. **Start something that gives you satisfaction** and makes you feel good about yourself. This will support your **immune system**.
6. **Support yourself using one of the following affirmations** for this time of year: I am; stable, helpful, understanding, resourceful, sympathetic, reliable and steady, nourished in life, supported and supportive, considerate. I care for others and have respect for myself.
7. **Include activities that bring you nearer to the earth** such as; gardening, digging, walking, rambling, golfing, or jogging.
8. Like the stone in a piece of fruit, occasionally **allow yourself to feel a strong sense of centre in your life**, so that you can deal with all of life's challenges and be there for those you love.

Eight Things to Avoid for Summer

1. Avoid **overworking**, over studying or having long periods of concentration without taking a break. Taking regular breaks gives you time to digest information, just as relaxation and down time allow you to digest life's experiences.
2. **Overanalysing** things, people or situations.
3. **Becoming overdependent** on others or having unrealistic expectations.
4. **Worry**, obsession, self-doubt, overextending, meddling or being overprotective.
5. **Avoid leaving things unfinished** including sentences, conversations and projects. **Overburdening** yourself and taking on too much.
6. **Becoming obsessive** about food.
7. **Jealousy or low self-image**, or focusing constantly on what you are not.
8. **Avoid the sweet stuff.** If you are tired, your body will crave sweet, so try to satisfy yourself with a naturally sweet food *(not sweets!)*, e.g. snack on an oatcake with a little honey on it, banana, grapes or be sweet to someone!

Eight Daily Habits for Late Summer

Give yourself a morning flush

1. **Do something for yourself every day.** How much time do you have for yourself and your personal interests? Make sure you have enough, and if not, schedule it in as a very important appointment. Even a ten-minute nap will do it!
2. **Boost your lymph,** by including inversions in your yoga practice (unless there are blood pressure issues), getting on a trampoline or lying with feet up a wall.
3. **Upgrade your level of immunity.** Rub natural lotion or oils into the body upward towards the heart to stimulate the lymphatic system and to get the immune system to an optimum level. Buy a lotion with the least chemicals in it!
4. **Sit and read.** This is a good time for studying, digesting information and life. Do some informative reading (see habit (2) with legs extended up against a wall).
5. **Take time to plan and prepare nourishing meals**, and make changes to improve your life/work balance.
6. **First thing in the morning,** have a fresh grated ginger and lemon infusion. Using a parmesan or ginger grater, grate the ginger over a large mug, pour water over and add a squeeze of lemon. It aids digestion, and you can also add some rosemary for its fat burning quality.
7. **A morning shake up** gets your lymphatic system moving and supports the immune system. Begin by slapping the body with your open palm, not too hard as it is not supposed to hurt. Go down the inside of your arms and up the outside. Down the back and sides of the body and legs and up the inside, to cover the entire body. Finish by a flat palm stroke down each arm, back of the body and down each leg toward the floor. Ending with a deep breath in and long exhale with your hands crossed over your navel.
8. **Practice pulling in your stomach** and finding your centre. Tie a rope around your middle; keep pulling your waist off it at regular intervals during the day.

Eight Ways to Help Your Immune System

The immune system needs to be in its prime at this time of year to fight the infections that we come into contact with on a daily basis. Then energy can be conserved and used to make us stronger for the winter ahead.

1. **Maintain a high level of nutrition**, the dictionary definition reads as follows: 'to feed and nourish is the process of obtaining food necessary for health and growth'.
2. **Avoid antiperspirants**, as these seal in the toxins in the chest area where your lymph drains.
3. **Exercise regularly** as your lymph is moved by muscular contractions.
4. **Get a good sleep at night**. You should be going to bed a little earlier as the nights draw in!
5. **If you feel a little under the weather** or feel a cold coming, try to catch it with a high dose of vitamin C or herbal supports like Echinacea.
6. **Feel good about yourself** so your system knows you are worth defending.
7. **Cut down on caffeine, alcohol and other toxins** and avoid heavy clogging dampening foods such as sugar, wheat, yeast and dairy. **Avoid microwave cooking**, which is shown to cause measurable changes in the blood, indicative of a pathogenic process beginning, similar to those found in the early stages of cancer (*Journal of Natural Science*, 1998).
8. **If you feel light-headed and unsettled**, lie on your front, rest your head on your arms and breathe for ten minutes. Let the earth support you for that time; then come up slowly and you will feel much more in control afterwards.

So why do we need to do all of these things? To maintain our health, for apart from the obvious answer of wanting to feel great all of the time, we want to avoid illness because of it long-term effects on the system from all points of view.

- ❀ **How you look** is important. The inner glow of a happy healthy person beats a new outfit any day.
- ❀ **Maintain a healthy balance in your energy bank account**. *(This concept is explained in the introduction.)*
- ❀ Maintain your ability to **think clearly and stay focused**, so that you make healthy decisions and attract nourishing and supportive relationships.
- ❀ **Prime health** is a state of centred confidence.

Illness is a chain reaction of free radicals *(bad guys)* trying to take over the cells. Antioxidants *(good guys)* come in to prevent or stop this chain reaction. If free radicals are allowed to multiply, this increases the stress on the body's defence system, your immunity. So it is in your body's interest to keep up the antioxidant level.

The immune system is also weakened by trying to fight off the effects of allergens in the body. Sometimes complicated, over-cooked, processed or toxic food needs the body's immune system to process it, because partially digested food has leaked into the bloodstream where it does not belong. The digestive process has tried and not succeeded in doing its job, so the immune system kicks in when antibodies are sent to deal with this leakage, as the situation becomes toxic. It is therefore especially important at this time of year, and in our best interest, to keep the digestive system in an effortless state of comfort, and to make its job as easy as possible.

Food Section

Food for the Late Summer Energy

Yellow is the colour of the season, so yellow and orange fruit and vegetables are the thing to eat at this time; find examples in the food list. These fruit and vegetables are rich sources of the antioxidant beta-carotene and have some vitamin C and E, essential for nourishing the immune system. Eat food in season, and look in your local fruit shop or farmer's market for what is fresh and grown locally.

How you cook is also relevant as the cooking method has a direct effect on the energy of the food. Prepare and cook properly. The ideal way of cooking at this time of year is with a low flame to sauté or sweat. This brings a natural sweetness to foods, especially to root vegetables.

Do not eat too much raw as it adds to the dampness of the season. Take care not to overdo sweet foods as they can create mucus in damp conditions. Internal dampness is the result of a sedentary lifestyle and overconsumption, bringing about a backlog of unprocessed food, which results in the body's failure to burn off or transform moisture. Poor food combining, eating late at night and drinking too much water at meal times can also be contributing factors, and manifests in the body as congestion in the form of fluid, mucus or phlegm.

After fifty years of research in America it has been discovered that overeating is thought to be a major factor in premature ageing. *(Walford & Ross; Life Extension Magazine, 1996)*.

Food List

Naturally sweet foods support the system at this time, as the sweet flavour harmonizes all other flavours and forms the centre of our diet. It makes us feel nourished, which is one of the key seasonal words. They stimulate the circulation and nourish us, and late summer is all about nourishment. Lamb, trout, mussels, venison, are amongst the best animal protein foods suitable in the UK.

Apples	Parsnips	Nectarines	Stewed fruit
Apricots	Dates	Oats	Sweet potato
Blackberries	Duck	Peaches	Tomatoes
Carrots	Fish	Pears	Walnuts
Chicken	Millet	Pumpkin	Yellow squash
Chickpeas	Mushrooms	Red and yellow	
Courgettes	Mung beans	peppers	

Eight Food and Nutrition Tips

1. **Review your diet** and cut down on, or cut out, sugar and highly refined foods.
2. Late summer is a damp time of year, so **avoid processed or stale foods**, having too many ingredients in a meal, and eating late at night.
3. **Respect nature and your body** by consuming only what you need. The way you eat is an expression of who you are. Always eat in an open and relaxed posture, because being slumped or twisted impedes the digestive process.
4. **Look after your stomach**, and do not eat too quickly, while on the run, or too much. Chew well, because the stomach has no teeth! **Value breakfast** as the stomach and spleen are at their strongest between 7 and 11am.
5. **Do not flood the spleen** as doing this affects the capacity for clear thought. So not too much fluid while you are eating, particularly iced drinks; keep fluid for between meals.
6. **Include Jasmine and liquorice tea**, as these are spleen tonics and can be taken with meals.
7. **Introduce kind-to-the-stomach food** into your diet; yellow, golden and round foods such as butternut squash, peaches and apricots, which harmonize the system.
8. **Resolve dampness** with foods such as lemon, parsley, celery, bitter foods, small beans, onions, leeks and garlic and Jasmine and green tea.

Exercise and Movement Section

This section will show you various ways to stimulate the energy lines for this time of year. Each time of year has a pair of organs, which are complementary and are particularly in focus at this time. The stomach lines run down the front of the body and the spleen lines run up the body. The following sections will include exercises that move energy in these areas and therefore energize the stomach and spleen.

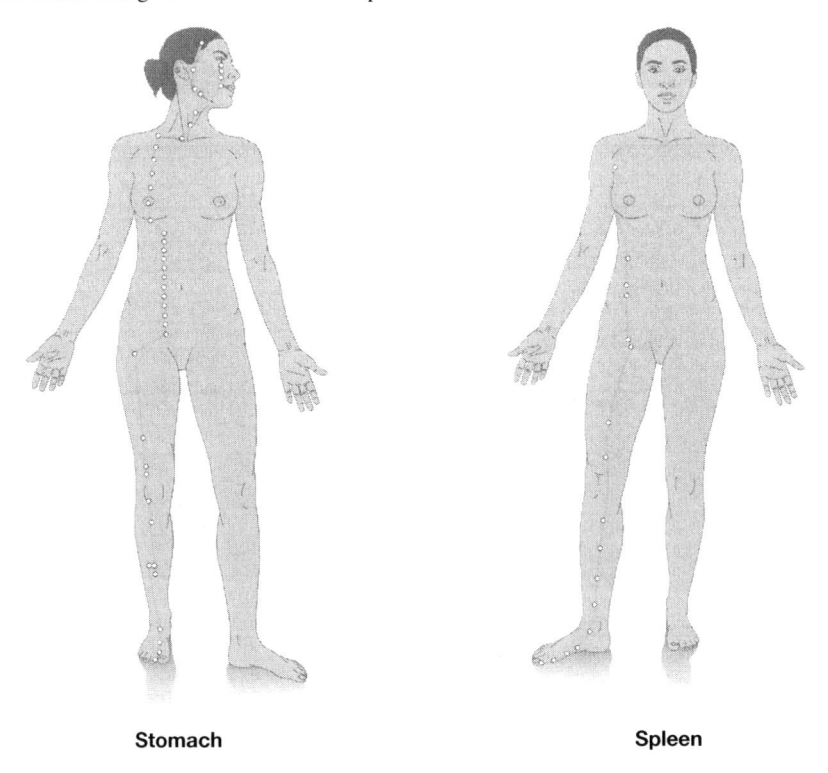

Stomach   **Spleen**

Exercise for Late Summer

The general guide for exercise at this time of year is a less frantic routine than in the summertime, as energy is slowing down. Try to be centred and focused on whatever it is you are doing in your exercise routine. Be content to do a little less than mid-summer, feel satisfied and nourished at the end of your session, whatever it is, and if you are not, then change it!

Take up exercise to develop muscle tone, improve balance and develop your centre. Feel in control when working out and include yoga, qigong or an exercise system such as Pilates, which works on your core stability. Particularly work on strengthening your legs, which support you and form your connection to the earth. Eight exercise classes in the gym would be:

- Pilates or a core stability class.
- Yoga, with the intention of feeling foundation and balance in the asana (pose).
- T'ai chi/qigong, ideal for meridian energy maintenance, self-awareness and self-control.
- Body conditioning, toning or strength class.
- Aerobics *(slightly less intensive than in summer if possible)*.
- Weight training or body pump, to build muscle tone. Walking on a treadmill if the weather is not suitable for outdoor walking.
- Step class, as it develops the leg muscles.
- Abdominal workouts, Swiss ball and any balance challenging classes.

Essential for earth energy:

- **Walk for at least 10 minutes a day**; long outdoor walks on balmy late summer nights are an ideal end to a long hard day at work. Walk a dog or if you haven't got one, borrow one, or go with a friend who has one. Walk briskly, don't stroll, head up, stomach in, lengthen in the centre of your body, shoulders down and stride out. Get into a good breathing rhythm and you will feel like a new person when you get home; it can be great for your social life too!
- **Golf gets you out in nature** if weather permits, and is perfect for replenishing earth energy. Focus on supporting and encouraging yourself between the shots.
- **Cycling**, for balance and leg strength: a great way of putting exercise into your life if you are struggling to fit it in. Use the bike to get to places instead of car (*and it's more environmentally friendly too*).
- **Tennis** for the last burst of summer energy.
- **Gardening**; get out there and you will feel a great sense of satisfaction when you are finished.
- **Go out to the park** and find the circuit-training course (*most good local parks have one*).
- **Outdoor gyms** are popping up all over the UK (*very common in better climates*), so search the internet to see if you have a local one. It is said to burn thirty per cent more calories than the same workout indoors. Worth a try and much greener!
- **If your immune system is compromised**, avoid exercises that create a lot of waste products, such as lactic acid. Instead, choose ones such as yoga, t'ai chi, qigong and Pilates that strengthen you from the inside out.

Qigong for Late Summer

Bo (or Collecting) points are located on the chest, abdomen or waist. They are used both for diagnosis and treatment, and are where the energy collects or gathers from each of the relevant organs. These points can become tender either spontaneously or on the application of pressure; in treatments they are used to regulate and balance the energy in their associated organs. The organ meridians are energy pathways that lead to and from a major organ, and pressure points along them are where the energy is particularly accessible from the surface. The initials and numbers refer to the particular acupressure point along an organ meridian. You can gently massage these points using the tips of the thumb, index and middle fingers.

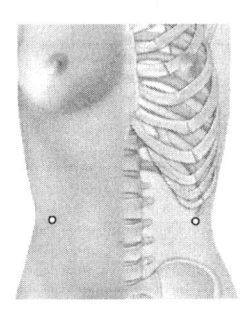

Zangmen (Completion Gate, LR 13) at the end of the eleventh floating rib. It is used for testing and balancing the function of the spleen.

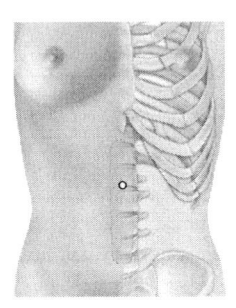

Zhongwan (Stomach Centre, Con 12) midway between the end of the breastbone and the umbilicus. It is used for strengthening and improving the function of the stomach and pancreas.

Massage the Stomach

Stand with feet hip-width apart as if holding a ball in front of your abdomen, with the left hand above the right. Inhale and raise the right hand up over your head, palm up, fingers pointing backward, and your left hand pressing down with equal pressure, fingers pointing forward. Exhale and draw the hands back to hold the imaginary ball with the right hand above the left, slightly by compressing the Stomach point. Then repeat, raising the left hand and lowering the right. Repeat eight times on both sides.

To energise the stomach you can reverse the breathing; exhaling as you stretch up and inhaling as you draw the hands back to hold the ball. Focus on bringing energy to the area of the body level with your hands.

Do this between 7 and 9am to get your digestive system moving

Massage the Spleen

Now inhale raising the right hand up and lowering the left. On the exhalation, twist around to the left keeping your hips facing forward and turning in the waist, creating compression in the left Spleen point. Inhale as you turn to the front and exhale as you come back to hold the circle, left hand above the right. Now repeat the exercise twisting to the right. Repeat eight times on both sides.

Do this between 9 and 11am to re-energize your spleen

Strengthen the Legs

Stand with your feet wide apart as if holding a ball in front of your abdomen with the left hand above the right. Inhale, and raise the right hand up above your head, palm up fingers pointing backward, and your left hand pressing down with equal pressure, at the same time lifting your left knee level with your groin, and sinking down slightly more onto your right leg. Exhale, and draw the hands back to hold the imaginary ball with the right hand over the left, stepping out to the left sinking down deeply, now repeat, raising the left hand and lowering the right and lifting the right leg. Perform this eight times on both sides *(remembering to keep your back straight)*.

Improve Balance and Centre

Stand with your feet hip-width apart with your palms facing inwards and fingers pointing towards each other in front of your abdomen. Inhale, and raise the right and left hands up in front of the chest as if holding a ball with your palms facing inwards and lifting your left knee level with your groin, sink down slightly more into your right leg. Exhale, and whilst rotating your palms outwards, turn in your waist to take the hands around to the left. Inhale, and return to the front and exhale as you lower the leg and the arms. Repeat on the other side. Perform this eight times on both sides.

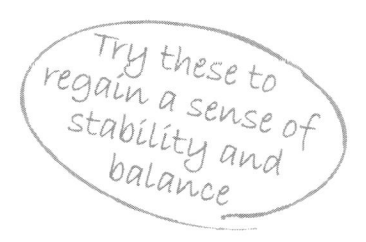

Try these to regain a sense of stability and balance

Qigong for the Immune System

Practicing poses or exercises for the eight Extraordinary Meridians encourages full health and a lively balance of energies in our body. These eight Meridians act as reservoirs of energy for the twelve Organ Meridians. They can be used to treat physical ailments by flushing and re-activating the flow of vital energy through the body. Take your time learning one sequence a day/week until you can perform the complete set.

These exercises have a role to play in preventative treatment by ensuring that blocked energy is dislodged, so protecting the body from imbalances and stagnation. Exercises involving the Extraordinary Meridians are especially helpful for those with sleeping problems, cold hands and feet, and those suffering from stress, fatigue and low immunity. It is advisable to do the qigong exercises or stretches every morning to draw on the rising energy of nature, and also in the evening before going to bed, to rid the body of the tiredness or negative energy accumulated during the day.

- Focus of the mind is important.
- Do not perform moves after a heavy meal, operation, or when you have a fever.
- Avoid forcing or straining.
- The stretch is made on the inhalation and you exhale as you return, unless otherwise stated. This allows the energy to flush through the meridians.

Repeat the exercises three, six or eight times.

To centre yourself, start by crossing your hands over Qihai *(two finger-widths below navel)* and breathing into the lower Dantian. *(Women left hand over right and men right over left.)*

Establish your centre

Spiralling Energy Up and Around the Spine

Hold the ball with the right hand above left *(palms facing each other)*. Spiral the right hand round to the tip of your tailbone *(GV1 between the tailbone and the anus)*. Spiral the left hand up above your head, rotating the fingers backward, and look up into Yintang, the third eye. Inhale; feel the stretch and gentle twist in the spine massaging the nervous system. Exhale and return the hands to hold the ball, with the left hand above the right. Repeat spiralling the left hand palm down, around to GV1 and the right palm up to the sky. Repeat eight times.

This sequence is an invaluable daily routine to build up immunity and keep bugs and low self-esteem at bay

Energizing the Waist and Thymus Gland

Start with holding the imaginary ball in front, with your right hand over the left. Now reach the left arm in front, rotating the palm to the left, and extend the right hand to the back, rotating the palm to the left. Turn in the waist to gaze at the back hand. Inhale and feel the stretch and twist in the waist, massaging the organs and the digestive system. As you exhale rotate back to the front, holding the circle with the left hand over the right. Next bring your right hand up inside the left. Then extend the right arm in front, rotating the palm to the right, and the left hand to the back, turning the left palm to face right. Look to the back, inhaling into the stretch. Exhale to the front, bringing your left hand inside the right. You can focus on bringing the in-breath into the thymus gland above the heart for immune support.

Flushing the Energy System and Strengthening Your Centre

Face the front, feet in a wider horse stance, palms facing forward at Qihai *(a point two fingers-width directly below your navel)*. Inhale and press palms forward away from the body, exhale and rotate palms to face the body, and bring them back to Qihai. Turn to the left on the ball of the right *(back)* foot, keeping the left foot facing forward, and press palms away, level with Qihai. Inhale slightly, lifting the front of the body to feel the stretch. Exhale, and return to face the front, bringing the palms back to the navel. Inhale, press forward as before, exhale, and bring the hands back to the navel. Then turn on the ball of the left *(back)* foot to face the right, pressing the palms forward and keeping the right foot facing the front. Inhale into the stretch, lifting the front of the body. Exhale, and return to the front, bringing the hands back to the navel.

Rebalancing Your Energy Centres

Bring the feet closer together about hip-width apart. Inhale and draw your hands above your head with the backs of the hands touching, then exhale as you separate the hands out and down to the sides, flexing the wrists. Inhale, draw the hands into the chest, palms touching and continue to draw them above your head. Exhale, and bring your hands down the midline, palms still touching, as you sink into a low squat.

In this low position, lift Huiyin *(the point in the centre of the pelvic floor)* and rock back onto your heels as you lift your big toes. Bring your third eye *(Yintang; the point between your eyebrows)* down to the tips of your fingers. Inhale, and push down through your feet, and rise to standing, uncurling your spine bone by bone. Take your hands above your head, palms still touching.

Exhale, and as you separate the palms of the hands, pressing them away in front to fold forwards to touch the ground. Inhale, and uncurl the spine bone by bone, keeping the head down until the very last, bringing the backs of the hands together. Repeat the cycle eight times. On the last cycle come up, bringing the hands into soft fist.

Particular Focus on Strengthening the Liver, Muscles and Tendons

Step out again into the wider horse stance, exhale as you bring your hands into soft fists, squeezing your elbows slightly in toward the navel, and drawing your navel firmly back to your spine. Rotate to the left, turning *(on the ball of the back right foot)* but keeping the left foot facing forward. Extend your arms in front of you with the backs of the hands together, making leopard's claws by flexing the ends of your fingers. Now draw your left arm back, keeping the elbow in line with the shoulder *(opening SI 10 at the top of the axillary crease in the shoulder)*. Inhale into the stretch with equal weight in the feet, and stretch in the arms. Exhale, and return to the centre, making soft fists and drawing navel to spine. Then repeat on the other side.

Now repeat turning to your right　　　　　**This position as seen from back**

Strengthen the Aura and Defensive Chi

Finish with this last sequence by inhaling, drawing the hands up the midline of the body, rotating the palms up, and exhaling, taking the hands out to the sides and down. Visualize your defending energy *(Wei Qi)* circulating out to the periphery of the body and also strengthening your aura.

Balancing Yin and Yang

End with a bow, placing the fist of the right hand in the open palm of the left. This symbolizes the balance of Yin and Yang energies, maintaining health and strengthening resistance to disease.

Tai Chi Moves for Late Summer

Movements in the form should focus on:

* Being grounded and stable in the legs.
* Poses and kicks that encourage balance and leg strengthening.
* Moving from your navel centre.
* The rising and sinking movements.

Waving hands like clouds is a series of moves that encourage co-ordination and movement from, and building power in the centre. Please note that there are many variations of this sequence depending on your style.

Stand with your feet shoulder-width apart with your hands crossed over your Qihai point, two fingers-width below your navel *(men right over left and women vice-versa)*.

Drawing the mind back into your centre: Inhale, and with intention *(Yi)* draw the mind back into the third eye area *(the Yintang point)*. As you exhale, guide the energy *(Qi)* down to the point below your hands *(Qihai)*. Draw the navel slightly inwards, and lift in the centre of the pelvic floor *(the Huiyin point)*, at the end of the exhalation. Stay with this for seven more breaths; this is both calming and centring.

Now raise your hands palm facing inwards in front of the body, the left hand above the right. Keeping the arms still, turn your waist to the left and right to feel the movement coming from the centre.

Now turn your torso and waist to the left (left hand above right) and then raise the right palm up and the left palm down rotating the palm out, as if wiping your palms a few inches away from each other. Feel the energy (Qi) between the middle of the palms (the Laogong points), which are important energy centres. In some yogic traditions these points are often referred to as two extra chakras.

Now move the hands, right above the left, to the right by turning in the waist. Now wipe the palms a few inches away rotating the right palm away. Repeat these moves several times turning to the right and left. Each time you turn to right the right hand is on top, and as you turn to the left the left hand is uppermost.

Next time, as you turn in the waist to the right wiping the palms to bring the right hand below the left, transfer the weight onto the right leg. As you turn in the waist taking the hands to the left, step out to the left.

Then cross the palms to bring your right hand above the left, transfer into the left leg, and then as the waist rotates the hands to the right, step in with the right foot. Repeat this stepping out to the left several times and then repeat the opposite way, stepping out to the right.

End the sequence with the stance of Single Whip. Inhale, when your weight is in the right foot, and circle your left hand up to the right shoulder. Bring your right fingertips to the right thumb, sucking the centre of the palm up, the Laogong point, extending the right arm forwards and slightly out to the right. Step out on to left foot into Single Whip, with your weight sixty per cent in the left leg, which is bent to ninety degrees in line with the second toe, extending the left arm in an arc to the left, with the palm forwards and angled slightly to the right diagonal, so that you can look at the back of the hand.

Yoga for Late Summer

Late Summer Yoga Poses

The emphasis is on connection to the earth or root. Use the feeling of navel to spine to emphasise core strength. The feeling for the spleen is rising, lifting and supporting. Work on stability in the poses. Return back to the centre after each pose for earthing and balancing. If someone is weak, they should do more coming back to the centre and less dispersing outward movements.

Tadasana

1 & 2. Find your centre and balance, feel the foundation under the feet

3

4. Lie down flat and stretch arms out

5

6

7

All over the place? Do this sequence to feel more grounded

Prostrations

Start on the back end of your mat, ease your body into effortless opening, no strain, stay in each pose as long as you want, feeling the body becoming more earthed and grounded. Repeat three, five, seven or nine times. **Perfect for feeling more grounded!**

The one ideal simple yoga poses for creating energy through the stomach and spleen meridians.

Feeling a bit worthless? Try this

8. Breathe and hold for five breaths

9. Inhale and turn right

10. Then stretch up

11. Five breaths again

12. Inhale and turn left

13. Inhale and stretch up

14. Back to the centre for five breaths

Practise this sequence five times sinking deeper into the legs each time, making sure in each pose that your knee does not extend beyond your toes.

Standing Flow for Late Summer

Simple poses to find balance and foundation. Stay for three breaths in each pose.

1. Start here to find your centre. Pull navel to spine as you inhale

2.

3.

Feeling buffeted by life's waves? Try this to surf over it all!

4.

5.

6.

7.

8.

Then when you are more confident, try the more difficult balances, keeping your eyes focused and the standing leg slightly bent to add foundation and balance.

9
10
11
12
13
14
15
16
17
18
19

This whole sequence can be done lying on the floor for a more grounding energy

Work with the Spleen energy and remove the need for sugar.

Lacking in abdominal vitality? Work on the core

2

3. Right leg forward first

4   Variation

5

6. In plank, stay for five breaths

8

9. Now left leg forward

10   Variation   11

Part 4: The Season of Late Summer 187

16. Keep the side of the foot pushing into the floor

18. Push left foot into the floor

19. Keep knees soft

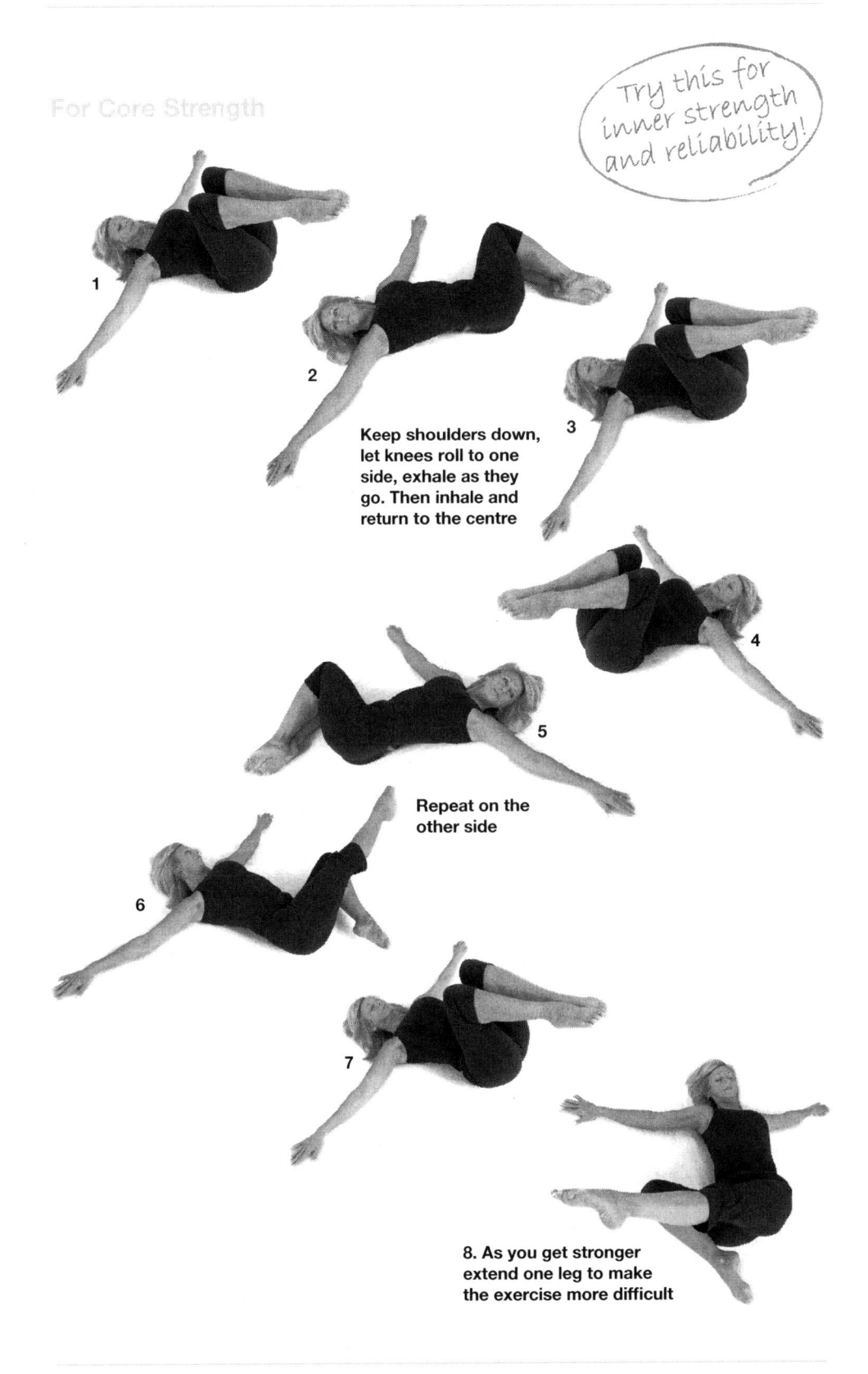

188 Seasonal Yoga: A fusion of yoga and tai chi combined with lifestyle tips for every season

For Core Strength

Try this for inner strength and reliability!

1

2

Keep shoulders down, let knees roll to one side, exhale as they go. Then inhale and return to the centre

3

4

5

Repeat on the other side

6

7

8. As you get stronger extend one leg to make the exercise more difficult

9. Practice reverse curl lifts for lower abdominal strength

10. Take care to keep the head and neck on the floor. The nearer the legs are to the chest, the easier it is!

11. Pulse as you gently lift the tailbone off the floor, repeat 4 x 10 times if possible

12. Counter pose to stretch extended bridge

13. If this is too difficult or uncomfortable, try it from a kneeling position, for five breaths

Relaxation Sequence

Baddha Konasana *(Bound Angle Pose)*

Surrender to the earth and feel supported

7. Keep both arms bent... it makes your arms longer!

Finally, stretch from side to side. Drop both bent knees to the right side, arms to left side, look toward hands then change sides. Stretch out and relax.

Meditations and Contemplations for Late Summer

In these sections, we use the controlling cycle of the five elements. Just as one element supports the next (the supporting cycle), its energy also has a controlling effect on another. Here we use the Wood element (the tree) to control Earth (the soil) by giving it substance through strong roots and foundation.

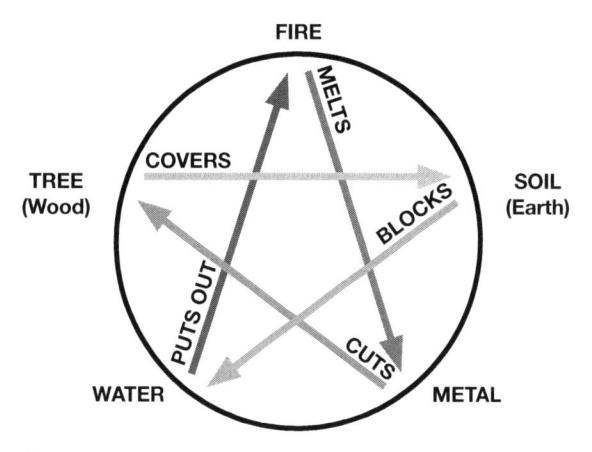

Standing Meditation

Zhang Zhuang (pronounced Jan Jon) means standing like a pole/tree. It is a method of Qigong thought to be about four thousand years old, involving little or no movement. It can be used to build strength, for self-healing, reducing stress and pain, improving health and increasing overall energy levels, as well as being an important part of martial arts training. It can also be done standing, sitting, or in some cases lying down.

Just as a tree experiences growth all over every year as the sap rises, we too can enhance and maximize the flow or Qi (prana) throughout our network of meridians (nadis). It strengthens the nervous and cardiovascular systems and has a beneficial effect on the various muscle groups, especially in helping to develop postural muscle. It enhances the connective tissue and, thereby, the flow of Qi and information throughout the body and to your extremities. In fact it fuses your whole being into a powerful and balanced force field.

First position – Wu Chi (Empty Pose) – this is the position of primal energy, as it aligns the forces of heaven and earth using the body as an open meridian or conduit:

- ❀ Feet shoulder-width apart, toes pointing forward and parallel. The weight is evenly distributed on the right and left sides, and between the ball and heel.
- ❀ The knees are soft, to lower the buttocks two inches, as if sitting on a bench.
- ❀ The pelvis is hanging loose, suspended between the hip joints. The tailbone is drawn down and the abdomen relaxed.
- ❀ The spine is light, secure and supported as if the whole body is hanging from a string from a point between your ears on the crown of the head, with the chin dropped a little in order to lengthen the back of the neck. Feel a stream of energy flowing down from the crown of your head, though your whole body, and into the earth.
- ❀ The shoulders are drawn down, with a broadness and relaxation between them. The elbows and hands relax; the inner elbow joint rotates in towards the body. The fingers are apart and gently curved, with the centre of the palms open and facing slightly backwards.
- ❀ Open the eyes to look forwards, not down, and the gaze is soft focused. The tip of the tongue rests on the roof of the mouth, to connect two major energy meridians. It empowers Yi (intention) and the ability to feel inner sensations, through kinaesthetic imaging.
- ❀ Inhalation and exhalation is through the nose, and the abdomen expands and contracts respectively. For the first few breaths you can open the eyes as you inhale and close them to exhale. Imagine you are conducting energy down from the crown of your head and up through the soles of your feet and gathering it in your lower Dantian or abdominal cavity.

Second position – Embracing Pose – move slowly into this position with intention (first visualizing the arms in the position and then letting the arms float up into it):

- ❀ One you have settled and feel calm, slowly bring your arms upwards and forwards to form a circle in front of your chest, palms inwards. Imagine them sticking to a fragile helium balloon which rests between your inner arms and chest. If you press too much it will burst, and if you press too little it will float away.
- ❀ Keep a space between your fingertips, about the size of a fist, with the top of your thumbs no higher than your shoulders. Feel as if your armpits and upper arms are resting on two small pillows, and sink lowering your buttocks down four inches as if you are sitting on a huge balloon, which is taking your weight behind you.
- ❀ Maintaining this position will build up mental and physical stamina. By creating kinaesthetic images such as the balloon you can now explore how the body feels changes as well as being supported and light.

Third position – Holding Ball in Front of Face – move slowly into this position with intention (visualizing the arms in the position and then letting the arms float up into it):

❁ Sink down deeper in the legs about eight inches, without extending the knees over the toes.
❁ Raise you arms level with your cheeks, extending the palms outwards, as if pushing a ball away from your face. Keep the crown of the head over the centre of the pelvis and the weight in the centre of the feet.
❁ This is a demanding position so use the mind to tell the muscles to relax to extend your endurance. The mind can focus on a sense of broadness and opening in Yintang, the third eye area.

Fourth position – Standing in the Stream (Covering Pose) – move slowly into this position with intention (visualizing the arms in the position and then letting the arms float down into it):

❁ Come up about four inches from the previous pose, or if practicing alone, sink down four inches as for the embracing pose. Maintain your elbows in the same position, and lower your forearms, with the palms down and out to the sides. The fingers are separated and angled slightly inwards. Feel as if your arms and hands are resting on a plank of wood that is floating on the surface of a running stream in which you are standing.
❁ You can feel the plank float slightly away from you and follow the motion with your body, but do not allow any change in the position of your arms. Then feel the plank float towards you and follow the motion.

Mentally and physically exhausted? Try this.

Fifth position – Holding the Balloon in Front of the Belly – move slowly into this position with intention (visualizing the arms in the position and then letting the arms float into it):

✿ Here you are sinking onto a large balloon behind you, by bending the knees two inches, as for the Wuji position, making sure your knees do not come over your toes. Imagine you are holding another large balloon in front of your abdomen. Your palms are inwards and open, and your fingers gently spread apart pointing towards the opposite knee. Relax your arms, forming a long sweeping arc from each shoulder, down the arms to the hands. It should feel like you are holding an enormous belly.
✿ This is a powerful exercise that helps you to gather energy in the lower Dantian, which is seen as the energy field for your physical energy and also where your constitutional energy resides.

Lastly, gather the qi you have generated in the practice into Qihai (CV6) the major point for the sea of qi. The location of this point is on the midline, two finger-widths below the navel. Its action is to tone qi and it is used for cases of extreme mental and physical exhaustion and depression. It regulates original qi and is used for coldness, weakness, fatigue, lack of willpower, impotence, hernia, oedema, irregular menstruation, asthma and abundant pale urination. Also dispels stagnant qi in such cases as constipation, abdominal pain and distension.

Weight Shifting

As your practice continues over time and your endurance grows, you should aim to hold the positions for longer periods of time. You can build on them by shifting your weight first to the left for a period and then to the right.

In the embracing pose, turn your torso slightly to the right and allow your right heel to lift slightly off the ground but keep the toes in contact with it; they turn with you as you shift your weight. Each knee should point in the same direction as the respective foot. Keep a quarter of your weight on the front foot and feel a slight push from the front foot to the back one, and vice-versa. Sense an elastic band between your front toes and your forehead, and one between your front knee and opposite hip and keep them slightly stretched. Hold for two minutes. This helps you to build a strong root and foundation in your practices.

Mental Contemplations for Late Summer

Late summer is about nourishment, support and transitions from one season to the next, time to return to the centre, a midpoint co-ordinating between seasons ending and beginning.

- What do you enjoy as your down time, time for you? Reflect on this and list twelve things and then schedule them in.
- Are you managing your current bank account of energy or are you drawing on your reserves and depleting your deposit account? List twelve ways to put energy back.
- What or who gives you support in your life; do you need more?
- Is your home environment nourishing you, and is it a place you want to come back to? If not, reflect on what changes you would like make.
- Do you need to re-vamp your diet or do a late summer detox?
- Are your thoughts and emotions sustaining you? Remember your brain is fed with a five star diet of nutrition (try to avoid processed sugar), oxygen, information, relaxation and affection.

Home and Lifestyle Section

Eight Home and Lifestyle Tips

Home is the centre of your universe, so it is very important at this time to enjoy and maintain it. The tips below can help you feel more earthed and centred.

- **Feel at home in yourself!** It will help you relate better with others.
- Try to build a high sense of **self-esteem** at this point of the year. Be around people who love you and make you feel good.
- Do a few things **just for you** this month. Have a regular massage, shiatsu, reflexology or aromatherapy treatment.
- Are you getting the **support** you need from those around you? If not, ask for it!
- Recreation **time with family and friends** is very important, as well as doing home-based things.
- **Take life at a slower pace**, and dine out occasionally with friends. Do some entertaining, which involves looking after others, but balance it with doing things just for you.
- **The moods to create are** comfort, stability and balance.
- **The atmospheres to be in and around are** peace, harmony, and unity. Focus on your relationships and well-being; have natural crystals, ceramics and other objects that come from the earth around you. To balance your home environment include objects in pairs, and keep your environment clutter-free.
Oils — rosemary to boost morale, and frankincense to alleviate worry and a troubled mind.

Late Summer Summary

- ☑ Have you managed to stop yourself eating on the run, and do you stop, sit down and relax before you eat? If you have been troubled by indigestion, have you successfully found the foods or eating habits that were causing it?

- ☑ Have you made the changes to your home so that it is more welcoming and cosy, in preparation for the coming winter months?

- ☑ Do you really feel that your immune system has become stronger?

- ☑ Have you now found the right diet to satisfy you and to sit comfortably in the stomach?

- ☑ Are you feeling slimmer around your middle, and have you become more creative and imaginative with your cooking?

- ☑ Are the sweet cravings you had now under control most of the time? Have you got a list of 'good for you' snacks that you have put in your store cupboard to replace any sugar-filled ones?

- ☑ Have you stopped worrying so much, or are you doing less overthinking?

- ☑ Are you feeling more earthed, grounded and centred in your approach to life?

- ☑ Has your ability to concentrate and general self-confidence improved?

- ☑ Is your life filling up with things or people that make it interesting and give you a feeling of being fulfilled?

- ☑ Have you found the appropriate food intake and exercise balance for this time of year? It is very important to avoid feeling stuffed or bloated.

- ☑ Do you keep exercising outdoors, weather permitting?

- ☑ Do you now have time and energy for other people because you have taken the time to nourish yourself?

The season of autumn

Autumn is the Metal element, a time when the nights are drawing in, and nature is slowing down with shorter days and longer nights. With the arrival of autumn, the first thing you notice is the beautiful array of colours with leaves starting to fade through the lack of energy they are receiving. The smell of a smoky atmosphere pervades the air…the smell of autumn. Crisp, cold autumn days are beautiful in sunlight, yet often foggy and grey in the mist as transmutation takes place. In nature, autumn reflects dryness, which is visible in the leaves as they lose their moisture, shrivel up and separate from the branches they have hung on to since the spring. There is a feeling that earth's energy is truly gathering inward and preparing to 'let go' for the winter.

The Feeling of Autumn

Structured, disciplined, ordered, virtuous, discrete, a sense of authority and principles, high standards, sound judgement, beauty, precision and the capacity to shape and refine. As temperatures fall and the evenings draw in, the motivation to exercise is less apparent. Nature is setting an example by slowing down, demonstrated by shorter days, longer nights and dropping temperatures. We can now relax and enjoy the results of our intensive months and adapt to a slower, gentler regime. A time to bring things to a conclusion, get rid of anything or anyone that is upsetting or annoying, leaving you with a sense of clarity and a clear mind.

If autumn was a person, their nature and energy would be more restrained. They would be dignified and serene, a person who can evaluate what is useful and what is not, and who can maintain or discard appropriately. The Metal element infers someone of high values, principles and standards, one who guards and maintains them like precious metals. One who has an ability to mine the hidden truths out of life's experiences, learn from them, and apply them to life in order to refine themselves. They are leaders, good at discerning what is worthy and meaningful, they can work well alone, and have the capacity to think clearly and make sound judgements.

They must guard against becoming over-serious, insular, or sinking into depression; shunning fun and pleasure so they become too restrained, dreary and aloof in their quest for perfection, or having unrealistic expectations of others or themselves.

> So it makes sense to develop the positive qualities, and watch out for the negative at this time of year in order to match the energy of the season. If you are out of balance at the moment, these are the issues that might come up in autumn to be dealt with:
>
> - Do you regularly avoid doing things that make you breathe deeply or suffer from breathing problems?
> - Did you ever smoke to lose weight or control an addiction?
> - Do you frequently get colds, sinus congestion, or mucus conditions?
> - Is your alimentary system sensitive or easily upset when you travel?
> - Did you give up exercise early in your life or did you ever do it at all?
> - Do you tend to put on weight in areas of most movement, i.e. hips, lower back, love handles or ankles?
> - Is your chest collapsed or do you tend to hunch forward?
> - Do you have any skin problems?
> - Do you find it hard to let go of things and move on, and do you constantly talk about the good old days?
> - Do you have issues about self-discipline?
> - Do you have grey cheeks, or a bluish tinge around the base of your thumbs?
> - Do you find it difficult to receive compliments?
> - Do you set standards for yourself or others that are too hard to reach?
> - Are you harbouring grief and not letting it pass?

Eight Priorities for Autumn

1. This is the time to **practise breathing properly** because it balances the emotions and clears the mind.
2. Assume **total responsibility** for how you feel on a daily basis.
3. **Get it off your chest**: sort out anything that is bothering you, or find a friend to talk to.
4. It is time to **let go** of relationships or things that are no longer serving or benefiting you.
5. Introduce **pungent flavours** into your diet such as ginger and horseradish, because they stimulate the lungs and intestines.
6. Do you have sound judgement, strength, structure and discipline in your life? Are you **maintaining high standards and principles** in order to value yourself?
7. Activities for autumn require control and proper use of the breath, so cardiovascular exercise is beneficial, but not in excess. Activity in the home is also important so **have a good clear out**, getting rid of all those things you no longer need.
8. It is a time to **clear your mind** of negative thoughts and to think positively keeping your mind open to new ideas.

Eight Things to Avoid for Autumn

1. **Dampening foods** like wheat *(bread)* and cow products: use sheep and goat products instead.
2. **Clutter and congestion** in every area of life.
3. **Constipation** by keeping the system moving, with the fibre in vegetables and fresh fruit.
4. **Bearing a grudge**; open yourself up and tell the person how you feel.
5. **Addictive habits**.
6. **Getting stuck** in the same old routine, so try changing it.
7. **Becoming isolated**, inhibited, disillusioned, autocratic, or obsessed with detail.
8. **Becoming melancholic**, negative, depressed or filled with constant regret. Avoid prolonged periods of sadness and grief, if possible, as they harm and weaken the lungs.

Eight Daily Habits for Autumn

1. **Start the day with eight full breaths** to energize yourself and your brain; it needs thirty per cent more oxygen than other organs.
2. **Mucus control!** Mucus is overproduced by the body at this time of year when it is aggravated by weather conditions and diet. Keep as mucus-free as possible by starting the day with a ginger and lime infusion, and by cutting out mucus-forming foods such as; meat, eggs, dairy products, oily foods and nuts, and concentrated sweeteners. Also avoid eating late at night, or too many highly processed foods.
3. **Dry skin body-brushing/moisturising.** Buy a long handled body brush, and use it for dry brushing from the soles of the feet and the palms of the hands, upward/inward towards the heart. This is essential at this time of year because the skin can become dry as the weather changes. You can also rub lotion or oils into the body afterwards to pamper the skin and to stimulate the lymphatic system. Be sure to buy the lotion containing the least chemicals. Remember the skin is involved in the process of ridding the body of wastes. It is seen as the third lung, and breathes just as surely and necessarily as the lungs themselves, so try to avoid close fitting synthetic clothing.
4. **Sit for ten minutes every day and meditate!** Just count the breaths, inhaling through the nose for three slow counts, and exhaling through the nose for six slow counts. It will increase a feeling of relaxation and letting go. Set your oven timer or alarm for ten minutes so that you are not distracted by repeatedly looking at your watch. Every time you notice your mind has wandered off, just let go of the thought and return to observing the breath; this is a great mind clearer!
5. **Tune into the seasonal energy.** The energetic theme of a typical autumn day is one of doing less. The focus is about breathing the energy of life in and out of the body, thus opening oneself to all that the universe has to offer!
6. **The quality of your breath** defines the quality of your movements and experiences, as well as the quality of your thoughts and moods. Hold on to your principles and keep your commitments. Be consciously more enthusiastic and positive at this time of year.
7. **Start to wear more warm clothes**, keep wrapped up; too many skimpy clothes in the winter encourages your body to put on additional fat to keep itself warm. You only have to look and see this in the huge rise of low-slung jeans and muffin tops!
8. **Continually monitor** any areas of your life where you might be pushing yourself too much by setting or expecting unreasonable standards of others or yourself.

Read it if you need it?

The Menopause

The menopause is covered in this section as it usually comes in the autumn of life! For some women it is not a problem, but for others it becomes an all-consuming one. There is no doubt that exercise of any kind is good, but t'ai chi, qigong and yoga are particularly helpful as they work on the endocrine system which helps against the various symptoms which can occur.

What is it?

It is a time when the levels of oestrogen and progesterone decline to a point where a woman is no longer menstruating and will therefore not bear children. This is welcomed by some women and mourned by others.

What happens?

- You can become more toxic; some women lose toxins through monthly bleeding.
- You can become tired, heavy, sluggish, put on weight or retain more fluid.
- Sleep patterns can become disrupted through night sweats, anxiety, etc.
- You can become more stressed and anxious due to lack of sleep and hormonal changes.
- Your immune and lymphatic systems may not function optimally.
- The adrenal glands work overtime, causing stress or a feeling of being constantly overwhelmed.
- Regular feelings of depression, or a feeling of low self-esteem can be evident.
- Losing your waist or developing fat around the navel area.

What can you do to help against these symptoms? Eight ways to fight the symptoms of the menopause:

1. **Keep your body less toxic** by cutting down on toxic foods and drinks. Carefully examine the labels on creams and suntan lotions; in fact, on all things that you are applying to your body, because the skin is the largest organ of the body and will absorb whatever you put on it. Women often become more sensitive and develop allergic reactions at this point in their lives.
2. **Exercise is very important**, such as walking if the weather suits, or going to the gym. Start taking the stairs instead of the lift, and take up t'ai chi, Pilates, yoga or meditation.
3. For sleeping issues **cut down on caffeine**, or try to cut it out altogether, especially in the late afternoon or evening. Make the caffeine rule one cup before midday and not afterwards.
4. **Do not eat too late** and when you do eat, make it quality food, as near to the way it was originally grown as possible.
5. **Write things down that are on your mind.** Start keeping a diary if you haven't already because it saves the tension of becoming forgetful.
6. **Spend time relaxing** before you go to bed. Avoid late night computer work or anything that overstimulates your mind.
7. **Take time out for yourself**, and try to introduce a ten-minute catnap into your life, as this will invigorate you and reduce stress.
8. **Take vitamins to supplement your diet**; liquid vitamins are great, especially if you have been sweating. Good quality flower remedies are also very effective for the edgy times!

The 'Man-o-pause'?

Bear in mind that you may not be the only one in the house who is suffering from these feelings. There is a male version, some believe, which usually appears later in life than women. The Man-o-pause's proper medical name is *Andropause* or *Viropause*, and although there may be no obvious sign of the cessation of anything, as with a woman, men can still suffer from symptoms.

Typical symptoms are:

- A new Ferrari or sports car in the drive.
- Low libido, less keen on sex than he used to be *(testosterone reduction)*.
- Feeling constantly tired or lacking motivation.
- Irritability and low mood/depression, grumpy, stressed or more anxious than usual.
- Weight gain, especially around the middle.
- New wardrobe of hip and trendy clothes.
- Lack of strength or endurance.

To help with the symptoms, follow the same advice as the menopause which can be combined with a visit to the doctor for more advice on the subject.

Food Section

Food for the Autumn Energy

'The secret of our daily diet is finding balance and the correct fuel that is suitable for our constitution, condition, activity and lifestyle.'
Taken from Healing with Whole Foods, Paul Pitchford.

Look in your local fruit shop or farmers market for what is fresh and grown locally. **Eat healthy comfort foods**. Yes...there is such a thing!

For example, start the day with a large bowl of porridge, made with half water and half soya or goat's milk for a creamy taste. Then sprinkle a generous portion of ground seeds on the top. Use flax, sunflower, pumpkin and hemp *(two tablespoons of flax to one tablespoon of the others)*. Grind them in a coffee grinder and keep in a sealed jar in the fridge. Top the porridge with organic honey which is comfort food for any time of day!

Food for the Autumn

Autumn is the time when the external temperature is changeable, and you should be introducing hot foods back into your diet. The lungs also appreciate the essence of foods through the sense of smell. Pine kernels are specifically good for the lungs and nettle tea is a useful tonic. The lungs are the most vulnerable organs to external conditions, hot is treated with cooling pungent flavours such as elderflower, and cold with hot and pungent spices such as ginger.

Top tip
Enjoy more spices to keep up the internal temperature and to stop mucus forming.

How you cook is also relevant, as the cooking method has a direct effect on the energy of the food. The ideal cooking style for autumn is to prepare and cook for longer, using methods such as roasting, pressure cooking, steaming or boiling.

Autumn Food List

Apples	Grains	Tangerines	Pungent and spicy
Apricots	Mushrooms	Turnips	foods
Carrots	Olives	Walnuts	Cinnamon
Celery	Onions	Water chestnuts	Garlic
Chestnuts	Pears	Watercress	Ginger
Chinese cabbage	White radishes	Wine	Ginseng
Egg whites	(mooli)		

Eight Food and Nutrition Tips

1. Review your diet and **cut down on refined white foods** such as white flour products, white sugar and white rice.
2. **Include flora-enhancing foods** such as; yoghurt, Miso, sauerkraut, Acidophilus[1], Spirulina[2] and chlorophyll rich foods such as; leafy greens, spinach, cabbage, etc.
3. Sluggish digestion can result from either a sedentary lifestyle or a lack of dietary fibre, so **add some pungent foods** and get things moving. Garlic clears the lungs of mucus, improves digestive activity and improves a sluggish liver. Mint, ginger, cinnamon and cayenne pepper are good for sluggish people but beware of too many pungent flavours as they can knot muscles, making them tight.
4. **Autumn recipe**: chop a selection of fresh autumn vegetables, preferably organic, e.g. butternut squash, pumpkin, sweet potato, turnip, parsnip, red/white onions and red/yellow peppers. Drizzle with some good olive oil and sprinkle with sea salt and pepper then roast in a hot oven until golden and sticky for about forty minutes. Add to brown rice or quinoa and grate or roast goat's cheese on the top, adding a few fresh herbs if you prefer.
5. **Avoid dry environments** and too much baked or dry food, dried fruit or white flour. Too much bread can also cause internal dryness and constipation.
6. **Eat fewer cold dairy products**, such as ice-cream, and avoid orange and tomato juices which can increase mucus production.
7. **Eat in a calm and relaxed environment** and take your time with a breather in between courses.
8. **Do not be obsessive** about your food or too precise with your eating times; eat when hungry because you actually need less food than you think you do.

(1) Acidophilus is a natural bacteria and is available from health food shops. It can help protect the body against harmful bacteria, parasites, and other organisms. It also plays an important role in digestion, helping to produce a number of chemicals that aid in the digestive process.

(2) Spirulina is a blue-green algae, one of the few plant sources of vitamin B_{12}, usually found only in animal tissues. It also provides high amounts of nutrients and is very easily digested. Commercial spirulina is available in powder, tablet and capsule form, or can be found added to food as a health tonic.

Exercise and Movement Section

This section will show you various ways to stimulate the energy lines for this time of year. As you have read earlier, each time of the year has a pair of organs that are complementary and particularly in focus to the time of year. As you can see, the Lung lines run from the front of the chest and the Large Intestine lines run across the back of the arms and shoulders. The following sections will include exercises that move energy in these areas and therefore energise the lungs and large intestine.

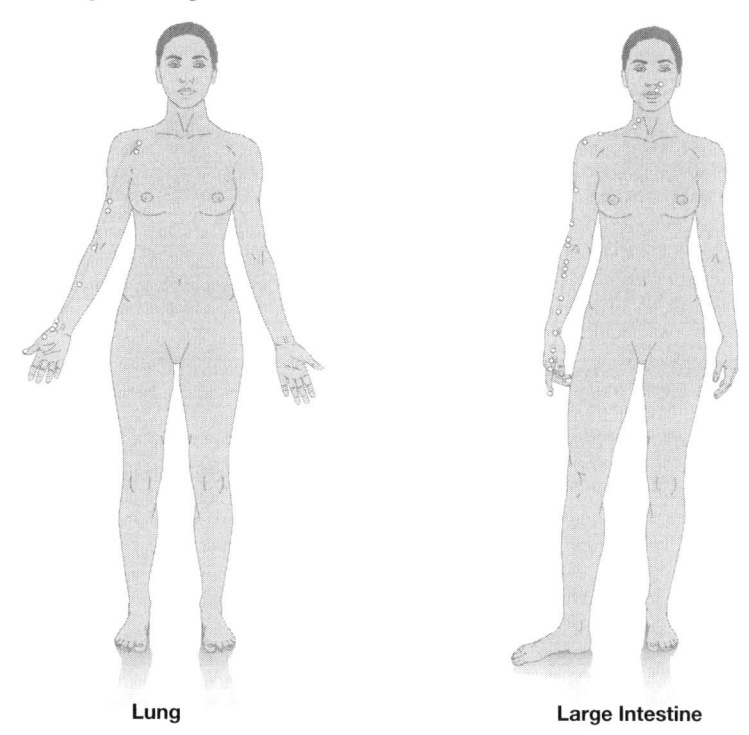

Lung　　　　　　　　　　　**Large Intestine**

Exercise for Autumn

Make your autumn routine a little slower. Choose a routine or class which has the capacity to shape and refine the body, or has movement techniques that maximise power with the minimum effort. Learn to conserve energy and move more efficiently.

Structured and disciplined is the order of the day, and whatever you decide to do, keep at it for this season. Discipline yourself to work out regularly; doing it with a friend can help. Demand high standards from your teacher or gym; find a class or a trainer who has a good plan or structure to their class; fluffy won't do it! Eight exercise suggestions would be:

1. **Be more enthusiastic** about your workout at this time of year. Have high standards and be precise in your approach to your chosen regime. Manage your exercise programme into a regular pattern or routine, and refine it more.
2. Go to an **Alexander Technique** or **Feldenkrais** class and learn the art of how to use your body correctly and to release any habitual tensions. These will give you techniques which reduce effort in movement and increase your body awareness.
3. **Work on the breath** and look into yoga breathing techniques (see pages 164). Practice them daily at this time of year and feel the difference.
4. Make sure you do **plenty of wide arm opening stretches** at the beginning of your session to maximise lung capacity.
5. **Balance** outward activities with inward activities; search out a t'ai chi, Pilates or yoga class which focuses the mind and builds reserves of power. Use yoga back bends to increase lung capacity; these are ideal for the autumn.
6. **Look out for depression**, it often happens at this time of year so breathe well, don't collapse your chest, and hold your head up high; remember that the neck is the bridge to the brain.
7. Go for **regular walks** and have plenty of fresh air in your environment, both at home and at work. Occasionally give yourself permission to be spontaneous.
8. **Take up exercises that focus on concentration, strengthening the abdomen and increasing your breath awareness**.

Avoid:
- Sitting still or slumped for long periods.
- Long walks in cold and wet weather.
- Getting chilled (so wrap up well).

Learn to Meditate on the Breath

This is a special practice for the autumn season, which can be used for yoga, t'ai chi and mediation. We are usually only aware of our breath when it is abnormal, such as when we are stressed, have an asthma attack, or when we have been running hard.

Try this exercise by using your ordinary breath as the meditation object. Do not try to make the breath long or short, or control it in any way, but simply stay with the normal inhalation and exhalation.

At first, the mind wanders off. Once you are aware that you have stopped focusing on the breath, gently return to it. If the mind wanders on the exhalation, then put more effort into that. Keep bringing it back with patience, like training a naughty child, always being willing to start again. Eventually you will be able to sustain your attention a little longer and begin to understand what concentration really is.

A deep, focused breath makes the process of breathing a conscious activity. The aim of such conscious breathing practice is to encourage full use of our lungs, train the mind and stabilise our emotional state. It allows you to become the silent watcher of the mind, so you become aware of its wandering and your ability to re-direct it. The Chinese say, *"Where the mind goes, the energy follows."*

Start your yoga poses in an upright comfortable seated position so that you become composed and focused on the present, and practice the above simple breathing meditation. Then repeat this at the end of your practice while lying down on your back to relax in Savasana. This deep breathing involves even, rhythmic breaths through the nostrils. On the inhalation, three things happen:

1. The lungs expand, causing the abdomen to expand outwards, the lower back to fill and as the diaphragm draws down, it gently massages the digestive organs, adrenals and kidneys.
2. The rib cage expands laterally to fill the middle parts of the lungs.
3. The collar bones lift to fill the top part of the lungs so that the rib cage lengthens.

Feel the breath like a wave, starting from the bottom and rising to the top. On the exhalation:

1. The collar bones lower.
2. The ribs move inwards and downwards.
3. The diaphragm rises into the chest. As the air is pushed out, the muscles of the ribs (intercostals) contract to squeeze the lungs inwards and expel the air out of the nostrils.

Try consciously pausing between each of the above six stages for a few complete breaths. Then return to a smooth wave as you completely fill and empty the lungs.

Deep, Rhythmic Breathing

Most people only use the top part of the lungs to breathe, whereas deep yoga breathing uses the lungs fully.

The physical benefits are:

1. Increases oxygen to the lungs.
2. Heart function improves because of a richer oxygen supply, not just to the heart but to all parts of the body. The movement of the diaphragm aids the heart's pumping action making its job easier, which in turn lowers blood pressure.
3. It helps the digestive process and assists in nourishment through improved cellular health.
4. The muscles, skin, and the organs generally work and repair more efficiently.

The mental benefits are:

1. When we learn to consciously control the breath, we have the ability to tap into the unconscious mind, the place of intuition. This happens as breathing, which is normally controlled by involuntary parts of the brain, is brought into conscious awareness.
2. Helps alter our emotional state and reduce stress.
3. Improves mental awareness of the body and the control of movement and co-ordination.
4. Our brain is supplied with oxygen-rich blood, improving concentration and clarity of thought.

Qigong for Autumn

Bo points or collecting points are located on the chest, abdomen or waist and are used both for diagnosis and treatment. These are where the energy collects or gathers from each of the relevant organs. They can become tender either spontaneously or on the application of pressure. In treatments they are used to regulate and balance the energy in their associated organs. The ones for the lung and large intestine are shown on the diagram. The initials and numbers in the brackets refer to the particular acupressure point along an organ meridian, (an energy pathway that leads to and from a major organ), and is where the energy is particularly accessible from the surface.

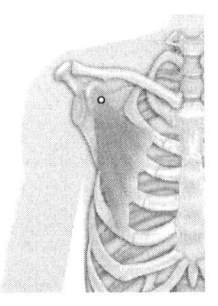

Zhongfu (Lung Bo Point, LU 1, The Central Residence): between the first and second rib, six cun (thumb-widths) lateral to the midline of the chest.

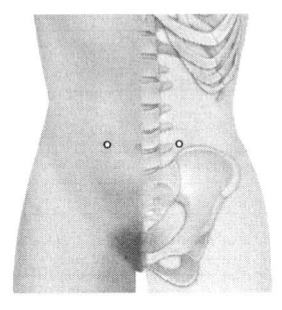

Tianshu (Large Intestine, ST 25, The Celestial Pivot): two thumb-widths to the side of the navel.

You can gently massage these points with the tips of the thumb, index and middle fingers. The lung points can also be thumped with soft fists to decongest and stimulate the lungs.

Squeezing the Ball to Strengthen the Intercostals

Stand with feet shoulder-width apart as if holding a ball in front of your chest, with the palms of your hands facing each other, and your elbows slightly bent. Inhale, moving the hands out to the sides, no more than the width of your chest *(the elbows can lift slightly)*. Exhale, and draw the hands back as if to squeeze the imaginary ball using the muscles of your rib cage to apply the pressure on the invisible ball.

Improve your breathing capacity

Massage the Lungs

Now cross your hands in front of your chest with your left hand inside your right. Inhale, and extend the left arm out to the left side, palm facing outwards with the thumb and index fingers extended upward and the other fingers softly curled. The right hand, with elbow bent, draws along the collar bone on the right lung point, as if pulling a bowstring with extended thumb and bent fingers. The focus is on breathing into the right lung.

Exhale, drawing the left hand in front of the right and crossing the arms in front of the chest. The focus is to exhale and massage the lungs as if squeezing the imaginary ball. Now repeat the exercise, extending the right arm, palm away, and pulling the bow with the left, as your attention is on filling the left lung.

Feeling weak or congested? Stop and take a breather!

Alternating the nostril variation

Inhale extending the left arm and drawing the bow with the right, with the focus on filling the right lung and right nostril, and then exhale turning the extended left arm around to the right by turning the waist, focusing on exhaling from the left lung and the left nostril and then reverse. Let the gaze follow the tip of the extended index as you turn in the waist, massaging the lungs as you turn.

Strengthen the Diaphragm

Here the breathing is reversed so that as you inhale and draw the imaginary bow, the diaphragm is tightened and lifted into the chest. As you exhale, the diaphragm is released and relaxed as if releasing an arrow from the bow. With this exercise draw the bow several times just to the left and then change and repeat several times to the right. Only use reverse breathing for short periods and avoid completely if you suffer from high blood pressure.

Massage the Kidneys

Inhale drawing the bow to the left.
Exhale turning in the waist to take the extended left arm in an arc behind you to the left.
Inhale rotating the torso to bring the extended left arm back to the midline in front of the chest.
Exhale and continue to draw the bow in an arc around to the right. Then repeat the exercise drawing the bow with the left hand and extending the right arm and turning around to the right. The hips and feet remain facing forward all the times, and the turn is in the waist and the chest.

Anxious, fearful or lacking energy? Recharge with this!

Massage the Intestines

Interlace your fingers behind your back extending the index fingers. Inhale, and lean slightly back to open the chest, sliding your index fingers down your back toward the base of your buttocks on the midline breathing into the lung points under each collarbone (see the previous pages).

Exhale, bending forwards and extending your arms back and over your head, then inhale into the Large Intestine points located two fingers-width either side of the navel. Exhale, while drawing your navel (and the Large Intestine points) back towards your spine. You can remain in this stretch for several breaths. Inhale, while returning to the upright position.

To increase the range of this stretch, a counter pose can be used before repeating it. This counter movement accentuates the opening and closing action of the Metal element's energy.

As you inhale, expand the torso and draw both arms out to the sides and above your head with palms facing forwards. At the same time take one leg straight back behind you, while rising on to the ball of the foot on the weighted leg. As you exhale, lower your leg and heel, drawing your hands down in front of your hips. Replicate this several times using alternate legs.

Then repeat the previous exercise folding forward by interlacing the fingers with the other thumb on top.

Feeling blocked or toxic? Get things moving!

The Turbulent Wave

Here the hand positions are important in order to stimulate the LI 4 pressure point (Hegu) which is located at the V formed by the thumbs and index fingers and is tender to the touch. To find it, press underneath the root of the index finger. It can also be used to relieve headaches, colds and sinus congestion. (Avoid the use of the LI4 in pregnancy.)

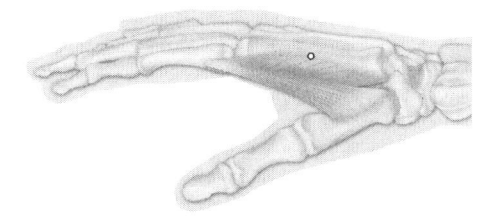

As if sitting back into a chair, bring your chest forwards to place your hands palms down on your thighs, with the thumbs on the outsides and fingers pointing in. Take a deep breath in, and then exhale fully emptying your lungs as much as possible. Maintain the exhalation, drawing your pelvic floor up and the abdomen in towards the spine, and the diaphragm up. Then release them in reverse order. Without inhaling, perform this lift and release another two to five times. Then inhale and come up.

The best time to perform this exercise is between 5 and 7am in the morning and always on an empty stomach. **Avoid if you suffer from high blood pressure.**

A morning exercise to tone the alimentary system

Stretches to Open Up the Lung and Large Intestine Meridians

The Lung meridian runs from Zhongfu, the Lung point below the collar bones, as mentioned previously, and down the inside of the arms to the thumb. Bring your hands to the starting position in front of your navel with the palm facing the body. Inhale drawing them up and out above your head, rotating the thumbs back to bring the palms upwards and slightly backwards, feeling the energy stream down to your thumbs or visualising a white light. Hold the inhalation for a few seconds. Exhale lowering the hands back to the starting position by rotating the thumbs down and slightly under. Repeat this several times.

Open up your lungs and grab some oxygen

The Large Intestine meridian runs from the index fingers up the back of the arms to the far side of the nose. To connect the Lung and Large Intestine meridians, bring the index fingers to the thumbs and extend the arms out to the sides at shoulder height. Inhale as you rotate the thumb and index fingers of your left hand down and back. Bring the V from between the thumb and index finger on the back of the right hand to the side of your right nostril. You should feel a stretch along the back of the arm and top of the shoulder as you draw the energy up the Large Intestine meridian, or continue to visualise white light coming up to the right side of the nose.

Exhale and return the hands out to the sides. Then inhale as you rotate the thumb and index fingers of your right hand down and back and bring the V from between the thumb and index finger on the back of the left hand to the side of your right nostril.

Regulate your elimination

Revitalize and Oxygenate Body and Mind

Inhale through the nose, lifting your arms above your head with palms facing forwards and the fingers stretched. Exhale through the nose, rotating the palms inwards folding your fingers over your thumbs to form soft fists, and drawing them down to the Zongfu points just below the collar bones. Focusing more on the strong exhalation and repeat up to one hundred and twenty times slowly or quickly, feeling the breath go right down into the bottom of the lungs as you raise your arms to inhale.

Revitalise the body and mind

Increase Your Personal Boundary

The Lung and Large Intestine meridians are all about exchange and elimination across boundaries. By placing your thumbs in the palms of your hands and squeezing them with your fingers, this stimulates the Lungs, Hegu and Laogong points and protects your personal space, which can be useful if you are going into a negative environment.

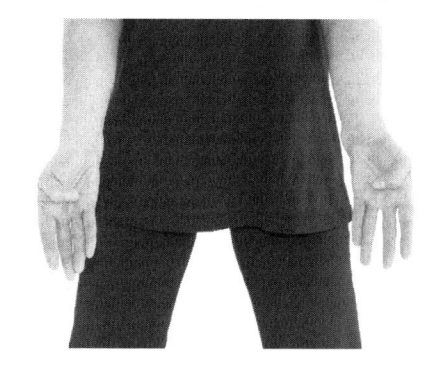

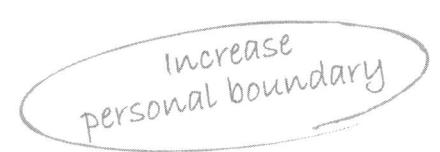

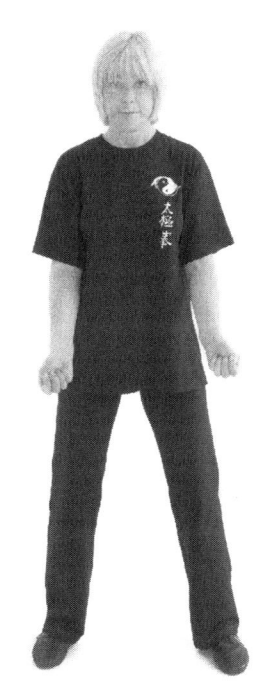

Increase personal boundary

Cleansing the Three Dantians

To spring clean your energy systems, try this

The three dantians are seen as the three fields of energy and correspond to the Western understanding of the three major cavities. The dantians also have major acupressure points where access to its physical energy is on the surface. They can also be used to direct the focus of the mind or for postural awareness. Chi/qi in these cavities can become depleted, excessive or rebellious which suggests imbalance. These imbalances can result from negative thoughts and emotions or through poor eating habits, posture and lifestyle. If the balance of chi becomes irregular or disrupted, illness or disharmony occurs.

- The lower *(Xia)* Dantian relates to the physical body, abdominal cavity and organs within this region *(Qihai is a point two finger-widths, below the navel)*. It is also seen as the place where the essence or constitutional energy resides.
- The middle *(Zhong)* Dantian relates to the emotions, thoracic cavity and the heart and lungs *(Shanzhong is the point in the centre of the breast bone)*. It is also known as the centre for dispersing chi.
- The upper *(Shang)* Dantian relates to the mind and the cranial cavity housing the Shen or spirit *(the point called Yintang is level with the third eye between the eyebrows and two finger-widths above the bridge of the nose)*.

How to cleanse these areas and eliminate mental, emotional or physical stress or pent up energy:

- Lower Dantian. Inhale and draw soft fists to the sides of the waist palms up, focusing on the kidneys and lower back. Exhale and spiral the fists forwards rotating the palms downwards slightly rounding to open the lower back. Feel you are eliminating any stress or fatigue from the kidneys and lower back area as you draw the area around the Qihai point, just below the navel, in towards the back.

- Now release the fists rotating the palms up, and draw the soft fists back to the waist as you inhale. Repeat this movement seven more times.
- Middle Dantian. Inhale, drawing your hands up level with the Shangzhong point in the centre of the chest, bringing the palms to face each other. Exhale throwing the hands forwards as if throwing out any negative emotions from the heart/chest. Keep the wrists soft so that you can feel the qi (chi) going right through to the ends of the fingers. Repeat seven more times.

- Upper Dantian. Inhale, drawing your hands up the midline, rotating the palms outwards at throat level as far as the point called Yintang, between your eyebrows. Now separate your hands out towards each temple. As you exhale, draw your hands out and down to the side as if discarding any negative thoughts or doubts from the mind. This can be done either slowly or faster up to a further seven times.

Eliminate mental, emotional and physical stress

T'ai Chi Moves for Autumn

Movements in the form should focus on:

- ❁ Co-ordinating breath and movement.
- ❁ Let the breath lead the movement.
- ❁ Focus on the moment of change between postures/positions.
- ❁ Keeping a sense of space or personal boundary.

Shooting the Arrow

Increase your breathing capacity

A vital part of the health maintenance of the lungs is that the diaphragm and the intercostal muscles of the rib cage are kept mobilised, flexible and strong.

Inhale raising your arms up in front of the body, palms up and with middle fingers pointing in towards each other, and flexing your elbows to the sides. Once they reach throat level, rotate the palms outwards as you bring your hands level with the Yintang point at the third eye, between the eyebrows.

Exhale and without moving your hips to the side, move the left side of your rib cage in, to bring the left elbow down to the side of the waist, as the right elbow lifts up to the right.

Inhale as you return to the central position. Repeat several times, alternating the sides.

Repeat the previous exercise but bring the palm of the left hand to the back of the right hand and place your weight on to the right foot. This time as you exhale, sink your weight down into the right leg and step out to the side on to your left foot. With feet slightly more than hip-width apart, bend your left knee to ninety degrees with your toes in line with the left knee. Extend your left arm out to the side, feeling as if the rib cage is like a bow, and the energy flowing down the arm like the force of a shooting an arrow. The weight is now sixty to seventy per cent in the left leg and thirty to forty per cent in the right leg, and your shoulder-blades open like a fan.

Now place the weight back in the right foot and bring the left foot in, placing the palm of the right hand behind the back of the left and repeat to the other side. This is a good exercise to illustrate how the movement of the body and breath co-ordination is crucial in the force of a deflection in t'ai chi.

Strum the Lute and Stamp the Foot

This sequence is a useful illustration of how the study of qigong and the skill of working with energy was always considered an invaluable precursor to the study of t'ai chi.

Having learned the earlier exercise of squeezing the ball on page 153, this can be applied to a martial art application by locking an opponent's elbow and wrist with your hands, while at the same time drawing them down and stamping on their foot.

Inhale as you raise your hands up and out to the sides, lifting your left knee to hip height and sinking the weight down in your right leg. Exhale and bring your hands towards the midline, as if to grip an opponent's elbow with your left hand and wrist with the right. Also bring your left heel down to the ground by sinking down and bending the right knee. Then as you inhale again, place the weight into the left leg and lift the right knee, repeating the move on the other side.

Yoga for Autumn

Withdraw and find your space

Autumn Yoga Poses

Metal is about gathering energy inwards with the focus on breathing *(Pranayama)* using opening and closing poses in the upper torso to stimulate and increase lung ventilation. Use Pranayama exercises to focus and balance gathered energy to cleanse, regulate and stimulate the respiratory tract, gently encouraging the whole system to detoxify and 'let go'. Do not compromise the breath to go into a posture, and work with opening the rib cage.

Warm up first

Pull the navel to the spine as you stretch your hands forward, move the chin into the neck, (1) **exhale**. Take the hands behind the back, move the head back, and try to arch the back. **Inhale**, (2) then pull the navel in. **Exhale** as you bring the shoulders round and in towards the centre, (3) then bring the hands forward to relax and stretch. Do this five times every morning at the start of your day if possible and before practice.

1

2

3. Keep sitting bones on the floor as you lean away from side to side, providing an anchor to stretch from

4

We are applying the knowledge of length before rotation; the flow of energy in yoga is foundation-length-rotation, so we lengthen the spine before twisting it.

5

6

7. Breathe in as you stretch up

8. Exhale as you come forward

9. Take a deep breath and lengthen the spine before you rotate

10. Breathe and lengthen before rotation

11. Breathe in as you stretch up

12. Exhale as you come forward

13

14

15

Warm-up for Spine Mobility Before the Next Sequence

Make full use of a complete breath.

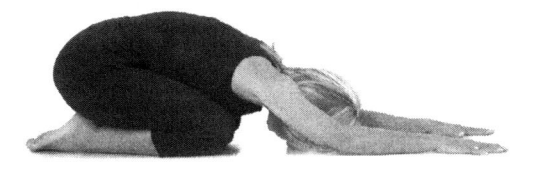

Collect and calm yourself with this series

1. Open armpits, breathe and lengthen spine

2. Inhale. Open the spine and heart in a wave of movement, mobilising the spine, vertebra by vertebra, and finally opening the heart

3. Exhale

4. Inhale

5. Exhale. Reach hands a little further forward

Get the flow into your life in preparation for winter, slowing the pace and the mind.

6. Roll through your toes

7

8. Then pull inwards, rise in a wave and finish in downward dog, (adho mukha svanasana) then into child's pose, which is calming for the heart

9. Roll back through your toes

Repeat the sequence several times until you feel warmer and more flexible.

10. Head just off the floor

11. Knees apart, feet together, breathe deeply

Easy Moon Salute

To warm-up or use as an autumn morning sequence. Link the movement to the breath flow, feeling the breath moving the body, one breath per pose.

1. Inhale

2. Exhale

3. Inhale

4. Do not bend your arms in the autumn flow by keeping them straight as you transition from plank to up dog. It is more restorative, conserving energy and strength.... exhaling

5. Finish the stretch by lifting chin up to top jaw, creating a full stretch in the neck. Inhale

6. Knees apart and feet together for a comfortable balasana (child's pose). Exhale

Inhale with the upward stretches, and exhale with the folding moves, going at your own pace, quite slowly, feeling the spine opening with each movement.

Move the energy through your spine, in and out of the stretches, being exact and thorough with the moves. Breathing in and out with each move, the breath and movement are united ... yoga!

Do you feel you need a change in life? Exchange and eliminate

7. Long inhale

8. Long exhale

9. Long exhale

10

11

12. Flowing with the breath uniting the movement from one move to the next

13

Metal Element Flow

Intermediate. Practice below sequence five times. Maintain focus on breath. The practice below is for experienced practitioners.

Breathe into these twists and get your practice moving!

1. Inhale as you reach up

2. Ankles and knees together

3. Five breaths each side

4

5. Parivrtta utkatasana, (finger point pose), push down on the top hand, lengthen the whole spine as the body rotates. Breathe

6. Bring hands to either side of the foot and step back into a lunge

7. Utthita parsvakonasana. Drop the right arm inside the foot and allow the knee to support the shoulder. Extend the left arm with a full in breathe

8. Fold the top arm behind the back, reach for the other arm to get binding

These moves are more advanced, so only do these if you have a yoga practice, but miss out if too difficult

9

10. Back to lunge

11. Then to downward dog

12. Then change leg and repeat the five previous poses

13. And finally Balasana (child's pose)

Opening the Autumn Channels With Breath and Meridian Work

Here the focus is on opening and closing the meridians by using hand and arm positions synchronised with the breath. Start in utkanasana, push the feet into the floor, with the ankles and knees together to stabilize the lower body. Pull navel to spine or uddiyana bandha, extend the upper body towards the ceiling, and expand the ribs with full breaths.

Twist and lengthen the spine right side, with the left arm to the outside of the right leg, bending the elbow to increase the foundation on the outside of the right calf. Now bend the right arm and press the hands together, pushing gently down on the bottom palm with the top one, see (3) for hand position. Breathe and lengthen as you do this. If you can reach the floor with the left hand, put the palm on the floor (4) and lengthen the right hand to the ceiling (5), curving the fingers as the hand goes up, and inhaling as the arm extends.

Do this five times with full breath awareness, exhaling as the arm comes down, and inhaling as the arm goes up. Return to the start pose. Now change sides and repeat.

1

2. Knees and ankles together

3. On the top hand push elbow into the outer calf, then put on the top hand

4

5. Right arm and hand move up towards the ceiling as you breathe in

The following poses are using the same breathing technique.

For trikonasana (triangle pose), move the feet about two feet apart, inhaling as you extend the arm to the side. Reach down to the floor, grip the big toe or reach down to place the palm on the floor, whichever feels right. You can bend your knee to get there, and bring the top arm down, curl the fingers, then inhale as your arm comes up, extending the fingers at the top and repeat five times. Then come up, pulling navel to spine to help you up there, turn to face the opposite way, then reach to the side and repeat the same as above for five breaths.

Allow the breath to penetrate deeply with each move, making breath the main focus of these poses

For the autumn season at work, or in the autumn season of your life, yoga in a chair will increase the oxygen in your lungs.

1. Spine rolling to warm up

2. Inhale

3. Exhale

4.

5. Exhale as you turn

6. Follow with rotations, while keeping sitting bones firmly on the chair

7. Exhale

8. Inhale

9. Exhale, with the knee and ribs resting on each other

One leg deep stretch, with ribs resting on thighs, right first then left, into back bend between, then to full both leg forward stretch

Older, injured, at work or in a chair? Try these

Part 5: The Season of Autumn 235

11. Sit on the edge of a chair, but check to make sure you are balanced

12. Inhale and exhale as you come up

13. Virabhadrasana 2. (warrior 2) on chair with back lean and then forward stretch for waist, then change sides. Inhale and reach

14.

15. Virabhadrasana 1 (warrior 1) one side, then turn to supported Prasarita Padottanasana, then Virabhadrasana 1 on the other side

16. Inhale as you twist

17. Exhale back to the centre

18. Parivritta Trikonasana, back to the centre, then on the other side. Exhale as you twist

Be creative but exact with these moves; use the objects around you

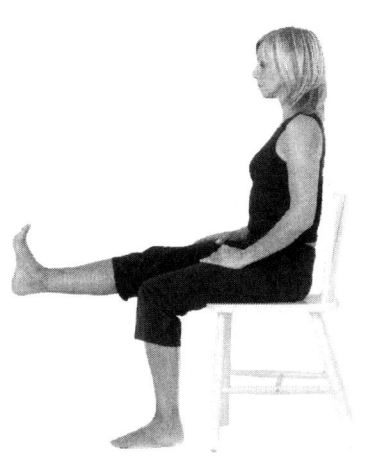

19. Leg stretch, purvatanasana, then other leg

20. Inhale

Exhale in transition

21. Inhale as you turn

22. Inhale and turn

Supported standing rotations as an extra if needed.

Alternate Nostril Breathing (Nadi Sodhana)

With the right thumb covering the right nostril, inhale through the left nostril for four counts. Remove the thumb, cover the left nostril with the ring finger, and exhale through the right nostril for eight counts. Inhale into the right nostril for four counts, keeping the left nostril covered. Now cover the right nostril and exhale through the left nostril for eight counts. Repeat the whole sequence slowly seven times.

Meditations and Contemplations for Autumn

In these sections we use the controlling cycle of the five elements. Just as one element supports the next (the supporting cycle), its energy also has a controlling effect on another. Here we use the Fire element (the mind) to control the Metal by using conscious awareness to focus on the breath.

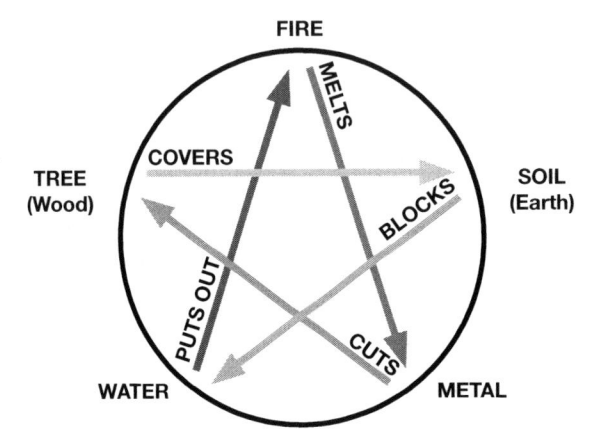

Standing Breathing Meditation – 'Where the Yi goes Chi Flows'

Intention or Yi can be applied to anything and everything we decide to do, such as setting an intention at the start of a day, new project or relationship, or using its effect to move energy for healing or to enhance energy flow. Meditation on directing chi flow has been used for centuries to strengthen the power of intention, as well as training the mind and eliminating stress.

Find a quiet place and after sinking the weight into your right foot, step out on your left so that your feet are shoulder-width apart. Balance the weight evenly between both feet with your weight slightly forwards on the Yongquan points which are in the soles, one third of the distance from the base of the second toe to the heel.

Inhale pulling in your abdomen, to reverse your normal abdominal breathing, to create a change in the intra-abdominal pressure, while raising your arms out to the sides with the palms down and puffing out your chest. Imagine chi flowing up from Yongquan *(the kidney points)* along the inner sides of your legs and up the front of your body to the inner ends of your collar bones, and then out to Zhongfu, the lungs points as described earlier.

As you **exhale** keep the abdomen pulled in and feel the Zhongfu points open and chi flowing down to your thumbs as you draw them up and back to open the Lung meridian. Stay there breathing in to the Zhongfu points and exhaling to direct chi flow down to the thumbs for several complete breaths.

Now **inhale** circling your hands in front of your chest with palms facing in, as if holding a large balloon between your hands and the front of your body. Soften your elbows and allow the weight of the arms to sink your shoulder-blades down. Visualize any negative or toxic chi being pulled out and clear white light expanding in your chest, while still keeping your abdomen drawn in. Stay in this stance for several breaths.

On the next inhalation, use the Yi to guide chi flow over the backs of your hands and up your arms to your shoulders. As you exhale, lower your arms down, relaxing the abdomen and guiding chi flow down the sides of the torso and legs back to the Yongquan points in the soles of the feet. Now return to normal abdominal breathing. The above can be repeated several times, but please note we only used reverse breathing for a limited period.

If you suffer from abnormal blood pressure or hypertension, avoid drawing your abdomen in, and just continue to do the exercise with normal abdominal breathing, expanding your abdomen as you inhale and relaxing it as you exhale.

Breathing Awareness Meditation

From ancient times, the breath has been recognised as the key to our life. In fact, in the root of language in many cultures, the word for breath is also the word for life-force or spirit. While normal unconscious breathing is controlled by the autonomic nervous system, the breath is also readily accessible to conscious control, and therefore provides a link between our conscious mind, our anatomy, physiology, deeper emotional states and our deepest spiritual potential. Awareness of the breath not only promotes relaxation and concentration but also awakens the higher energies, directing them to every cell in the body.

This practice can be practiced in Shavasana (corpse pose) lying on the back on a blanket or soft mat. Arms should be straight, palms up, about forty-five degrees out from the body to allow for a broadening of the lung points just below the last third of the collar bones. The legs should be straight and placed thirty-five centimetres apart to avoid contact of the thighs. Avoid using a pillow, unless the chin is lifted and neck is tight. If you have a tendency to fall asleep then sitting or standing may be preferable.

- Become aware of your breath, feeling the flow of your breath in and out of your lungs; try not to change the rhythm, just breath naturally.
- Now concentrate your awareness on the rise and fall of the abdomen, and after twelve to twenty breaths, shift you attention to…
- …the chest, feeling the ribs elevate and the body broaden on inhalation and then the intercostals relax on the exhalation; for twelve to twenty breaths.
- Now focus on the rise and fall of the collar bones as the body lengthens on the inhale and shorten on the exhalation; twelve to twenty breaths.
- Now sequentially focus on the abdomen (pause), ribs broadening (pause), collar bone rising (pause). Then reverse, pausing between each stage, collar bones, ribs and abdomen twelve to twenty breaths.
- Then smoothly and seamlessly in and out for twelve to twenty breaths.

This can also be used as a prelude to sleep, visualisation techniques or as preparation for meditation.

To take this three level breathing into the spine, it can be done in seated position in a more physical way by curling over the navel and lowering the forehead towards the pubic bone.

- Inhale to expand the abdomen, and extend and lift out of the lower back.
- Inhale to expand the ribs and extend the middle back.
- Inhale to lengthen and elevate the upper back and neck.
- Now exhale, allowing each area to empty from top to bottom, folding forwards to bring the head back towards the pubic bone, feeling the body empty of air.
- Repeat seven to eleven more times.

Spine breathing to engergise your nervous system

Mental Contemplations for Autumn

Separation and Liberation

The **art of separation** is one of the most difficult there is, because you have to know when the time is right. In the movement meditation of t'ai chi it is seen and experienced as the time when Yin changes into Yang, or vice-versa. When an inhalation changes to an exhalation, or when an inward move changes to an outward one.

Any premature separation is a wrench or tearing and we can learn the art of separation from nature itself: such as the separation of a nut from its shell, the leaves from the trees, or from fruits that ripen and fall away. It is a sign of change, of maturity, like a child leaving its mother's womb, so that the umbilical cord can be cut. We too must learn when the time is right to let go and move on. Is there something in your life that you can let go of to allow the new? Cultivate the art of this perfect timing.

The Practice of Authenticity

Just as you can have genuine or fake gems, or valuable and base metals, it is important in life to practice authenticity. Bad habits, dishonesty, and things we are not proud of develop isolation, making us feel unworthy so that we cannot be effective in life. Here are eleven tools to bear in mind and practice:

1. Make authenticity your top priority.
2. Consider what motivates you and what you value.
3. Practise honesty, and when you catch yourself telling a lie, stop, admit it and apologise; the embarrassment will make you think twice next time.
4. Make sure the self-improvements you are working on are not just to impress others.
5. Appreciate your attributes, make a list of them and read them when you are 'feeling less than'.
6. Consider what accomplishments and good decisions you have made in the past and when your gut feelings turned out to be the best.
7. Think independently and be mindful of what is suitable for you, regardless of the rest of the world.
8. Stop trying to be perfect and look super spiritual, every seemingly 'together' person has 'not so together' moments, falling apart is how you get put together.
9. Live with the genuineness others will want to emulate.
10. Honesty facilitates honesty, and people can tell when you are real.
11. Openness means living without pretence and giving others the chance to be transparent.

Home and Lifestyle Section

Eight Home and Lifestyle Tips

Adopt a style that will be comfortable and supports this element by creating structure in your life and order in your surroundings.

1. At home, **clear out the clutter** and make a rule: bring one thing into the house, then get rid of two things! Place a beautiful single object in a quiet place so that you can sit and meditate on it.
2. **Burn lots of spicy aromatherapy oils** in the house; it's the time when your sense of smell is at its peak. **Thyme** stimulates the lungs and opens the chest to improve shallow breathing as well as invigorating the spirit. **Eucalyptus** decongests, clears mucus and is great for sinusitis and the common cold. **Pine** cleanses, clears phlegm, is a tonic for the lungs and is used for asthma. **Tea tree** is anti-fungal and anti-viral.
3. **Get your finances in order**. Clear away unfinished projects by bringing things to a natural conclusion.
4. **Clear up any misunderstandings** and focus on what's important and what you value. So often conflicts or disagreements arise out of differing values or belief patterns.
5. Practise **letting go** of what you no longer need in life, to make more room for what sustains you.
6. **Bach flower remedies**, which are particularly helpful. **Crab apple** is useful for getting rid of impurities in the body and mind. **Honeysuckle**, if you are stuck in the past, as it dissolves grief and helps focus on the now. **Pine** is used for regret or guilt. **Walnut** helps you to move on.
7. **Keep your environment functional, practical and simple**. Is your central heating on too high? Apart from being expensive and burning valuable energy, it is also too drying for the body, especially the skin, lungs and mucous membranes *(a humidifier can help this)*.
8. Use recreation time to go sightseeing or take an educational holiday, instead of chasing the sun. **Join clubs or debating groups** which involve relating to others and expression on a more intellectual level. Therapies such as acupuncture, hypnotherapy and psychotherapy are helpful if you are under the weather.

Avoid

- Exposure to nicotine, carbon dioxide, lead and nitrogen dioxide.
- Becoming autocratic, strict and pernickety, distant, too intense, formal or self-righteous.
- Putting yourself under intense pressure, or feeling trapped in situations.
- Becoming isolated in your life or indifferent to the world outside yourself.
- Being dominated by perfectionism or becoming obsessed with details.

Autumn Summary

- ☑ Have you taken up a dynamic breathing exercise to give your brain a new boost of energy on a daily basis?

- ☑ Have you noticed that you have managed to avoid colds, flu and chesty coughs this season?

- ☑ Does your life have more discipline, order and structure?

- ☑ Is your skin looking healthier and in better condition than it was at this time last year, and are you doing your dry skin brushing every day?

- ☑ Are you more positive and open because you are able to let go of the negativity of the past and the things that no longer serve you?

- ☑ Do you find you are feeling more optimistic, approachable and enthusiastic, and are you more fun to be around?

- ☑ Are you openly accepting compliments and becoming less hard on yourself?

- ☑ Have you managed to give up a habit that you never thought you could?

- ☑ Are you currently practicing some yoga, qigong or stretching exercises to move and open the chest?

- ☑ Are pungent foods now a big part of your autumn diet? They should be heating your insides nicely!

- ☑ Are you including more root vegetables in your diet to give you a concentrated form of fuel?

- ☑ Have you taken time to re-evaluate or re-structure your belief patterns, to rectify any problem areas of your life?

The season of winter

Traditionally, December the 21st, the time of the winter solstice is the start of the winter, the shortest day and the longest night. It is the coldest time of year when the sun is at its lowest, nature is still, and the trees are bare; a time for getting all wrapped up before you go outside. Whereas indoors, winter has different meanings; the family season, log fires, long cosy nights. In this inward withdrawing period you may be feeling a little more emotional and sensitive, or have a desire to be alone, to go deeper into yourself and reflect on your life. Use this natural time of storage and rejuvenation to replenish and recharge the batteries.

The Feeling of Winter

A time of retention, reflection and introspection in order to regenerate and develop the imagination, yet retain a sense of curiosity and adventure. The Water element is all about stillness and contemplation, invaluable in order to see where life is taking us, and to develop a sense of inner peace in the hectic pace of modern life. Flowing gently in the path of life while knowing in which direction you are heading, is the key to a stress-free winter and how to increase longevity. Then you can enjoy life's journey and not just rush from one thing to the next. It is time to confront our fears and regain our courage; and also to withdraw to replenish our energy and vitality, and in doing so gain answers from our inner wisdom to all the questions life poses. Winter will teach us how to flow with the tide of life and not struggle against it so we can discover new directions and purpose. Then we can attain our goals and fulfil our destiny.

Water is linked to body fluid, and bathes the brain, cleanses the mind and enhances memory: the kidneys and bladder regulate water in the body. Energy also comes from the adrenals, which are linked to the kidneys, so it makes sense to conserve that energy at this time of year.

The colour of the winter is blue: did you know that colours directly affect mood? Blue is associated with a cool, calm, hopeful, protected, cleansed, relaxed, and reassuring state. Blue inspires mental control, creativity and clarity, and has a beneficial and calming effect on the nervous system. Subconsciously, because we associate blue with the night sky, it makes us feel we are more relaxed. Blue is also an appetite suppressant. As nature does not create blue food *(other than blueberries)* we do not have an automatic appetite response to this colour.

Part Six

If winter was a person, their nature would be someone with emotional and spiritual depth; appearing to be outgoing, likeable, easy to be around, but difficult to know what they are truly thinking. They have no problem in retreating into themselves to regenerate, but at the extreme can also be very shy and retiring with a more brooding nature. They have the capacity for deep love and strong sexuality with the power of attraction, yet can keep their true nature hidden. When they feel safe they trust totally. Seeming soft, like water, they can create a path through any terrain or environment with a sense of adventure, but they need to know their limits. Because of their capacity for stillness they are good listeners; being philosophical, reflective, receptive and passionate. They are flexible and adaptable to circumstances, to some this can appear as lacking direction (but they can be privately involved with some venture or activity later to be revealed). They can float between an active social life and the need for solitude. They tend to internalise their emotions and are easily affected by what others feel around them. They become fearful if they do not have their space for privacy. If they cultivate natural wisdom they can benefit others greatly.

So it makes sense to match the energy of the season by developing the positive, and watching out for the negative qualities at this time of year. If you are out of balance at the moment, these are the issues that might come up in winter to be dealt with:

- ☐ Do you lack direction or become easily fatigued, lethargic or yawn a lot?
- ☐ Do you drive yourself and work through tiredness seeming indefatigable?
- ☐ Are you emotionally tense on a regular basis and find it hard to lighten up?
- ☐ Do you sometimes feel introverted, withdrawn or anti-social?
- ☐ Do you have fluid retention, poor bladder control or get frequent cystitis or bladder infections?
- ☐ Do you crave salty foods?
- ☐ Do you suffer nervous system or bone disorders?
- ☐ Do have lower back pain or stiffness?
- ☐ Is your skin sunken, dark or puffy below your eyes, or are your ears red?
- ☐ Do you often become anxious, apprehensive or fearful, or have issues around trust?
- ☐ Is the quality of your head hair poor?
- ☐ Are you regularly staying up late working on the computer?
- ☐ Do have difficulty with short-term memory?
- ☐ Do you lack willpower?

Eight Priorities for Winter

1. **Winter is a time for hibernation** with lots of opportunities to rest. Retire early, rise late and sleep for 1–2 hours longer. Health can be greatly enhanced in the winter by going to bed earlier. Stay in more. Avoid stressful situations and have regular periods of respite during the day.
2. **Start winter in a relaxed state of mind**. It is a time of reflection to look back over the year. Did you meet your goals? What lessons did you learn?
3. **Keep warm** and wrap up well, be cosy. Keeping your back and feet warm is crucial at this time of year.
4. **An opportunity to slow down** and conserve your energy. Look on this as the time for storing power for the next thing you want to do, so you can do it more powerfully.
5. **Take total responsibility for how you feel** on a daily basis. Understand it is natural to feel fear, notice threats, assess risks and respond appropriately. Find ways to discover courage, or just feel the fear and do it anyway.
6. **Be careful and take care of yourself**, work on self-trust and learn to discriminate when it is appropriate to pull back and when to engage.
7. When you are concerned about something in the future, imagine going beyond that point and looking back at it so you can **learn to dissociate from scary situations**, and visualize changing outcomes.
8. Be aware of any fears or apprehensions which are preventing you from moving forward and deal with them, **give others and yourself re-assurance**.

Eight Things to Avoid in Winter

1. Work which includes **sitting at the computer all night**!
2. **Aggressive activities** such as high intensity aerobics or punishing exercise regimes.
3. **Too much sex**.
4. **Not enough sleep**.
5. **Procrastination**.
6. **Stimulants** and continually elevated stress levels which draw on high levels of adrenaline; this drains and damages the kidneys.
7. **Becoming over-tired**.
8. **Becoming obsessive** about secrecy.

Eight Daily Habits for Winter

1. **Winter is a time for conserving energy**. Meditate or rest more. Schedule in space for yourself and reflection time, and try to have an occasional massage.
2. **Start the day with a five-minute meditation**, or lie in bed for five minutes before you get up, thinking positive thoughts of calm and peace. Combine with eight full breaths to energize yourself and as you inhale and exhale, repeat the thought of calm and peace for the day.
3. **Regularly re-evaluate** your values and priorities. Tell your loved ones and colleagues what you value and appreciate about them.
4. **Time management**: Try not to leave things so late that you are continually fighting against tight deadlines.
5. **Monitor the quality of what you drink**, and how much, because this is especially important in winter. Avoid cold, icy drinks as they chill the kidneys.
6. **Make friction fitness your morning practice.** Rub oils into the body after your morning shower or bath. Use almond oil, or thicker more viscose oil, concentrating on each part of the body and rubbing the oil into the skin to create heat and friction. Tense the muscles under the hands while you are rubbing to create more heat. It will stimulate the lymphatic system, warm the body, boost the blood flow and improve tone and elasticity. Add a few drops of essential oil as well, if you want.
7. **Re-charge your batteries**, go to bed before 10pm, and, for a few days, fit in with the hours of daylight.
8. **Maintain your body temperature** by wearing the appropriate clothing in winter and keeping your home well heated. Avoid exposure to extreme cold which is very depleting for the kidneys. Rub them one hundred times every day with the backs of your hands made into soft fists.

The Art of Meditation

How to live in the eye of the storm

'I think when tragic things happen, it is on the surface; it is like the ocean. On the surface a wave comes and sometimes the wave is very serious and strong. But it comes and goes, comes and goes, and underneath it the ocean .... always remains calm.'
H.H. the 14th Dalai Lama

Why would I want to meditate?

Life has changed dramatically throughout the world over the last hundred years. Values and social systems are no longer the same as they used to be in ancient times. This has brought about a dispersion of human energies on all levels, and the mind of man has lost a point of balance and harmony in every sphere of existence.

Are you ever stressed?

We are faced with a new epidemic of stress-related disorders, caused by our inability to adapt to the highly competitive pace of modern life and the influx of information, most of it negative, from the media. Modern medical science has been trying to tackle these problems, but is failing because the real problem does not lie in where the symptoms are manifesting *(the body)*, but originates in our ways of thinking and feeling, our values and ideals. With such dispersal of energy, fluctuating degrees of pressure and increased quantity of information now coming at us, how can we expect to experience harmony in body and mind?

When did you last experience a real state of harmony?

Where were you, what were you doing and who were you with?

In order to subconsciously deal with this rise in stress related problems and mental overload, there has been a huge rise in interest and demand for exercise systems that unite mind and body together, such as yoga, t'ai chi and Pilates, as well as relaxation and meditation techniques to train and clear our over-active and scattered minds.

Have you ever had an over-active mind?

Regular practice of any of the following techniques to slow the mind down will bring us back into a relaxed and calm state.

Training the Mind

'The mind is sometimes like a motor car; if you don't learn to handle it properly you will have an accident, but if you are a good driver, it can take you to new and wonderful places.'

The Chinese texts often refer to the mind as a monkey darting from one branch to another in the forest of life. The ancient masters would refer to the following techniques as giving it a banana!

These simple practices have the capacity of penetrating into the depths of the human mind, creating a real sense of peace, oneness, focus and tranquillity.

Learn to become the detached observer

This is where the mind is trained to focus on external sounds, moving from one sound to another, and then back to the original sound, with the attitude of a detached observer. So gradually the mind lets go of tension. You discover that you can begin to direct your mind to anything you want, such as changing from focusing on the negative to the positive, or from an irritating sound to a pleasant one.

You can also use this practice to detach yourself from distracting sounds or situations which may be going on around you, as you come to realize that you are viewing the distraction or friction as external to yourself, from a point of inner stillness and empowerment.

The great thing about this is it can be, and should be, practiced regularly so it becomes a powerful tool for any situation and reduce stress. You will gain the ability to re-direct the mind, from a worried or anxious state to one of confidence and calm.

Awareness of the breath

This is where the attention is drawn to the ingoing and outgoing breath
This can help to increase your breathing capacity and release tension.

- ✿ Watch the breath coming in and out of the nostrils.
- ✿ Watch it pass in and out of the throat.
- ✿ Feel the chest fill and empty.
- ✿ Feel it move the diaphragm downwards and upwards.
- ✿ Feel it fill the lower back and abdomen.

Stay and focus on each of the above areas for several breaths.

Alternate nostril breathing with mental attention
You could also mentally practice Anuloma Viloma (*alternate nostril breathing*) by focusing your attention on the breath as it moves in and out of the nostrils alternately:

- In and out of the left.
- In and out of the right.
- Now out of the left, then in the left and out of the right and in the right and out of the left and so on. Feel as if, for a few seconds after inhaling, you are suspending the breath in the mind to cleanse and re-energize it.
- A progression is to focus breathing into the left nostril and the right side of the mind, and then out of the right nostril and the left side of the mind, and vice-versa. This is like practicing an internalized figure of eight to balance brain and nostril dominance. Then at end of this practice, centre yourself by returning the focus to the rise and fall of the abdomen.

The full version of physically closing alternate nostrils is in the autumn section. This uses the thumb and ring finger to cover alternate nostrils as you breathe in and out.

In all versions always end with the exhalation out of the left nostril.

Body scan
Use the conscious awareness of the mind like a miner's lamp to mentally scan the body for areas of tension and then breathe relaxation into any tense area, feeling the muscles release as you exhale. You can also visualize healing light into weak or injured parts. *(**This can also be used as a prelude to sleep in cases of insomnia caused by an over-active mind.**)*

Visualization
This develops self-awareness and relaxes the mind by purging it of disturbing material. If the mind is dissipated, visualization can be difficult because the attention cannot be held long enough for an image to take form. So you can start by recollecting experiences associated with the image, and then gradually let the image arise effortlessly within the consciousness. Start practicing by simply visualizing familiar objects or events and then go to other images that may have made a strong influence on the mind. You can use powerful symbolic images such as:

- Burning candle.
- Egyptian pyramid.
- Snowcapped mountains.
- Birds flying in the sunset.
- Full moon.
- Imagine yourself in a park in the early morning.
- Being by an ocean or a lake.

Then go on to visualize:

- Doing something well.
- Achieving something that you have always wanted to do.
- Being at the peak of health or professional performance.

You can use this technique to access emotions you may need to face a particular challenge, e.g. 'remember a time when...' Feel the feeling you had at that time, release the image but retain the feeling and then transpose that feeling to the new situation. To end, gradually bring the mind's attention back to the natural breath flowing in and out of the nostrils.

Maintain your awareness of the breath while at the same time developing your awareness of physical relaxation. Now start moving your body and stretching yourself... Take your time, then when you are sure that you are awake *(sit up)* and slowly open your eyes.

Do you feel in a changed state? Does it feel better?

Food Section

Brief Guide to Seasonal Eating

Good nutrition is an essential part of your routine in the winter, because the body needs hearty hot food in order to keep itself warm. In short, eat properly in winter; simmering stews, warming soups, kidney and aduki beans, roasted root vegetables and warm drinks such as green, ginger or Jasmine tea. Add basil and black pepper to increase the warming effect, and use pungent spices such as garlic, ginger and cloves.

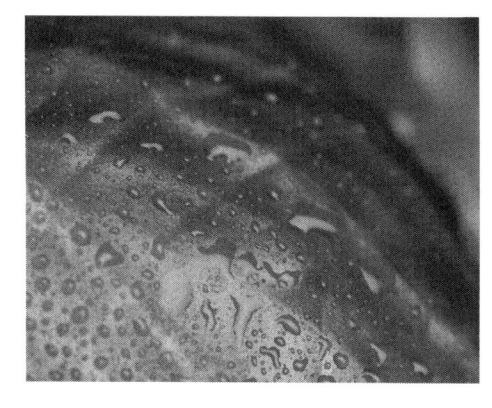

Beetroot and sea vegetables are very good for cleansing the blood and supporting the kidneys. For example, Kombu in soups and stews can add great nutritional value to meals, this is available dried in health food shops. Eat very little cold food at this time of year. Do not drink fluids to excess. Hot water is good as it flushes the kidneys and cleanses the system. Eat organic food as much as possible and filter your water.

Food for the Winter Energy

Eating cooked, salty, Yang foods *(root vegetables and fish)* is the way to replenish energy at this time of year. Eat food in season, and look at your local fruit shop or farmers' market for what is fresh and grown locally. There will be more root vegetables at this time of year, filled with concentrated goodness to support this inward energy. How you cook is also relevant as the cooking method has a direct effect on the energy of the food. The cooking styles should be casseroles, soups, and roasting. Prepare food that has a warming quality and cook it properly and slowly.

Winter Food List

Aduki beans	Chestnuts	Olives	Squash
Apples	Chinese cabbage	Onions	Swede
Apricots	Garlic	Parsnips	Tangerines
Artichokes	Ginger	Pears	Tofu
Beetroot	Grouse	Pheasant	Turbot
Black beans	Kale	Potatoes	Turkey
Brussels sprouts	Lamb	Red cabbage	Turnips
Carrots	Leeks	Rhubarb	Walnuts
Cauliflower	Mackerel	Scallops	Water chestnuts
Celeriac	Mushrooms	Seaweed	Watercress
Celery	Mussels	Spinach	Whole grains

Eight Food and Nutrition Tips

1. **Eat earlier** in the evening, because you need to go to bed earlier and the body needs to rest and not digest.
2. The kidneys hate the cold, so **avoid iced and refrigerated food and drink**, especially at this time of year. Caffeine and strong stimulants are also best avoided.
3. Balance is vital as excessive **salt**, including the overuse of such foods as soy sauce or miso, are harmful to the blood, harden the pulse, and are bad for the heart. They calm the thin, dry, nervous type of person, but must be restricted by those who are overweight, bloated, or with high blood pressure. Excess salt also dries out and toughens the body and mental atitudes as well. On the positive side it keeps up the mineral content in the body and also balances the water content. Use natural rock salt and not refined salt for all of your cooking.
4. **Keep your diet alkaline**, with lots of fruit and vegetables, and avoid too many acid-forming foods. Note the difference in acidic foods; normally these cause acid to flow into the muscles, drawing calcium out of the bones to neutralize it, they make muscles tighten, and build up debris which cannot be filtered. However 'alkaline forming' acidic foods like lemons and lime combine with the digestive juices/acids already present in the body, turn alkaline and are beneficial.
5. **Eat plenty of hot home-made soups and stews** to maintain the body temperature. Introduce seaweed to them, which will help mineralise the body and support the kidneys.
6. **Do not go on a diet** at this time of year, but simply clean up your act.
7. **Do not eat the Christmas leftover chocolate**, as excessive sugar makes your bones ache.
8. Poor nutrition is caused through an unbalanced diet or constant nibbling. So **avoid eating between meals** and reduce fluid intake in the middle of your meal, which dilutes your digestive juices.

Exercise and Movement Section

This section will show you various ways to stimulate the energy lines for this time of year. As you have read earlier, each season has a pair of organs which are complementary and resonate to a particular time of year. The organs linked with winter are the kidneys and bladder.

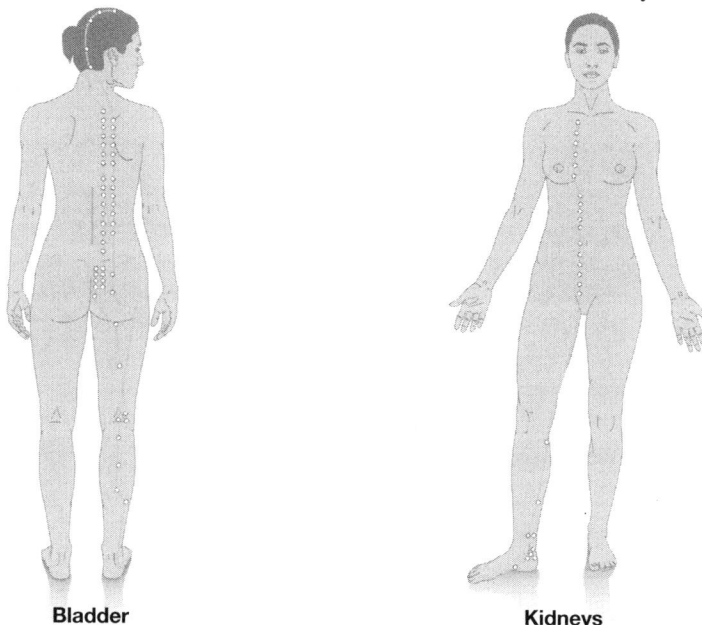

Bladder **Kidneys**

As you can see, the lines for the kidneys run up the front of the body and those for the bladder run down the back. The following sections include exercises that move energy along these pathways. These organs give us the mental and spiritual energy for; willpower, drive, ambition, skill, cleverness and ability. This is what your mental focus should be concentrating on in the wintertime.

Exercise for Winter

Stay balanced during the winter and curb your expenditure of energy. Restorative yoga, t'ai chi, qigong are best suited for this Yin season, as they safeguard and replenish your energy reserves rather than drain them. Think of these practices as investments in your energy bank account. Avoid too much outdoor activity like running or cycling in bad weather, as the dampness can chill the body. This time of year is also the time to think about the health of the skeletal system and joint mobility, so try to avoid stiffening up; a regular massage can help.

The kidneys are one of the most vulnerable organs at this time of year. Exercises that generate warmth and energy, such as certain Pilates, qigong, and yoga exercises, are extremely beneficial. Proper breathing also supports the kidneys, both in cleansing the blood and massaging them by the movement of the abdomen and diaphragm.

Cleansing the Seven Chakras to Give Your Entire Energy System a Boost

Meridians are the energy transportation system on the pranic level. However, the chakras (meaning disc, vortex or wheel) are on a slightly higher frequency and are seen as major centres of spinning electromagnetic activity and vital energy. So rather than be tied down to a specific anatomical structure, they are named after the areas over which they spin. An analogy would be to a storage disc for a computer, full of vital programmed information, the body being the hardware, the user the Self, and universal energy the electricity to power it. Here is where memories are energetically coded, and an imprint made of every important or emotionally significant event you have experienced. We did not write all the programmes, and some of them may be outdated, have viruses in them, or be inappropriate in our life. So part of our healing can be to re-write the programmes, making them more relative to the life we want to lead. It is important to keep them clear because if they become blocked, not only do they form obstacles to your personal growth, but they influence the organs, muscles, ligaments, and other systems within their energy field.

If you feel low in energy, sluggish, out of balance emotionally or unable to cope, it may be that a chakra has become blocked or toxic, and a simple test can detect this. Chakras can exhibit excess or deficient patterns, which can result from coping strategies designed to deal with stress, trauma or unpleasant circumstances, failing. Regular chakra clearing, in one of the ways listed below, can help bring about deeper levels of harmony at the heart of your life. This can have long-term positive cumulative effects on your health and well being.

Listed here from bottom to top are the seven major chakras named after the part of the body over which it spins, their anatomical position, their chief operating quality, area of life and their associated endocrine gland and colour. Some people like to work with colours to regulate their energy system and can visualize a colour bathing each chakra. This enables it to become purer and more luminous with each cleansing breath, as the stale energy or turbid colour is being released.

Chakra	Quality	Gland	Colour
Root chakra (base of spine)	Life force / Security	Sexual organs	Red
Sacral chakra (womb)	Creativity / Relationships	Adrenal glands	Orange
Solar Plexus chakra (navel/upper abdomen)	Assertiveness / Energy levels	Pancreas	Yellow
Heart chakra	Love/compassion / Equilibrium	Thymus	Green
Throat chakra	Expressiveness / Communication	Thyroid	Blue
Third Eye chakra (between eyebrows)	Comprehension / Sense of purpose	Pituitary	Indigo blue
Crown chakra	Universal connection / Practical spirituality	Pineal	Violet

Chakra Testing

- Lie down on your back with arms outstretched, at a ninety-degree angle to the body level with the shoulders, and with fingers pointed towards the ceiling. Turn your palms to face outwards and bring the backs of the wrists together.
- Your partner then lightly taps the chakra to be tested with their middle finger three times. Then slides their hands between your wrists to pull them apart as you resist. If this is easy to do, and there is little resistance, the chakra needs clearing, balancing and strengthening.
- Once you have detected the chakra that is the weak link in the chain and needs attention, imagine a clock face on this chakra. Rub the palms of your hands together to energize their magnetic energy, and then with both hands palms down, circle anti-clockwise four inches above and over the chakra. This is done for up to three minutes, keeping the circles no wider than the width of the body, to pull out any negative energy. Then shake off any excess energy from your hands, and rub them again to energize. Now rebalance the chakra, circling your hands in a clockwise direction. Then shake the excess off your hands again, at the end.
- Some people prefer to have their partner do this, clearing and energizing, working all the way from the root to the crown. Shaking the energy and rubbing palms together between each chakra.
- **There are two exceptions**:
1. In the case of a man, over the crown chakra only, the circling is clockwise to clear and anti-clockwise to rebalance. The rest are the same.
2. In the case of someone with headaches, work down from the crown to the root chakra. Listed below are several other ways of clearing, energizing and enhancing the chakras.

Are you low in energy, sluggish, out of balance emotionally or unable to cope? Test your chakras

Breathing with Yi to Clear and Cleanse the Seven Chakras

Step out into a narrow stance (feet shoulder-width apart) or into a wider horse stance, extending your hands forwards, palms facing downwards. Starting with the little fingers, circle your hands drawing them into soft fists rotating both palms upwards.

Now extend your arms forwards with hands palm down and place your mental attention into the area of the base or root chakra, which is level with the pelvic floor. Inhale, while suffusing the chakra with energy as you draw your fists back to the sides of the waist.

As you exhale, intentionally release any toxicity from the chakra and the hormonal glands at that level. This can be repeated two or three times as you feel is appropriate. Then move up to the next chakra and so on with your intention and conscious awareness at each level, but the level of the arms moving forwards and back remains the same.

To end the exercise and close down the purified chakras, draw your hands out to the sides and above your head whilst you inhale. Exhale rotating the fingers in and pressing the palms down using your intention to close down each energetic centre.

Give your entire energy system a boost

Regularly performing the wave will cleanse and clear the Penetrating channel (sometimes known as Chong Mai or Sushumna channel). This will free up the channel and positively influence the chakras which are aligned along it, and also will greatly benefit the craniosacral and endocrine systems.

The Chinese refer to the spine as having three doors, each of which govern the health and mobility of one of the three main areas of your spine. They also enhance our three Dantians, energy seas or oceans, which refer to our physical, emotional and mental energies housed in the abdominal, thoracic and cranial cavities respectively.

The lowest door is on the centre of the spine on the Du Mai (Governing Vessel); it is called Mingmen just below the spinous process of the second lumbar vertebra. As well as positively influencing the lumbar spine, it tonifies the kidneys and the genitourinary system. It is a major point for increasing vitality. This point is level with Shenshu BL23, the Shu points which can boost the energy of the kidneys by applying gentle pressure to them.

The middle door is level with the lower borders of shoulder-blades on the centre of the spine below the spinous process of the seventh thoracic vertebra. It is called Zhiyang (Reaching Yang) and harmonizes the chest and soothes the liver. It is level with points on the Bladder channels called Geshu 1.5 thumb-widths either side of the spine, at the same level. As well as positively influencing and relieving pain and stiffness in the thoracic spine, they invigorate the blood, relax the diaphragm and benefit the chest and skin.

The upper door forms the tip of a triangle just above the knobble on the midline of the back of the head; it is called Nahou (the Brain Window or Door), which regulates the blood and Qi and clears the mind. To locate it, find two important points on the outer edge of the descending border of the trapezius muscle. They are underneath the ridge of the skull and half a thumb-width below the hairline, and two fingers-width out from the centre of the neck. These points are BL10 referred to as Tainzhu (Celestial Pillars), which calm the mind and are used for neck pain, tension and stiffness. They also relegate energy and the blood to the brain and eyes. Then draw a triangle and where they meet on the back of the head will be Nahou.

Performing the Wave

Place your hands on the thighs and as you exhale, bring your head down towards your pubic bone. Now as you inhale, start by pushing your tailbone forwards, then the hips, solar plexus and then the centre of the chest leaving your head down. Next draw the chin in towards the throat to feel the back of the neck stretch and a lift in the Celestial Pillar points, as mentioned previously. Lastly feel Nahou, open and let the head lift upwards so that the base of your skull can tuck under and move forwards.

Now leading with your chin, exhale and bring the head down and taking the tailbone back. Inhale again and repeat the wave, leading with the tail and finishing with the head, drawing the energy up the core of the body to the mind. Do this eight to twelve times. See if you can feel all the points mentioned above, along the spine and back of the head, being opened and closed like doors. This will help maintain the health of the spine, nervous system while nourishing the mind and enhancing the cranio-sacral rhythm.

Feeling stiff, tense or anxious? Give your nervous system a tonic

Exercises or Asanas to Help Regulate the Chakras

Root Chakra
- Lifting the pelvic floor as you exhale.
- Knee to chest (Apasana).
- Seated Angel Posture (Upavista konasana).
- Standing or seated straight leg forward bend, with feet slightly apart.

Sacral Chakra
- Pelvic tilting, pelvic rotations or figures of eight (standing).
- Locust (Salabhasana) with hands under body and legs slightly separated.
- Fish (Matsyasana).

Solar Plexus
- Bow pose (Dhanurasana) especially if rocking.
- Boat (Navasana).
- Reclining Hero (Supta Virasana).
- Warrior poses.

Heart Chakra
- Cobra (Bhujangasana).
- Cow Face posture (Gomukhasana).
- Child's Pose with forearms level with the head (Yogasana).

Throat Chakra
- Head nods lying on back to lift head to look at toes.
- Shoulder stands (Sarvangasana).
- Throat lock (Jalandhara Bandha).

Third Eye Chakra
- Eye exercises, especially when focusing upwards between the eyebrows.
- Plough (Halasana).
- Balancing poses such as tree and eagle pose (Vrkasana and Garudasana).
- Candle gazing (Trataka).

Crown Chakra
- Head stand.
- Standing intense stretch (Prasarita Padottanasana) with head down to floor.
- Meditation focusing on Sahasrara (Crown).

Always return to abdominal breathing to end and return to the centre.

Eight Exercise Suggestions

1. **Slow down the pace of your training** and take a longer relaxation time.
2. **Ideal exercises** for this time of year would be t'ai chi, qigong, balancing hatha yoga, or a gently challenging body sculpt class but allowing plenty of time for deep relaxation afterwards.
3. **Yoga practice.** Include lots of forward bends and back bends in your practice. They send energy to the kidneys and bladder and support spinal health.
4. During this season, focus on repeating poses, exercises and movements, so that with each **repetition** the beneficial effects will go deeper into the body. It also builds confidence in your practice.
5. **Meditation**: winter is the best time to start practicing it! Plenty of nurturing meditation and breathing techniques throughout the winter season will have a rejuvenating effect.
6. **Spinal massage.** Bend forward with your hands on your thighs and have a friend place the sides of their little fingers in the meridians about two fingers-width either side of your spine, and then rub up and down in small movements down the back to the sacrum. Angling the pressure downwards will stimulate the Bladder meridian and all the lymphatic and Shu points along it. Shu points are powerful supportive points for the functioning of the major organs. If you angle the sides of the fingers slightly centrally and inwards towards the sides of the vertebrae you will stimulate the Huatuojiaji points. These are points closer to the spine, which have a regulating effect on the nervous system. The benefits of these points were first recognised by a renowned Chinese doctor Hua Tuo in the second century.
7. **Try flowing yoga** that involves moving from one asana to the next or experience the actions of a t'ai chi form, where the movements are linked together *(refer to the t'ai chi/qigong section)*. In form work, it is important to experience the complementary opposites in each *movement (referred to as Yin and Yang)*, i.e. the ebb and the flow, backward and forward, fast and slow, right and left, up and down, and so on.
8. Work on exercises that particularly build **spinal strength, maintain bone density and improve postural awareness**. Improve the lower back with lots of hamstring stretches, and enhance the way you move with an Alexander or Feldenkrais class, if you can find one locally. In the weight training gym keep it light with high repetitions to improve flexibility or try the cable machine if your gym has one.

Qigong for Winter

Bo points or collecting points are located on the chest, abdomen or waist. They are used both for diagnosis and treatment, and are where the energy collects or gathers from each of the relevant organs. These points can become tender either spontaneously or on the application of pressure; in treatments they are used to regulate and balance the energy in their associated organs. The **organ meridians** are energy pathways that lead to and from a major organ, and where the energy is particularly accessible from the surface. The initials and numbers refer to the particular acupressure point along an organ meridian. You can gently massage these points using the tips of the thumb, index and middle fingers.

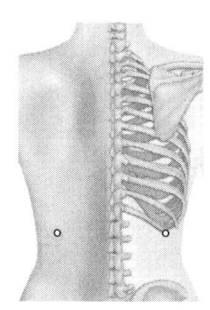

Jingmen (Capital Door, GB 25) between the free end of the twelfth ribs at the sides of your waist, and used for testing and balancing the function of the kidneys.

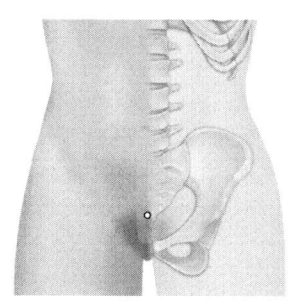

Zhongji (Central Pole, Con 3) about a hand's width below the navel or a thumb's width above the pubic bone, and used for testing and balancing the function of the bladder.

Massage the Spine and Release Tension and to Maintain Spinal Health

Stiff and tense? Flex your spine

Bend forward, placing your hands on your thighs, with your thumbs to the outside. **Inhale**, and lift your head to look up and tilt your tailbone up and back. **Exhale**, lifting your pelvic floor, pulling your tail between your legs and lifting your navel and internal organs up to the back. Bring your chin down on to your throat to squeeze the thyroid gland and look back up to your navel. **Inhale**, and reverse the curve lifting the head and eyes up, and the tailbone up and back. Feel the energy moving up and down the spine.

Release Anxiety, Fear and Tension, Mobilise the Lower Back, Massage the Bladder and Strengthen the Kidneys

Inhale, drawing soft fist, palms up, to the kidney points at the sides of the waist packing the kidneys with power. **Exhale**, and turn in the waist to the left and throw your arms forward, spreading your fingers and sinking low in the legs, flattening your back, keeping your arms beside your ears, and drawing them in an arc around to the right. **Inhale** as your back returns to the upright position, making fists at your waist. Then reverse. Repeat eight times.

A bundle of nerves? Regain your cool

Flush and Reinforce the Kidneys and the Adrenal Glands

Inhale, slowly raise your arms to the sides, then forward and upward. Then feel the stretch in your spine as you bend your knees as if to sit back in an imaginary chair. Keep the spine straight and the neck long and feel the Qi being drawn into the kidneys. **Exhale** as you bring your arms forward, and lower your hands to the sides of your knees, or to sweep over the tops of your feet. The palms of the hands face up for more of a reinforcing energy, or palms down for a release of stagnating energy.

Inhale, and sweep your arms backward and bring them back up above your head, sit back to stretch the spine and once again bring the Qi *(energy)* up into the kidneys.

- As your spine becomes more flexible, you can open the three doors, as mentioned earlier (one point on the spine below your waist, one on the spine level with the base of the shoulder-blades, and one at the base of the skull) while bringing your head toward the knees.
- You can also increase the power of the exercise by rising up on the toes as you inhale and sweep up, or by speeding up the movements.

Points to notes
- If your back is sensitive, keep it straight and just bring your hands down to the sides of the hips.
- If you have high blood pressure, keep your head above your heart at all times.

Opening the Bladder Meridian

This exercise will help to release pent up energy and stress from the nervous system and support the kidneys. This is because the energy pathways from the Bladder meridian flow into the Kidney's energy pathways. A particularly good time of day to do this sequence is between the hours of 15.00 to 19.00, when there is often an energy lull, or if the nervous system or kidneys are not at their strongest.

- Place your hands on your hips and extend your left leg forwards to rest on the heel, keeping the weight mainly in the right leg.
- As you **inhale**, lower your head and elongate the neck, sticking the chin out bringing it in towards the top of the breastbone. Curl your tongue to rest against the upper palate. **Exhale** as you draw your chin in and up, to raise your head and lengthen your neck.
- Perform the same movement by sticking the chin out but bring it down lower, in towards the centre of the chest. Then gradually lengthen the back from the base of the shoulder-blades, to extend upwards from the middle door, as mentioned previously.
- Lastly make an even larger circle, bringing the chin down towards to the navel, and feel the lift emanating from the door in the lower back. (Refer to the chakra section for the information on the three doors.)

Anxious and stressed? Try this

- ❖ **Exhale** to draw your arms forwards and up above your head, circling them back, round and down towards the extended foot. Sinking down as far as you can into the back leg.
- ❖ **Inhale** to bring your weight into the front leg while lifting the heel of the back foot to open the Kidney point. Feel as if you are scooping water up from the ground, lifting the water held in the palms of your hands, and throwing it over your head and down you back. Cleansing the nervous system of tension, anxiousness and stress.
- ❖ After eight circles, take hold of the left little toe side of the foot with one hand and with the other, rest the fingertips on the kidney point in the sole of the foot and stretch your torso over the extended leg for five breaths.

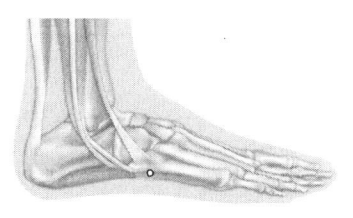

Kidneys

Flowing Sequence to Get the Qi Moving and Keep the Body Supple

For supple strength try this!

1. Figures of 8

Hold an imaginary ball in the left hand and rotate the tips of the fingers of the left hand (palm up) in toward the Kidney point (see previous diagram at the start of the Qigong section), this is at the side of the waist at the end of the twelfth rib. **Exhale** as you circle the hand to the back. **Inhale** as you draw it up and around the head. Repeat several times and then do the same on the right side using the right hand. Next do each side alternately, then both sides/arms together. Repeat eight times.

2. Wild goose flexes its wings

Inhale, opening the palms forward and draw your hands behind you expanding the chest. **Exhale**, bringing the little fingers together in front of the navel and taking your breastbone back, rounding your upper back. Then draw the hands back and down to the sides *(palms forward)* again to open the chest. This opens and closes the Kidney Meridian in the chest and has a very beneficial effect on breathing and the muscles of the chest. Repeat eight times.

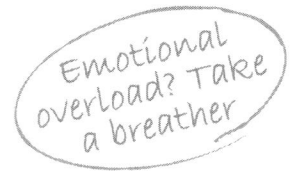

Emotional overload? Take a breather

3. Twisting dragon

Standing with the feet hip-width apart and imagine you are holding a large ball in the palm of the right hand, with the left hand on top. **Inhale** and as you **exhale**, draw the right arm forwards and in an arc around to the right and behind your back, resting the back of the hand on your left kidney and turn to look down to the left heel. The left hand follows and sweeps in front of the face with the back of your hand level with the third eye area between the eyebrows. **Inhale**, turning to the front, holding the ball in the left palm with the right palm down on the top. Repeat, exhaling and twisting to the left. Repeat eight times.

4. The tortoise

This is an exercise to smooth out the flow of Qi through the Bladder and Kidney meridians.

Inhale, lengthening through the spine with palms up and fingers pointing in toward the waist. **Exhale**, sitting back and bending forward, extending your arms straight backward, then in an arc forward, to either side of your ears. This lengthens the Bladder meridian, which runs down either side of your spine.

Get your life and energy flowing smoothly!

Inhale, drawing the hands out to the side and back to the waist, fingertips pointing in, then come up to standing.

Exhale bringing your forearms together in front of the chest and slightly rounding your upper back. **Inhale** keeping both elbows bent draw both arms out to the sides to open the chest and Kidney meridian that run either side of the breastbone. Rise up on to the balls of your feet. **Exhale**, bring the forearms together and lowering the heels to close the chest and the Kidney meridian.

Now repeat the whole sequence seven more times, to open and close the Kidney and Bladder Meridians and soothe your nervous system.

Warm and Re-energize the Kidneys Daily

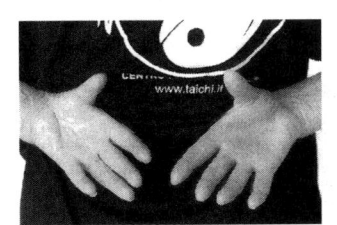

Rub your kidneys – either side of the lower back – *(with the backs of your hands made into soft fists)* in small circles one hundred times. Then release the fists and resting the 'v' between your thumb and index fingers on the kidneys. Inhale through your nose and draw your navel back to the spine to squeeze the kidneys. Exhale strongly through the mouth as if blowing out a candle, drawing your hands around the sides of your waist and throwing them forward to release any tension, tiredness or stagnation. Repeat this six to eight times.

T'ai Chi Moves for Winter

Snake Creeps Down

This help to develop the sinking energy we need in winter and strengthens the legs, and just like a shadow, trains the body to follow the mind.

Sink the weight into the right leg and lift the left. The left hand is resting with the thumb at the centre of the chest. The right arm is extended out to the right, level with the shoulder, with a soft elbow and shoulder-blade drawn down. The tips of the index and middle fingers lightly touch the pad of the thumb.

Sink down in the right leg and extend the left leg out to the side with the toes pointing forward. Draw the left hand down and then out towards the left foot, keeping it close to the body. As it reaches the left foot, the toes turn out to ninety degrees.

As the right hand draws down and passes the right knee, the right heel turns out to bring the right knee and hip to face to the left. Then the snake rises to become a golden cockerel. The left hand presses down towards the ground, and the right hand continues to rise, bringing the right knee up to the right elbow, the weight is now fully on the left leg.

Sink the weight into the left leg and lift the toes to swivel on the heel to bring the body to face forwards again. The right hand is drawn in, resting with the thumb at the centre of the chest. The left arm extends out to the left level with the shoulder, with a soft elbow and shoulder-blade drawn down. The tips of the index and middle fingers lightly touch the pad of the thumb. The moves are then repeated to the right. Repeat the moves another four times on each side.

For a modification

Place the back of the left hand in the small of your back, with the 'v' made between the thumb and index finger on the vitality point called Mingmen (which is on the middle of the spine, one vertebra below your waist). Have the other hand in front of your face, palm inwards, and the elbow bent.

With the toes pointing forwards or slightly to the sides, bend the right knee to ninety degrees in line with the toes, and extend the left leg. Exhale, and as you inhale, bring the torso over the bent right thigh, to bring the right arm forwards. Turn in the waist drawing the back of the right hand along the ground towards the straight left leg (keeping as low as you can, or as low as you feel is comfortable). Now bend the left leg and straighten the right. When the torso is over the left thigh, exhale straightening the back. Then turn the waist to the right, bending the right knee again and straighten the left leg. Perform the movement eight times and then change sides. Keep the extended arm as still as you can and let the movement come from the back and waist to get the full benefit.

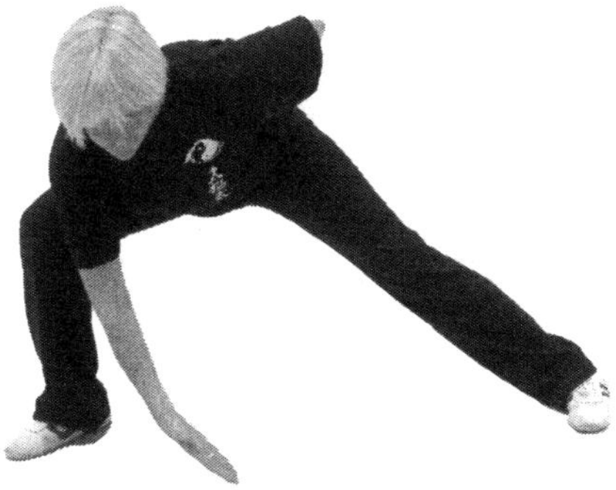

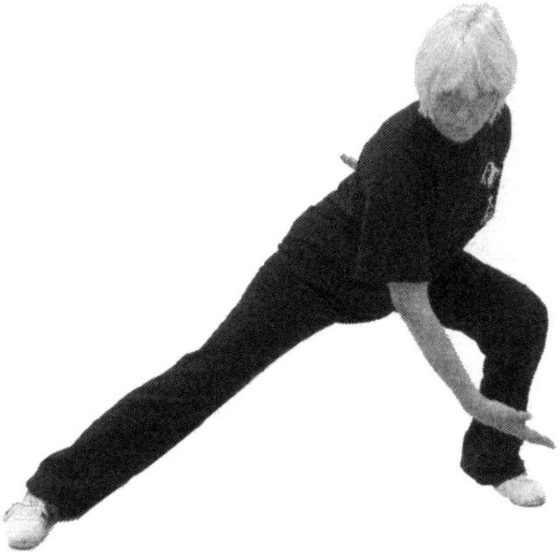

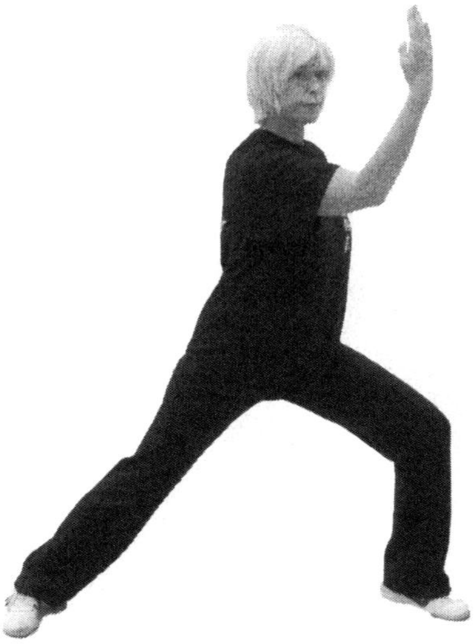

Yoga for Winter

The Focus is Flow

Like we have said previously in the book, winter is about rest, renewal, rejuvenation, depth and focus, so we should try to reflect this in our yoga practice. Repeating poses so that on each repetition they go deeper into the body.

Inverted poses consolidate and rejuvenate the brain and nervous system, and they return the thoughts from the muscles back into the mind from whence they came. Inverted poses work on the crown energy centre associated with the pineal and pituitary gland influencing the hormones. They alleviate tension and induce a state of relaxation. They allow gravity to lengthen the spine, keeping it elastic, enhancing the flow of spinal fluid, and allowing the nerves that stem from the spine to flow and communicate freely, delaying ageing, increasing willpower, and enhancing meditation and focus *(very important in the Water element)*.

The yoga practice works with awareness on three levels;

1. The physical level – to the different meridian lines, organs, and the systems they govern.
2. The emotional level – to the emotions we feel during the practice and learning to breathe through them.
3. The mental level – to our life challenges and ways of thinking.

Beginner Level

Breathe, relax, focus, and do not push yourself too hard. Rest between poses if you get tired. **A 10-minute practice designed to stretch the winter meridians and energize the Kidney and Bladder.**

1. Stand with feet together, stand tall, pull navel to spine, and stretch up arms as you inhale

2. Exhale as you fold forward, bending knees as you go, soften the spine to follow the shape of the bent knees, relax the neck. This pose enlivens the internal organs

Keep it simple and flowing.

3. Inhale, look up, lengthen spine, reach arms forward, come into a 'cat' position

4. Then stretch arms to 'upward dog', back bend

5. Lift your sitting bones toward the ceiling as in 'downward dog'. Stay and breathe for five breaths

6. Step right leg forward

7. Take hands behind your back, fingers pointing up, resting palms on the kidneys and breathe into your hands

8. Inhale, reach your arms up and stretch through the front of the body

9. Bring your hands back either side of your front foot and change legs

10. Place hands again on the kidneys and breath into them

11. Inhale, lengthen and stretch through the front of the body

12. Relax back into 'child's pose'

To make it stronger for the kidneys, keep the toes turned under for poses 8–12.

For better emotional accessibility

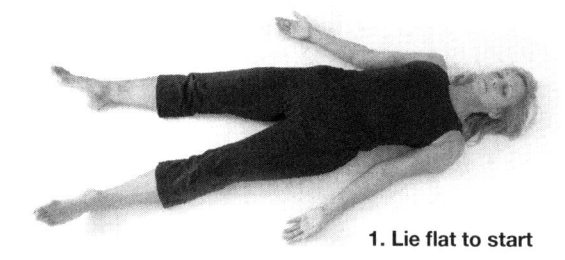

1. Lie flat to start

2. Inhale, and grab the big toe, ankle or calf, breathe into stretched leg while you feel the weight and foundation of the other leg, and stay here for three breaths

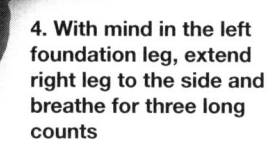

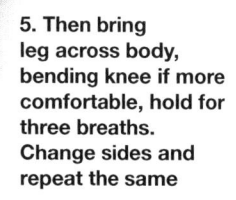

3. Inhale and lift nose toward knee for three breaths

4. With mind in the left foundation leg, extend right leg to the side and breathe for three long counts

5. Then bring leg across body, bending knee if more comfortable, hold for three breaths. Change sides and repeat the same

6. Dandasana

7. Paschimottanasana, for cooling and calming

8. Setu Bandasana (Bridge Pose)

9. Or if possible, Ardha Chandrasana (Full Crab)

10. Knees to chest to relax and stretch the spine

11. Find a position that suits you

Intermediate Flow

Here is another winter flow if you have more yoga experience. The aim again is to move the energy around the meridian lines of the Kidney and Bladder. These flows are designed for people with a yoga practice and do not have teaching points *(explaining what you should do)*.

Is life too hectic? Do you feel overstretched? Try this

1. Stand equally on both feet

2. Inhale and reach up

3. Exhale knees bent in line with the feet

4. Pull the navel in as you exhale round the spine

5. Straighten

6. And repeat

Stretch your legs and tip forwards with your feet parallel and facing forwards

Put your hands on the floor to balance and support you

Flow from pose to pose, and get into a rhythm of breath.

13. Do not go too deep too soon

14. Breathe deeply while you hold this position for several breaths

15. Inhale and lengthen

16. Lengthen the spine with the inhale and then twist on the exhale

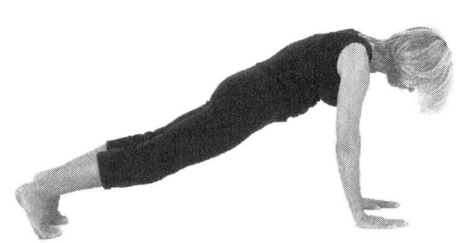

17. Hold the tummy in

18. If this is too difficult keep your arms straight

19

20

Keep flowing with breath and movement

21. Rest in the child's pose for as long as you need

22. Then change legs

In the winter concentrate on spending three to five breaths in each pose, going deeper into pose and finding the still point before moving on. Finish with shoulder stand, head stand and then a long relaxation.

25. Spend a long time in balasana (child's pose), breathe deeply into your rib cage so that you feel the ribs pressing on the thighs at the front and expanding either side if the spine is at the back. Breathe into the kidneys

For restoration and jet lag

1. Use a little momentum to get up there

2. Fold a mat for a little extra height, and make sure your neck hangs over the edge, stay here for five to twenty breaths and build it up

3. Pull in the navel to get a little more stretch in the spine, with toenails touching the floor. Five breaths

4. Use knees as earmuffs for cleansing effect. Five breaths

5

IMPORTANT NOTE
Do not practice this sequence if there is high blood pressure, if you are menstruating, or if there are neck and upper spine issues.

6. Then finally...

Meditations and Contemplations for Winter

In these sections we use the controlling cycle of the elements. Just as one element supports the next, the supporting cycle, its energy also has a controlling effect on another. Here we use earth and a sense of centre to control the water to stop it leaking away.

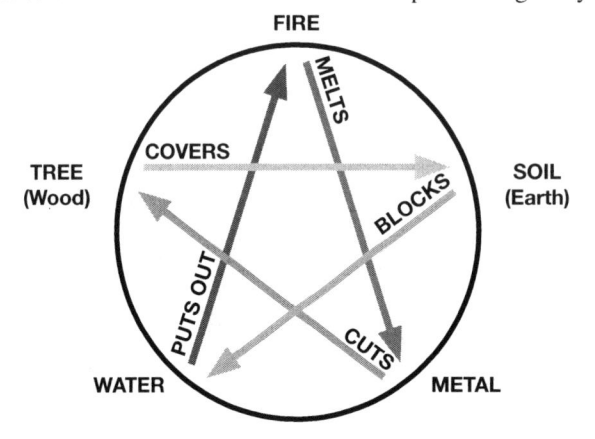

How to Centre Yourself

Normal abdominal breathing is good for calming, sleep or centring yourself. Place your hands just below the navel *(women with the left hand over the right, and men with the right hand over the left)*. Breathe in and out through the nose; this can be done standing or lying.

Rest and revitalize

How to Re-charge Your Batteries

Kidneys are thought of as our life-force batteries governing our vitality. Here we reverse our breathing, as compared with the abdominal breathing previously, by drawing the navel back to the spine as you inhale and releasing it as you exhale. Feel as if you are sucking energy into your centre on the inhalation, and on the exhalation, flushing it around the body. Breathe in and out through the nose.

1. Raise the right hand in front of the face, palm turned out, and the middle finger of the left hand pointing into the navel (palm up). Breathe the Yang energy *(Heaven's force)* from the palm of the right hand and spiral it through the heart clockwise into the left hand and then into the navel.
2. Then place the left hand palm downwards, and have the right middle finger pointing into the navel *(palm up)* and breathe the Yin energy *(Earth's force)*, spiralling it anti-clockwise through the heart into the navel.
3. Now raise the right hand up in front of your face, palm facing away, and breathe the Yang energy through the raised right hand and the Yin energy from the lower left hand, feeling the energy spiralling in both directions into your navel, refuelling yourself from both powerful sources.

Bone breathing is a meditative exercise for helping the mind to heal the body and keep the mind in the now. This can also be used to promote sleep, re-charge depleted energy levels or help with arthritis and bone diseases.

1. Imagine you have little holes in the end of your toes. On the in breath, breathe in light through all the bones and joints of the foot, and then up the right leg to the thigh. As you exhale, imagine all the tension and toxins being washed away. Repeat several times, taking as long as you like to gradually fill all the bones with light. Then do the same up and down the left leg.
2. Then breathe up the left leg and draw the light through the bones and joints of the pelvis, taking it down the right leg on the out breath. Repeat up the right leg through the pelvis and down the left leg.
3. Now imagine holes in the end of your fingers, and as you inhale, bring the light into the bones of your right hand, wrist and arm; as you exhale feel it wash away the tension and toxins. Then do the same up and down the left arm several times.
4. Then take the in breath up the left arm through the shoulders, shoulder-blades and collar bones and down the right arm, then up the right arm and down the left.
5. Now imagine a little hole at the tip of your tailbone and breathe the light up your spine to your head and as you exhale, feel it washing away tension, stress and any impurities down and out of the back.
6. Lastly take the light on the in breath round your ribs to the breastbone and on the out breath back to the spine.
7. Now become aware of all your bones and joints being filled with light. If there are any areas still needing light, take your attention to them and breathe light into them.

If you reach a point along a pathway on the in breath, such as an elbow, wrist or vertebra, through which the light cannot pass and it becomes blocked or there is an area of pain, you can either stay and focus on it breathing light into the area until it releases, or send the breath back down and draw it up again and again until it eventually clears. You can also use this technique, of breathing in light, to support any area or organ of the body.

A Mental Contemplation for Winter

Winter is a time of seeds being underground, hidden roots which are gathering energy to be reborn in spring, a time to feel what your inner changes need to be.

Sankalpa: Sowing the Seed of Change

Sankalpa is a Sanskrit word which translated means **resolve or resolution** and we can use it to reshape our personality, direct our lives along positive lines and create our destiny rather than being forced or pushed by this tempestuous life. This takes the form of a short mental statement impressed upon the subconscious mind, when it is receptive and sensitive to autosuggestion which is during the relaxation phase. The resolve is a **determination to become or do something in your life**, made at the beginning of a meditation practise, or before sleep. It is like sowing a seed in the fertile bed of a relaxed and clear mind. At the end of the session, or on waking, re-affirm the resolve to irrigate it, and then regularly affirm this statement so it grows well.

Many people make intellectual resolves which do not bring about results because the resolve is not planted deeply enough; it is done when the mind is not ready to receive it, when it is disturbed, distracted, full or stressed. For real success it needs to be created with strong willpower and feeling; made when the mind is relaxed and ready to acknowledge and absorb it. Once planted deep in the subconscious, it gathers the vast forces of a clear intellect, bringing about amazing changes in personality and self-realisation in many areas of life. It is a powerful technique and should be used intelligently, and not just for fulfilling desires or eliminating bad habits. If using it for the latter, then always state/affirm in the positive. It can also be used for therapeutic purposes, but it is best when used for a higher purpose that will transform your life, whether it is mentally, emotionally or spiritually. Choose ones which can act as a directing force for everything you do in your life, so that you transcend the behaviours of the external mind. What are televisions, radios, advertisements, newspapers, magazines doing to our brains everyday? This is why meditation is so good, enabling us to regularly spring-clean our minds and then correct any negative patterning.

* Be clear, precise and sincere.
* Always state in positive (not 'I will not') and do not rush.
* Choose only one to work on at a time, and do not expect overnight success as it may take time.
* Some people used 'I will' when stated at the beginning then 'I am' at the end of the session or on waking.
* Visualise it as having already happened.

Home and Lifestyle Section

Eight Home and Lifestyle Tips

1. **Burn** lots of scented candles or spicy aromatherapy oils in the winter. **Oils for winter are**; rosemary for low self-esteem, ginger for strengthening fire, geranium for calming the mind, also helpful for hormonal imbalance, and fennel is great for the kidneys. Use oils such as jasmine and sandalwood in your bath.
2. **Maximize** the quality and quantity of uplifting light entering your home in winter by placing a crystal in a sunny part of the house. **Enhance** those neglected dark corners by placing an inspirational picture or item there and illuminating it. **Avoid mirrors in the bedroom**, particularly facing the bed, as they can disrupt sleep and reflect back the negative energy you may discharge during the night.
3. **If there is too much impatience** in the home, include a few water features, glass, reflective surfaces, fish tanks, and pebbles.
4. **Enjoy relaxing** in the winter by a real log fire! **Get plenty of rest.** Try to fit in with the hours of daylight for a few days, or go to bed before 10pm, or have periods of relaxation in the day to re-charge so that you are not depleting yourself.
5. **Take time to go on a retreat or to a health spa.** Keep entertainment more restful such as going to the cinema (romantic films!). **Have a sauna** (*or steam bath*) to induce sweating, which can reduce the load on the kidneys.
6. **Communication** with others can be deeper and more profound, with a slower and more cautious approach to relationships.
7. **Learn to reflect and re-evaluate.** How do you react when under stress? Where, when and with who do you tend to get most stressed? Where does it go to in your body, and how can you deal with it? What specific behaviours/emotions/mental tendencies are you associating more strongly with at the moment? What are you good at, and what are your capabilities and skills? What do you value? List your values in order of importance, and make sure that you are including them in your life. (You can make a list of work and private life values and see how different they are). If you are working as part of a team, look for underlying motives, assess what is safe, and look deeper and notice any hidden agendas. **Write down the answers to the above questions and then any changes you would like to make in your life.**
8. **The state of water in your body** can reflect the state of your emotions. People can be more emotional at this time of year. Our lives and life force are able to have the same conditions of water as our planet. There are droughts and floods, still and stagnant pools, flowing streams and powerful oceans at different times. These are all natural happenings and should be ridden, like a boat rides on water. Hang on ... there will be a calm patch soon! Otherwise when things seem stuck believe that things will start moving when the time is right, if you are patient and wait.

Avoid

- Becoming over-tired.
- Cold or damp environments and rooms.
- Having too many changes at work, in relationships, and environment, until your energies are replenished.
- Becoming obsessive about secrecy.
- Having hidden agendas or underlying motives.
- Negative self talk.

Winter Summary

- ☑ Are you going to bed earlier and getting up later, when possible?

- ☑ Are you eating warming soups and stews on a regular basis, and having less cold foods and iced drinks? This also includes frozen foods which still contain the memory of having been frozen!

- ☑ Have you become more aware of the quality of your liquid intake and included more filtered water?

- ☑ Are you keeping your diet more alkaline by increasing your consumption of fruit and vegetables, and have you monitored your intake of salt?

- ☑ Have you noticed that you have more courage and an increased sense of adventure, and are less timid and fearful?

- ☑ Have the dark circles or puffiness under your eyes disappeared or becoming less so?

- ☑ Are you including time for stillness and contemplation in your day, and are you happy to stay at home a little more?

- ☑ Do you feel more receptive to things, more spiritual, or have you more emotional depth and generally look into things more deeply? Have you a more inward sense of oneness rather than feeling you have to wear your heart on your sleeve?

- ☑ Have you included exercises or treatments that work on the flexibility of the spine, or have you noticed any niggling back pain has disappeared?

- ☑ Have you noticed that you have found ways to conserve your energy and that you are not rushing around as much as you used to? Are you aware when you are tired and able to rectify it?

- ☑ Are you less stressed and anxious than you used to be?

- ☑ Are you finding it naturally easier to do a daily meditation at this time of year?

- ☑ Keeping warm is very important, so are you making sure that you are well wrapped up, especially around the middle of the back, the kidney area?

Quick Reference Guide for Body, Mind, and Emotions

Abdominal vitality 130
Accessibility 225
Adrenals 210
All over the place 126
Anxious 155, 212
Awareness 94
Aura 121

Back (lower) 218
Balance 30, 94, 113, 118
Balance personal power 122
Bladder 213
Blocked 156
Blood pressure 66
Body scan 48
Bones 234
Boundary (personal) 161
Brain (energize) 23
Breathe 174, 182, 184
Breathing capacity 153, 165
Buffeted 128
Build immunity 114

Calm 66, 74, 86, 170
Centre (self) 114, 117, 122, 234
Chakra regulation 205
Change 172, 235
Clear head 71
Compassion 81
Congested 154
Constipation 88, 157, 158, 159
Contentment 85
Cool (regain) 209
Co-ordination 31, 94
Core 130

Decision making 28, 46, 72
Defensive chi 121
Depressed 49, 81
Detoxify 14, 15, 23
Diaphragm 155
Digesting fats 24
Digestive system (recharge) 25, 111
Down to earth 37

Eliminate 159, 172
Emotional accessibility 225
Emotional overload 215
Emotions (toxic) 96
Energy boost 155, 202
Energy cleanse 117, 162
Energy flow 216

Energy system (re-balance) 118
Exchange 172
Extremes (balance) 79
Eyes 12, 28

Fat burning 26
Fatigue 72
Fearful 155, 210
Feeling stuck 40
Feel supported 134
Flat (feeling) 78
Flexibility (mind and body) 27

Gallbladder 24
Get moving 40
Get up and go 49
Grounding 126

Hangover 23, 39
Harmony with self 89
Head (clear) 29, 71
Head (too much in) 29
Heart 71, 72, 81
Heat 78
Hectic life 227
Highs and lows 89, 97
Humour 44

Immunity 105, 115
Indecisive 28, 46
Injured 178
Inner smile 42
Inner strength 132
Intention 182
Intestines 69, 156, 157

Jet lag 231
Joy 78, 97

Kidneys (energize) 218
Kidneys (flush) 210
Kidneys (massage) 155, 218, 224
Knocked off centre 114

Lacking energy 238
Left/right balance 181
Legs (strengthen) 113
Lethargic 43
Life energy
Liver boost 25, 49
Liver wake up 35
Lung massage 154

Lungs (open) 158

Massage 68
Meditation (walking) 91
Memory 28
Mental detox 14
Mental exhaustion 137
Mental focus 94
Mind into body 29, 122
Mind training 219, 234
Miserable 81
Morning after 39
Morning energy 160
Morning flush 104
Motivation 43,
Moving massage 68
Moving meditation 91
Muscles and tendons 120
Neck tension 71
Nerves (bundle of) 209
Nervous system 185, 204

Off centre 113. 114
Office 178
Older 178
Order 86
Overload (emotional) 215
Overstretched 227
Oxygenate 158

Peace 85
Perspective 44
Precision 31
Pressure 66

Re-boot (mind, body, and emotions) 200
Re-charge 155, 231
Re-energize 223
Re-group 30
Relaxation 47, 48
Reliability 132
Restoration 231
Revitalize 160, 232
Rhythm 67, 86
Rib cage strengthening 155

Self-esteem 115
Self healing 135
Self massage 68
Sharpen wits 31
Shoulder tension 70
Slouching 72
Sluggish 204
Small Intestine 72
Smile 42

Space 168
Spine massage 184, 206
Spleen (massage) 113
Spring clean 162
Stability 113
Stagnation 25, 36
Start the day 76, 77
Stiffness 204, 208
Stomach (massage) 112
Strength (build) 132
Stress 135, 164, 218, 212
Stretch yourself 36
Stuck 40
Supple strength 214
Support 134
Surrender 134
Swollen ankles 68
Sync (get into) 67

Tendons (strengthen) 120
Tension 31, 208, 204
Thymus 116
Tired 43, 72
Toxic, general 23, 156,
Toxic thoughts and emotions 96

Vision 28, 51
Visualization 49, 50
Vitality 218, 233

Waist (trim) 25, 112
Wake up 35
Warm heart 71
Warm up 71, 76
Wheelchair 178
Withdraw 168
Worthless 127

Yin and yang (balance) 121
Yoga for chakras 205

Zest for life 78

Printed in Poland
by Amazon Fulfillment
Poland Sp. z o.o., Wrocław